The Bioeconomy

The bioeconomy is steadily becoming more important in regional, national and European public policies. As it encompasses the transformation of agricultural, marine and organic resources into food, feed, fuels, energy and materials, the bioeconomy should become a major new industry, outlining the possibility of a post-fossil future. This book is the first attempt to depict the origins, formation and challenges of this new industry in terms of emerging institutions, innovation and economic strategies. The result of this work is that the substitution of raw materials alone is not enough to get out of the fossil economy.

This book develops a political economy of the ecological transition which theorizes the transition as a new crisis of capitalism. This phase is characterized by stakeholders' attempts to develop renewed rationales and strategies to take control of the reorganization of flows of natural resources, their outcomes and their evaluation. The proposed framework considers recent results in four complementary research strands: transition studies, institutional economics, ecological economics and the evolutionary economics of innovation.

The book will be of interest to researchers interested in the development of the bioeconomy, and both researchers and students seeking to understand the role of heterodox economics in the ecological transition.

Nicolas Befort is Associate Professor of Economics and Director of the Chair in Bioeconomy and Sustainable Development, NEOMA Business School, France. He is also Associated Research Fellow to LISIS (INRAE, CNRS, University Gustave Eiffel).

Routledge Studies in Ecological Economics

Anarchism and Ecological Economics
A Political Platform for Ecological Economics
Ove Daniel Jakobsen

Water Resources and Economic Processes
Edited by Tiziano Distefano

The Degrowth Alternative
A Path to Address our Environmental Crisis?
Diana Stuart, Ryan Gunderson and Brian Petersen

A History of Ecological Economic Thought
Marco P. Vianna Franco and Antoine Missemer

Radical Ecological Economics and Accounting to Save the Planet
The Failure of Mainstream Economists
Jacques Richard

Economics, Ecology and Policy for the Bioeconomy
A Holistic Approach
Sanja Tišma, Anamarija Farkaš, Anamarija Pisarović, Marina Funduk, and Iva Tolić

The Informal Sector and the Environment
Edited by Ranjula Bali Swain and Uma Kambhampati

The Bioeconomy
Institutions, Innovation and Sustainability
Nicolas Befort

For more information about this series, please visit: www.routledge.com/Routledge-Studies-in-Ecological-Economics/book-series/RSEE

The Bioeconomy

Institutions, Innovation and Sustainability

Nicolas Befort

Routledge
Taylor & Francis Group
LONDON AND NEW YORK

First published 2023
by Routledge
4 Park Square, Milton Park, Abingdon, Oxon OX14 4RN

and by Routledge
605 Third Avenue, New York, NY 10158

Routledge is an imprint of the Taylor & Francis Group, an informa business

British Library Cataloguing-in-Publication Data
A catalogue record for this book is available from the British Library

ISBN: 978-0-367-61040-1 (hbk)
ISBN: 978-0-367-61041-8 (pbk)
ISBN: 978-1-003-10301-1 (ebk)

DOI: 10.4324/9781003103011

Typeset in Bembo
by Taylor & Francis Books

Contents

Figures

Tables

Acknowledgements

The realization of this book was made possible by the Chair in Bioeconomy and Sustainable Development of NEOMA Business School (funded by NEOMA Business School, Greater Reims, the Paris-Reims Foundation, the Marne-en-Champagne Chamber of Commerce and the Caisse d'Epargne Grand Est Europe) and the "Young Researcher" (2017–2018) and "High Level Researcher" Grants (2020–2021) of the Greater East Region. Thanks to Sophie Raynaud for the assistance in the realization of the illustrations.

I thank Morgane for her unwavering support. This book is dedicated to her.

1 Introduction

1. Getting out of the fossil economy

Since the advent of Fordism after World War II, social movements have stood against the development of productivism, warning of the risks to biodiversity and the environment entailed by this mode of production. Just as the Club of Rome report pointed out in 1972 that the dynamics of the extraction of natural resources observed at the time were not sustainable, all the IPCC reports indicate an increase in greenhouse gas emissions responsible for climate change (Meadows and Club of Rome, 1972). The IPCC reports also expose the anthropic responsibility regarding climate change (IPCC, 2022). This idea of anthropic responsibility is expressed by the notion of the Anthropocene (Sarrazin and Lecomte, 2016). Humanity has now become a geological force, as shown by the layers of material formed by our waste. The merit of this notion is that it anchors the debate on climate change in the relationship that humanity has with nature. Nevertheless, there have been criticisms of this vision (Banerjee and Arjaliès, 2021; Malm, 2016).

From the point of view of political economy, the notion of the Anthropocene is problematic for two reasons. On the one hand, it tends to consider humanity as a homogeneous whole, denying both the conflicts generated by the appropriation of capital and the colonial past of Western countries. On the other hand, Malm bases his concept of the Capitalocene on the concept of the "fossil economy". According to Malm (2016), the fossil economy is rooted in the development of the steam engine associated with the development of the use of coal, which has structured this mode of production. The latter, unstable by nature, is oriented by its expansion based on the increasing consumption of fossil resources at the origin of greenhouse gas emissions. It is interesting to note with Figure 1.1 that the CO_2 emissions relating to fossil fuels were reported around 1770 and experienced a significant increase in 1900 and then a very strong increase from 1950. As this book will show, these three dates are not insignificant. Indeed, the turning point of 1770 illustrates the thesis of the emergence of the fossil economy as a choice guided by the interests of the British, French and American ruling classes (and other Western countries). Thus, extraction and increasing combustion are the result of the search for the

DOI: 10.4324/9781003103011-1

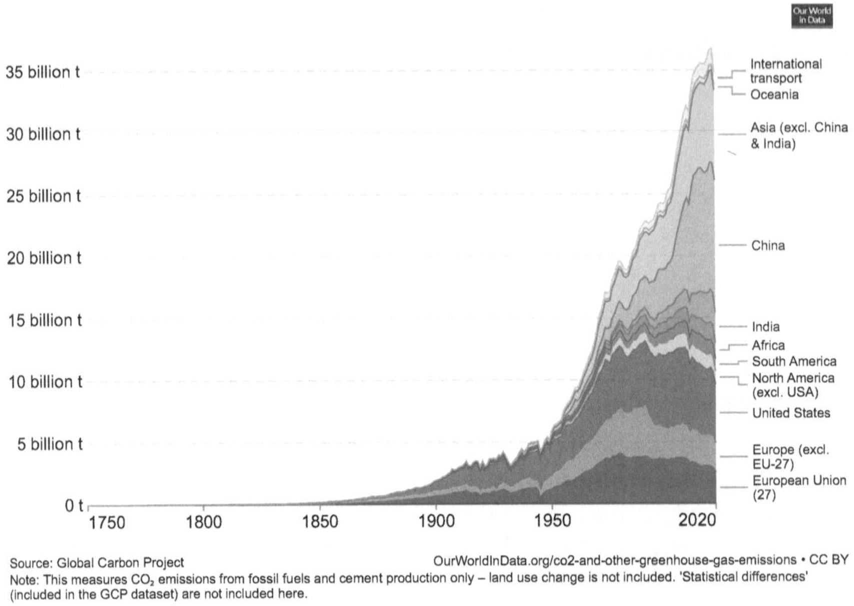

Figure 1.1 Annual emissions from fossil fuels, by world region

expansion of the sphere of capital accumulation. Malm's point is similar to that of Mitchell's (2013) considering that the expansion of fossil combustion was only possible through the expansion (or its imposition in colonial situations) of wage labor.

The notion of the Capitalocene points to the dialectical unity between the expansion of the production of the form of capitalism that was implemented during the industrial revolution and its need to expand its access to natural resources. Here, the mainstream economists, who believe in the innate virtues of innovation, defend the idea of a possible decoupling between production growth and a decrease in the use of natural resources. Three major objections are to be formulated here, underlining the aporias of neo-classical and neo-liberal economics, i.e. economics disconnected from the material relations guiding production. First, several systematic reviews identify no evidence for the possibility of such decoupling (Schröder and Storm, 2020; Vadén et al., 2020; Wiedenhofer et al., 2020). Secondly, this conclusion is in line with the founding works of ecological economics (Georgescu-Roegen, 1975; Martinez-Alier, 2002) which insist on the energy consumption necessary for any economic activity. Third, there is a dialectical relationship between capital accumulation and natural resources (Cahen-Fourot, 2020). On the one hand, the expansion of capital accumulation leads to an increase in the cost of the production of raw materials or the reproduction of natural resources, which affects the conditions of profitability of capital, generating the need to expand the exploitation of resources (O'Connor, 1991, 1988). On the other hand, the metabolic rift approach suggests that the exploitation of natural resources in the process of capital accumulation is not accompanied by a return to the nature of the resources exploited, leading to deteriorating conditions for capital accumulation (Foster, 2000; Foster and Burkett, 2017).

The ecological transition is therefore a transition from a fossil economy to a post-fossil economy. Whereas the fossil economy is based on the institutionalization of the extraction and consumption of natural resources to feed the accumulation of capital, the post-fossil economy designates an economy anchored in the planetary limits discarded from the mode of organization of the production of the fossil economy. This raises two questions. On the one hand, it is a question of determining the possibility and the conditions of capital accumulation in a post-fossil economy. Indeed, the history of capitalism is fueled by the increasing consumption of resources, especially fossil fuels. But does the imposition of planetary limits on production allow the continuation of capital accumulation? On the other hand, as the objective of a post-fossil economy is set as a horizon to be reached, the transition process towards this new economy is called into question.

However, even though these issues are analytically distinct, they are in fact related. Indeed, as the socio-economics of capitalism shows (Beckert, 2016, 2013), the answers that will be brought to these questions can only exist in hindsight. Indeed, the climate crisis has brought capitalism into a new emerging phase. The interpretative hypothesis of this book is that the dynamics of the emergence of this crisis questions the foundations of capitalism on its capacity to continue its expansion through the increasing consumption of resources. The responses provided by the actors are therefore aimed at reproducing their existence in this space where the crisis itself is an object of production of interpretation, as shown by the Anthropocene–Capitalocene debate. Therefore, the interpretation that becomes hegemonic will play a major role in structuring the responses to the crisis – without prejudging their sustainability or not. Consequently, this book proposes to study the processes by which the actors develop and transform their activities in the ecological transition. This approach includes both the classical dimensions of political economy (institutions, innovation, production) and the specificities of the issue of sustainability. That is to say, it is a question of studying the processes by which the actors revisit the issue of natural resource exploitation and how they construct representations of sustainability in regard to the exploitation of these resources.

2. The bioeconomy as a post-fossil economy

In this context, the subject of the bioeconomy has emerged since the 2010s (Aguilar et al., 2009; McCormick and Kautto, 2013; Schmidt et al., 2012) and carries the promise of a great transition towards the use of renewable resources to replace the use of oil, notably under the impetus of the European Commission, which has been interested in these issues since the early 2000s. Thus, the bioeconomy represents the emblematic economic space for the exit of the fossil era since it is about replacing oil in the production of all consumer goods (materials, chemistry, energy).

Before presenting the European position, let us recall that this promise of transition is part of the thinking of Nicholas Georgescu-Roegen (NGR) (Georgescu-Roegen, 1971), who was responsible for changing the term *bioeconomics*: since the 1930s, this term had been used to designate the economy of fisheries and natural resources. For NGR, a bioeconomic perspective sees economic development as an extension of biological evolution. That is to say that humanity is the result of evolution, and the economic sphere extends this evolution by developing techniques that allow the transformation of humanity's environment. NGR therefore speaks of humanity as an "exosomatic" species. The consequence of this exosomatic nature of the human species is to increase our dependence on objects and access to resources and energy. I invite you to look around you and observe all the goods and services you need. NGR is therefore developing a very long-term perspective by calling for a bioeconomic transition.

This transition is part of the continuation of two major historical periods generated by Promethean technologies. In mythology, Prometheus is the titan who stole fire from Zeus and gave it to humans. NGR takes up this image by defining Promethean technologies as technologies allowing access to energy that was not then available, and allowing the generation of an innovation cluster that further increases access to energy. Prometheus 1 was then fire, and Prometheus 2 was the invention of the steam engine. However, the steam engine that generated the thermo-industrial revolution caused environmental damage. The challenge then is to find a technology capable of providing access to a significant amount of energy while respecting planetary limits. The study then points to three options: either to continue without changing anything that would lead to collapse, possibly to growth or to decline. That is to say, a reduction in useless consumption and production in order to switch to a new ethic. Prometheus 3 would therefore be a return to the use of biomass, a renewable resource, abandoning fossil resources.

Thus, this vision of the bioeconomy describes a post-fossil economy where the fundamental organizing principle is based on the balance between the flows of renewable natural resources and the flows resulting from production. The economy is considered as a constituent element of the social sphere whose function is to ensure the sustainable satisfaction of material needs of human societies (Polanyi, 2001). Therefore, by being (1) motivated by expected profits, (2) dynamically unstable and generating strong uncertainty, (3) distinguished from other economic systems by its need for constant growth that is not decoupled from the use of natural resources, the fossil economy is not able to ensure a sustainable satisfaction of material needs (Beckert, 2016; Befort, 2021). The bioeconomy described by NGR has three principles. First, it positions the degrowth of fossil or unsustainable activities as the principle guiding the transition to a post-fossil economy. Secondly, this dynamic translates into the inscription of economic activities in the constraint of planetary limits. The evaluation then translates into a necessary reflection on the indicators to be used in the transition and to evaluate the sustainability of the post-fossil economy. Thirdly, the ethic issue that is emerging from the transition to a post-fossil economy and that should structure it is that of *sufficiency*.

These principles lead us to the three questions that structure the reflection in this book. First, the notion of the Capitalocene explained above highlights that the ecological transition today represents a crisis of capitalism. Consequently, is the fundamental dynamic of capital accumulation compatible with a necessary inscription within planetary limits? Secondly, the transition process is not independent of the form of the fossil economy, nor of the visions of the future held by the actors in the way they perceive the outcome of the ecological transition. Therefore, what are the futures drawn by the activities that fall under what the actors call "transition" (innovation projects, public policies, etc.)? Third, how do these activities and futures actually develop the perspective of a post-fossil economy?

3. Where is the bioeconomy today?

Since the emergence of the bioeconomy in the public policy sphere, many studies (Bauer, 2018; Bugge et al., 2016; D'Amato et al., 2019; Giurca, 2018; Holmgren et al., 2020; Levidow et al., 2019, 2013; Vivien et al., 2019) have questioned the realities and futures drawn by the dominant conceptions of the bioeconomy.

3.1 The bioeconomy of biotechnologies

The OECD has invested heavily in participating in the diffusion of biotechnology throughout the economy (OECD, 2017, 1996; OECD International Futures Programme, 2009), equating bioeconomy and biotechnology (Birch et al., 2010). For example, Patermann and Aguilar (2018, p.22) wrote "biotechnology is the core lever of the bioeconomy". This drive to match biotechnology with the bioeconomy began in 2005 with the launch of the *Knowledge-Based Bioeconomy* concept (European Commission, 2005) following the Lisbon Strategy. For example, the German Bioeconomy Strategy of 2010 mentioned the development of a *Knowledge-Based Bioeconomy* relying on the transformation of biomass for the production of molecules for the chemical and energy industry (Schmidt et al., 2012). Thus, this bioeconomy of biotechnologies corresponds to an alliance between part of the biotechnology industry and part of the agro-industry.

The development of biotechnologies is part of the extension of "traditional biotechnologies" from fermentation processes to genetic manipulation and synthetic biology made possible by the discovery of the structure of DNA in 1953 and the synthesis of proteins in 1961 (Bud, 1991). The promoters of biotechnologies consider that they have the potential to generate a Schumpeterian technological breakthrough which would generate a new industrial revolution and then produce a new growth cycle. Thus, the development of biotechnologies is based on the promise of a technological breakthrough thanks to biotechnologies.

This expansion has been presented as a paradigmatic revolution based on a new knowledge base, and as an industrial revolution for pharmacy, medicine, agronomy and chemistry, thanks to the constitution of biotechnology as a general purpose technology. That is to say, biotechnology, such as information technology, will profoundly transform all sectors.

To this end, the development of biotechnologies has relied on an original institutional architecture, described by Coriat et al. (2003) as helping to form a *finance-driven* innovation regime. Here, *start-ups* are seen as the key organizations for generating new knowledge (Audretsch, 2001). These companies can be either academic *spin-offs* or strictly private firms (Arora and Gambardella, 1990; Audretsch, 2003). The emergence of these *start-ups* was encouraged by the Bayh Dole Act (1980) authorizing the patentability of living matter. In order to encourage the development of these companies specialized in the production of knowledge, new financial regulations were introduced. In 1984, the "Alternative 2" market of the NASDAQ authorized the financing of unprofitable companies on financial markets. Finally, this movement of commodification of knowledge has also been supported by the development of *markets for technology* (Arora et al., 2001; Mowery and Sampat, 2005) aimed at facilitating the exchange of intellectual property rights between firms.

In parallel with this mobilization of capital for the development of biotechnologies, public authorities have launched massive support programs. For example, one of the first European research programs focused on the development of these biotechnologies (Aguilar et al., 2009). These firms have also received subsidies under the US biotech development policy.

The development of biotechnologies forms part of the emergence of an economy of promises (Befort, 2021). The rationality of the actors carrying a technology aims at demonstrating the radicality of the innovations they are implementing, justifying investments on financial markets and public support for the financing of the demonstration and industrialization of biotechnologies. White biotechnologies are therefore an extension of biotechnologies, more than 80% of whose turnover is generated by red biotechnologies[1] (Festel, 2010). According to this vision, the bioeconomy is hence a sub-sector of biotechnologies. Nevertheless, the development of this bioeconomy aims at the industrialization of biotechnologies under conditions that make economies of scale possible in order to compete with thermochemical processes. However, this development model suffers from blockages generated by intellectual property rights, resulting in the need to develop innovation systems and organizations capable of ensuring the change of scale.

3.2 The bioeconomy of biorefineries

This bioeconomy of biorefineries is built as a promise for a major transition towards the use of biomass as a substitution for the use of fossil resources for the production of food, chemical molecules, materials and energy. The European Commission is very active in promoting that vision of the bioeconomy:

> The bioeconomy provides a useful basis for such an approach, as it encompasses the production of renewable biological resources and the conversion of these resources and waste streams into value added products, such as food, feed, bio-based products and bioenergy. Its sectors and industries have strong innovation potential due to their use of a wide range of sciences, enabling and industrial technologies, along with local and tacit knowledge.
>
> (European Commission, 2012)

Biorefineries are defined as complex systems based on the transformation of biomass of agricultural, forestry or marine origin, and ensuring economic and environmental sustainability. The biorefinery, beyond being a "technical" object, is also a "transitional object" (Nieddu and Vivien, 2015), i.e., the biorefinery constitutes a framework of thought which orientes and structures the actors' visions of the future, guiding their resource allocation choices in the process of reorganizing the value chains that are underway in the bioeconomy. Biorefineries have been around for a long time, and the issue is the possible industrial link between food and non-food uses of plants. During the 1990s, chemical companies such as Dupont and agricultural companies such as Roquette developed R&D projects aimed at exploring opportunities for valorization in biofuels and bioplastics (Nieddu, 2000). From an institutional point of view, this exploration of new opportunities has taken the form of *backcasting* projects in the United States and Europe (BIOPOL and EUROVIEW in Europe) from 2005 onwards. These projects mobilized the actors in the agro-industrial, wood-pulp, biotechnology and chemical industries. The aim of these projects was to make an inventory of the types of biomass available, the knowledge bases to be mobilized and the potential markets.

The development of this bioeconomy has not been supported by an institutional architecture based on the commodification of knowledge. The production and dissemination of knowledge have been stimulated by calls for multidisciplinary projects aimed at structuring interactions between actors drawing on heterogeneous knowledge bases. These projects are carried out by alliances of actors in research projects, but also in *joint ventures* and, to a lesser extent, by *start-ups*. The *Bio-Based Joint Undertaking* (BBI-JU) public–private partnership, launched in 2014, illustrates the dynamics of recomposition of the division of labor underway. One-third of the funding (€975 million) is public, the other two-thirds is private (€2.7 billion). The BBI's calls for projects are based on the definition of five value chains (SIRA, 2013), for which it is possible to identify a leading actor. For each of them, the objective is to finance a *flagship* project or the financing of industrial scale-up. These projects aim to finance segments of the value chain, involving suppliers and outlets. Moreover, these projects must take into account impact and sustainability assessments used by actors as tools to legitimize their products (Morone and D'Amato, 2019; Vink et al., 2003).

4. Heterodox economics and the ecological transition

The diversity of work on the definition of the bioeconomy (Bauer, 2018; Bugge et al., 2016; Giurca, 2018; Holmgren et al., 2020; Levidow et al., 2019) illustrates this issue of the futures shaped by the processes of transition to a bioeconomy. In this perspective, the approach of this book is to develop a political economy analysis of the transition to a post-fossil economy. This approach studies how the actors in conflict seek to resolve the problem of reproducing accumulation by integrating (or not) planetary limits and how they claim to respond to this new crisis of capitalism. To do this, this book will study the concrete forms taken by the projects developed by the actors to respond to the challenge of the emergence of a bioeconomy. These concrete forms are of two kinds. On the one hand, they are the narratives that the actors produce around their innovation or production actions (Borup et al., 2006; Geels and Raven, 2006). The production of these narratives reflects the visions of the future that guide actors' resource allocation choices but are also structured by the interests that actors seek to preserve (Beckert, 2016). On the other hand, it is a matter of studying innovation projects and production start-ups in the bioeconomy to understand how actors develop space and value chains of the bioeconomy.

To address these issues, it is necessary to turn to the potential contributions of heterodox economics, which is marked by its openness to other social sciences. Political economy approaches aim at characterizing the configurations and contradictions of capitalism over time by focusing on institutions and power relations. Thus, the field left aside the question of the ecological transition. It is notable, for example, that the massive work of Shaikh (2016) does not mention ecological issues. Nevertheless, the common ground of political economy analyses provides sound principles.

From this perspective, the field of ecological economics is a good benchmark, especially because of the key role of NGR's reflections on the bioeconomy in the emergence of this field of research (Mayumi, 2001). This field is divided between three traditions (Buchs et al., 2020; Douai and Montalban, 2012; Spash, 2020, 2012): the new resource economists, the new environmental pragmatists and the social ecological economists. The first pursues the mainstream agenda by using methodological individualism, which aims at achieving allocation efficiency through market-based instruments to solve ecological issues. Whereas the second tradition is mainly developed by non-economists trying to develop "useful knowledge" through the quantification of ecosystem services and natural capital, the latter has embedded the various traditions of heterodoxy, i.e. Marxism, post-Keynesianism, socio-economics and institutional economics. Nevertheless, even if ecological economics seems to be the most advanced research stream in economics regarding ecological issues, its focus mainly remains on such topics as natural resources or biodiversity. This leads such authors as Spash (2020, p.10) to call for an analysis of "the real operation of the current system" in the frame of political economy and in dialogue with allied research streams.

First, the framework draws on the multi-level perspective of *transition to sustainability* studies (Markard et al., 2012) with its strong meso level focus on regimes (Geels, 2004, 2002). Regimes are conceived as the expression of the structure of the system, analyzed as configurations of institutions and material relations embedded in historical trajectories (Sorrell, 2018; Svensson and Nikoleris, 2018). This approach joins institutionalist political economy here in considering that the meso level is not necessarily a sector, the form of which is historically dated to the Fordist period of the Glorious Thirties (Tickell and Peck, 1995). Post-Fordism paved the way for diverse meso forms, taking the form of innovation systems unfolding at different scales (Schot and Steinmueller, 2018). Research into the diversity of accumulation forms has shown an increasing diversification of the forms of capital accumulation. Thus, post-Fordism has given way to a neo-liberal accumulation regime driven by finance (Amable et al., 2021; Boyer, 2009). Today, capitalism seems to be transformed by (Allaire and Daviron, 2019; Beckert, 2019; Marchi et al., 2013; Montalban et al., 2019; Mazzucato, 2021, 2018):

- the development of a platform economy based on the production of value through intermediation, thereby responding to the growing differentiation of markets
- the development of a quality economy (labelled products, etc.)
- the development of strategies to meet the challenge of ecological transition (green growth, degrowth, etc.).

These transformations are reflected at the meso level either by the conversion of existing spaces (the transition of agriculture, for example) or by the emergence of new spaces that do not correspond to already existing spaces. The case of the bioeconomy is emblematic of this dynamic. The numerous research projects aimed at defining and measuring it bear witness to the difficulties of identifying its stabilized boundaries (Pyka et al., 2022). To account for this, this study defines economic spaces as fields in the sense of Bourdieu (2005, 2000, 1997). That is to say that these spaces are constructed by the actors who try to define their meaning and their borders. At the time of the emergence of these fields, the actors maintain conflictual relations aiming at defining the hierarchical positions which organize the functioning of the field. As a result, there may be multiple boundaries and the current activities of the actors must be read as revisiting past trajectories and projecting them into the future in order to deploy the space. This particular dynamic is specific to a transitional phase, since it involves questioning the past productive division of labor (the emergence or transformation of meso spaces), the organization of production, its evaluation and its goals.

The transition is also the moment of the emergence of a new institutional architecture. Second, the framework draws on institutional economics, with its notion of institutional change (Amable, 2016, 2009). Institutions are defined as the "rules of the game" imposed by a coalition of actors sharing common interests (Amable and Palombarini, 2009). In this perspective, the ecological transition is theorized as a period of institutional change toward a new institutional architecture. During this period, the actors attempt to impose competing frameworks by using institutions to shape their field (Franceschini and Pansera, 2015; Hoppmann et al., 2020). These institutions also pertain to the organization of the use of natural resources (Dupuy et al., 2015).

As *transition studies* show, innovation is at the heart of the transition dynamic and plays a major role in structuring the institutional architecture. In order to do so, this book draws on evolutionary economics of eco-innovations to study material relations, and particularly here, innovation strategies. This strand considers products as "compromises" between sustainability claims and inherited techno-economic constraints which generate irreversibility and rebound effects (Arfaoui et al., 2014; Belis-Bergouignan et al., 2004; Cecere et al., 2014; Lancaster, 1966; Oltra and Saint Jean, 2009).

5. The bioeconomy of today and tomorrow: a reproduction of the fossil economy?

5.1 *Objectives and book methodology*

The development of today's bioeconomy outlined above has been analyzed as *hijacking* the original conception developed by N. Georgescu-Roegen (Vivien et al., 2019). This reading considers that the principles of sustainability advanced in the vision of an ecological bioeconomy are contrary to the models developed today. Nevertheless, the analysis of the emergence of the bioeconomy offers a key perspective for studying the relationship that capitalism in transition maintains with the fossil economy. Indeed, the bioeconomy of biotechnology or biorefinery is developing very far upstream in the value chains, since it involves substituting the use of biomass for the use of oil. Consequently, the study of the development of today's bioeconomy, in relation to its contribution to the emergence of a post-fossil economy, invites us to study the strategies by which the actors seek to recompose their economic space. More specifically, the aim of this book is to study whether the strategies that have led to the emergence of the bioeconomy and its structuring involve the substitution of fossil resources by renewable resources, or whether the development of the bioeconomy is part of an expansion of production through the development of new productions considered to be sustainable because they are produced from renewable raw materials.

The data used in this study were collected within the projects "Managerial practices of biorefinery platforms" (Chair in Bioeconomy and Sustainable Development, 2017–2021), "Innovation platforms in the bioeconomy" (Greater East Region, France, 2017–2018), "Innovation communities for a sustainable bioeconomy" (Greater East Region, France, 2020–2021) and "Productive heritages, stakeholders' strategies and appropriation of knowledge in doubly green chemistry" (Champagne-Ardenne Region, France, 2013–2016). These projects led to 60 interviews with economic actors, policy makers and natural science researchers. These interviews were completed by the collection and analysis of heterogeneous data (patents, academic publications in natural sciences, reports, press releases of the companies studied, press articles) constituting a database of 434 documents.

5.2 General outline

Chapter 2 aims, on the basis of the theoretical currents outlined in the previous subsection, to highlight the analytical tools of a political economy of the ecological transition. To this end, a critical discussion of the notion of regimes developed within *transition studies* is presented so as to underline that the question of the study of ecological transition processes concerns conflicts between actors over the form of the regime, conflicts fuelled by the mobilization of heterogeneous resources. These conflicts participate in the production of institutions aiming (1) to organize the conflict over the form of the regime, the objective of which is to draw future borders, and (2) to make the future space emerge and exist. In this context, innovation strategies play a role in the transformation of companies and the production of symbolic objects that help organize the transition.

Chapter 3 proposes a review of the long history of the bioeconomy by showing how it is rooted in the history of chemistry. More specifically, this historical approach highlights the need to think in terms of *substitution* in the transition, since the products and services must offer better functionalities than their petroleum-based equivalents. This chapter shows that a product, in its transition, is part of a more global mode of production and helps to structure it.

Chapter 4 is devoted to the formation of the institutional architecture of the bioeconomy. To do this, the book details the formation of the European bioeconomy space based on the analysis of structuring projects carried out by the actors. This analysis shows that the question of product identity and the reconstitution of the division of labor are two major issues for the actors. Finally, this analysis is conducted at the level of the United States of America. Indeed, this country has a long tradition of thinking about non-food uses of plants and has been a pioneer in the development of biotechnologies and biorefineries. This perspective highlights the dynamics of political compromise between different forms of bioeconomy.

Chapter 5 draws on the results in terms of alliances between actors to reconstitute value chains by integrating the territorial issue. In doing so, the diversity of firm models and territorial anchoring strategies allows us to draw a landscape of the bioeconomy where firms must deal with localized innovation ecosystems and globalized value chains. While this perspective is relatively common in contemporary capitalism, the novelty lies in the question of the diversity of possible raw materials and the trade-offs that actors must make.

Chapter 6 applies an economics of techno-economic promises approach (outlined in Chapter 2) to study the long-term development of biodegradable plastics. This perspective highlights that beyond the promises, whose role is to anchor products in an emergent economic field, the actors need to develop learning processes in order to succeed in developing the production of their products.

The final chapter builds on the approach of Chapter 6 to study two emblematic molecules – succinic acid and levulinic acid – which are the two structuring products for the field of the bioeconomy.

Note

1 Red biotechnologies refer to medical biotechnologies such as techniques using messenger RNA. White biotechnology refers to industrial biotechnology (production of plastics, materials or energy).

Bibliography

Aguilar, A., Bochereau, L., Matthiessen, L., 2009. Biotechnology as the engine for the knowledge-based bio-economy. *Biotechnol. Genet. Eng. Rev.* 26, 371–388. https://doi.org/10.5661/bger-26-371.

Allaire, G., Daviron, B. (Eds.), 2019. *Ecology, capitalism and the new agricultural economy: the second great transformation*, Critical food studies. Routledge.

Amable, B., 2016. Institutional complementarities in the dynamic comparative analysis of capitalism. *J. Institutional Econ.* 12, 79–103. https://doi.org/10.1017/S1744137415000211.

Amable, B., 2009. *The diversity of modern capitalism*, Reprinted ed. Oxford University Press.

Amable, B., Palombarini, S., 2009. A neorealist approach to institutional change and the diversity of capitalism. *Socio-Econ. Rev.* 7, 123–143. https://doi.org/10.1093/ser/mwn018.

Amable, B., Palombarini, S., Broder, D., 2021. *The last neoliberal: Macron and the origins of France's political crisis.* Verso Books.

Arfaoui, N., Brouillat, E., Saint Jean, M., 2014. Policy design and technological substitution: investigating the REACH regulation in an agent-based model. *Ecol. Econ.* 107, 347–365. https://doi.org/10.1016/j.ecolecon.2014.08.013.

Arora, A., Fosfuri, A., Gambardella, A., 2001. Markets for technology and their implications for corporate strategy. *Ind. Corp. Change* 10, 419–451. https://doi.org/10.1093/icc/10.2.419.

Arora, A., Gambardella, A., 1990. Complementarity and external linkages: the strategies of the large firms in biotechnology. *J. Ind. Econ.* 38, 361–379.

Audretsch, D., 2003. The role of small firms in US biotechnology clusters, in: Fuchs, G. (Ed.), *Biotechnology in comparative perspective.* Routledge, pp.14–32.

Audretsch, D., 2001. The role of small firms in US biotechnology clusters. *Small Bus. Econ.* 17, 3–15.

Banerjee, S.B., Arjaliès, D.-L., 2021. Celebrating the end of enlightenment: Organization theory in the age of the Anthropocene and Gaia (and why neither is the solution to our ecological crisis). *Organ. Theory* 2. https://doi.org/10.1177/26317877211036714.

Bauer, F., 2018. Narratives of biorefinery innovation for the bioeconomy: conflict, consensus, or confusion? *Environ. Innov. Soc. Transit.* 28, 96–107. https://doi.org/10.1016/j.eist.2018.01.005.

Beckert, J., 2019. Markets from meaning: quality uncertainty and the intersubjective construction of value. *Camb. J. Econ.* https://doi.org/10.1093/cje/bez035.

Beckert, J., 2016. *Imagined futures: fictional expectations and capitalist dynamics.* Harvard University Press.

Beckert, J., 2013. Capitalism as a system of expectations: toward a sociological microfoundation of political economy. *Polit. Soc.* https://doi.org/10.1177/0032329213493750.

Befort, N., 2021. The promises of drop-in vs. functional innovations: the case of bioplastics. *Ecol. Econ.* 181, 106886. https://doi.org/10.1016/j.ecolecon.2020.106886.

Belis-Bergouignan, M.-C., Oltra, V., Saint Jean, M., 2004. Trajectories towards clean technology: example of volatile organic compound emission reductions. *Ecol. Econ.* 48, 201–220. https://doi.org/10.1016/j.ecolecon.2003.09.010.

Birch, K., Levidow, L., Papaioannou, T., 2010. Sustainable capital? The neoliberalization of nature and knowledge in the European "knowledge-based bio-economy". *Sustainability* 2, 2898–2918. https://doi.org/10.3390/su2092898.

Borup, M., Brown, N., Konrad, K., Van Lente, H., 2006. The sociology of expectations in science and technology. *Technol. Anal. Strateg. Manag.* 18, 285–298. https://doi.org/10.1080/09537320600777002.

Bourdieu, P., 2005. *The social structures of the economy.* Polity.

Bourdieu, P., 2000. *Les structures sociales de l'économie.* Éditions Points.

Bourdieu, P., 1997. Le champ économique. *Actes Rech. en Sci. Soc.* 119, 48–66. https://doi.org/10.3406/arss.1997.3229.

Boyer, R., 2009. *Feu le régime d'accumulation tiré par la finance.* Rev. Régulation.

Buchs, A., Petit, O., Roman, P., 2020. Can social ecological economics of water reinforce the "big tent"? *Ecol. Econ.* 169, 106553. https://doi.org/10.1016/j.ecolecon.2019.106553.

Bud, R., 1991. Biotechnology in the twentieth century. *Soc. Stud. Sci.* 21, 415–457. https://doi.org/10.1177/030631291021003002.

Bugge, M., Hansen, T., Klitkou, A., 2016. What is the bioeconomy? A review of the literature. *Sustainability* 8, 691. https://doi.org/10.3390/su8070691.

Cahen-Fourot, L., 2020. Contemporary capitalisms and their social relation to the environment. *Ecol. Econ.* 172, 106634. https://doi.org/10.1016/j.ecolecon.2020.106634.

Cecere, G., Corrocher, N., Gossart, C., Ozman, M., 2014. Lock-in and path dependence: an evolutionary approach to eco-innovations. *J. Evol. Econ.* 24, 1037–1065. https://doi.org/10.1007/s00191-014-0381-5.

Coriat, B., Orsi, F., Weinstein, O., 2003. Does biotech reflect a new science-based innovation regime? *Ind. Innov.* 10, 231–253. https://doi.org/10.1080/1366271032000141634.

D'Amato, D., Korhonen, J., Toppinen, A., 2019. Circular, green, and bio economy: how do companies in land-use intensive sectors align with sustainability concepts? *Ecol. Econ.* 158, 116–133. https://doi.org/10.1016/j.ecolecon.2018.12.026.

Douai, A., Montalban, M., 2012. Institutions and the environment: the case for a political socio-economy of environmental conflicts. *Camb. J. Econ.* 36, 1199–1220. https://doi.org/10.1093/cje/bes046.

Dupuy, R., Roman, P., Mougenot, B., 2015. Analyzing socio-environmental conflicts with a commonsian transactional framework: application to a mining conflict in Peru. *J. Econ. Issues* 49, 895–921. https://doi.org/10.1080/00213624.2015.1106200.

European Commission, 2012. *Innovating for sustainable growth: a bioeconomy for Europe* (Communication from the Commission to the European Parliament, the Council, the European Economic and Social Committee and the Committee of the Regions No. SWD(2012) 11 final).

European Commission, 2005. *New perspectives on the knowledge-based bioeconomy.*

Festel, G., 2010. Industrial biotechnology: market size, company types, business models, and growth strategies. *Ind. Biotechnol.* 6, 88–94. https://doi.org/10.1089/ind.2010.0006.

Foster, J.B., 2000. *Marx's ecology: materialism and nature.* Monthly Review Press.

Foster, J.B., Burkett, P., 2017. *Marx and the earth: an anti-critique*, Historical materialism. Haymarket Books.

Franceschini, S., Pansera, M., 2015. Beyond unsustainable eco-innovation: the role of narratives in the evolution of the lighting sector. *Technol. Forecast. Soc. Change* 92, 69–83. https://doi.org/10.1016/j.techfore.2014.11.007.

Geels, F.W., 2004. From sectoral systems of innovation to socio-technical systems. *Res. Policy* 33, 897–920. https://doi.org/10.1016/j.respol.2004.01.015.

Geels, F.W., 2002. Technological transitions as evolutionary reconfiguration processes: a multi-level perspective and a case study. *Res. Policy* 31, 1257–1274.

Geels, F.W, Raven, R., 2006. Non-linearity and expectations in niche-development trajectories: ups and downs in Dutch biogas development (1973–2003). *Technol. Anal. Strateg. Manag.* 18, 375–392. https://doi.org/10.1080/09537320600777143.

Georgescu-Roegen, N., 1975. Energy and economic myths. *South. Econ. J.* 41, 347. https://doi.org/10.2307/1056148.

Georgescu-Roegen, N., 1971. *The entropy law and the economic process.* Harvard University Press.

Giurca, A., 2018. Unpacking the network discourse: Actors and storylines in Germany's wood-based bioeconomy. *For. Policy Econ.* 101754. https://doi.org/10.1016/j.forpol.2018.05.009.

Holmgren, S., D'Amato, D., Giurca, A., 2020. Bioeconomy imaginaries: a review of forest-related social science literature. *Ambio.* https://doi.org/10.1007/s13280-020-01398-6.

Hoppmann, J., Anadon, L.D., Narayanamurti, V., 2020. Why matter matters: how technology characteristics shape the strategic framing of technologies. *Res. Policy* 49, 103882. https://doi.org/10.1016/j.respol.2019.103882.

IPCC, 2022. *Climate change 2022: Impacts, adaptation and vulnerability, summary for policymakers.* United Nations.

Lancaster, K.J., 1966. A new approach to consumer theory. *J. Polit. Econ.* 74, 132–157. https://doi.org/10.1086/259131.

Levidow, L., Birch, K., Papaioannou, T., 2013. Divergent paradigms of European agro-food innovation: the knowledge-based bio-economy (KBBE) as an R&D agenda. *Sci. Technol. Hum. Values* 38, 94–125. https://doi.org/10.1177/0162243912438143.

Levidow, L., Nieddu, M., Vivien, F.-D., Befort, N., 2019. Transitions towards a European bioeconomy: life sciences versus agroecology trajectories, in: Allaire, G., Daviron, B. (Eds.), *Ecology, capitalism and the new agricultural economy: the second great transformation.* Routledge, pp.181–203.

Malm, A., 2016. *Fossil capital: the rise of steam-power and the roots of global warming.* Verso.

Marchi, V.D., Maria, E.D., Micelli, S., 2013. Environmental strategies, upgrading and competitive advantage in global value chains. *Bus. Strategy Environ.* 22, 62–72. https://doi.org/10.1002/bse.1738.

Markard, J., Raven, R., Truffer, B., 2012. Sustainability transitions: an emerging field of research and its prospects. *Res. Policy* 41, 955–967. https://doi.org/10.1016/j.respol.2012.02.013.

Martinez-Alier, J., 2002. *The environmentalism of the poor: a study of ecological conflicts and valuation.* Edward Elgar.

Mayumi, K., 2001. *The origins of ecological economics: the bioeconomics of Georgescu-Roegen.* Routledge.

Mazzucato, M., 2021. *Mission economy: a moonshot guide to changing capitalism.* Harper Business.

Mazzucato, M., 2018. Mission-oriented innovation policies: challenges and opportunities. *Industrial and Corporate Change* 27, 803–815. https://doi.org/10.1093/icc/dty034.

Mazzucato, M., 2018. Mission-oriented innovation policies: challenges and opportunities. *Ind. Corp. Change* 27, 803–815. https://doi.org/10.1093/icc/dty034.

McCormick, K., Kautto, N., 2013. The bioeconomy in Europe: an overview. *Sustainability* 5, 2589–2608. https://doi.org/10.3390/su5062589.

Meadows, D.H., Club of Rome (Eds.), 1972. *The limits to growth: a report for the Club of Rome's project on the predicament of mankind.* Universe Books.

Mitchell, T., 2013. *Carbon democracy: political power in the age of oil.* Verso.

Montalban, M., Frigant, V., Jullien, B., 2019. Platform economy as a new form of capitalism: a Régulationist research programme. *Camb. J. Econ.* 43, 805–824. https://doi.org/10.1093/cje/bez017.

Morone, P., D'Amato, D., 2019. The role of sustainability standards in the uptake of bio-based chemicals. *Curr. Opin. Green Sustain. Chem.* 19, 45–49. https://doi.org/10.1016/j.cogsc.2019.05.003.

Mowery, D., Sampat, B., 2005. The Bayh-Dole Act of 1980 and university–industry technology transfer: A model for other OECD governments? *J. Technol. Transf.* 30, 115–127.

Nieddu, M., 2000. Science et dynamiques économiques, le cas des biopolymères. Sci. Société 87–104.

Nieddu, M., Vivien, F.-D., 2015. La chimie verte, une fausse rupture? Les trajectoires de la transition écologique. *Rev. Fr. Socio-Économie*, 2, 139–153.

O'Connor, J., 1991. On the two contradictions of capitalism. *Capital. Nat. Social.* 2, 107–109. https://doi.org/10.1080/10455759109358463.

O'Connor, J., 1988. Capitalism, nature, socialism a theoretical introduction. *Capital. Nat. Social.* 1, 11–38. https://doi.org/10.1080/10455758809358356.

OECD, 2017. *Biomass for a sustainable bioeconomy: technology and governance.* OECD.

OECD, 1996. *The knowledge-based economy.* No. OCDE/GD(96)102. OECD.

OECD International Futures Programme (Eds.), 2009. *The bioeconomy to 2030: designing a policy agenda.* OECD.

Oltra, V., Saint Jean, M., 2009. Variety of technological trajectories in low emission vehicles (LEVs): a patent data analysis. *J. Clean. Prod.* 17, 201–213. https://doi.org/10.1016/j.jclepro.2008.04.023.

Patermann, C., Aguilar, A., 2018. The origins of the bioeconomy in the European Union. *New Biotechnol.* 40, 20–24. https://doi.org/10.1016/j.nbt.2017.04.002.

Polanyi, K., 2001. *The great transformation: the political and economic origins of our time*, 2nd ed. Beacon Press.

Pyka, A., Cardellini, G., van Meijl, H., Verkerk, P.J., 2022. Modelling the bioeconomy: emerging approaches to address policy needs. *J. Clean. Prod.* 330, 129801. https://doi.org/10.1016/j.jclepro.2021.129801.

Sarrazin, F., Lecomte, J., 2016. Evolution in the Anthropocene. *Science* 351, 922–923. https://doi.org/10.1126/science.aad6756.

Schmidt, O., Padel, S., Levidow, L., 2012. The bio-economy concept and knowledge base in a public goods and farmer perspective. *Biobased Appl. Econ.* https://doi.org/10.13128/BAE-10770.

CSL_BIBLIOGRAPHY Schot, J., Steinmueller, W.E., 2018. Three frames for innovation policy: R&D, systems of innovation and transformative change. *Research Policy 47*, 1554–1567. https://doi.org/10.1016/j.respol.2018.08.011.

Schröder, E., Storm, S., 2020. Economic growth and carbon emissions: the road to "hothouse earth" is paved with good intentions. *Int. J. Polit. Econ.* 49, 153–173. https://doi.org/10.1080/08911916.2020.1778866.

Shaikh, A., 2016. *Capitalism: competition, conflict, crises.* Oxford University Press.

SIRA, 2013. *Bio-based and renewable industries for development and growth in Europe.* European Commission.

Sorrell, S., 2018. Explaining sociotechnical transitions: a critical realist perspective. *Res. Policy* 47, 1267–1282. https://doi.org/10.1016/j.respol.2018.04.008.

Spash, C.L., 2020. A tale of three paradigms: realising the revolutionary potential of ecological economics. *Ecol. Econ.* 169, 106518. https://doi.org/10.1016/j.ecolecon.2019.106518.

Spash, C.L., 2012. New foundations for ecological economics. *Ecol. Econ.* 77, 36–47. https://doi.org/10.1016/j.ecolecon.2012.02.004.

Svensson, O., Nikoleris, A., 2018. Structure reconsidered: towards new foundations of explanatory transitions theory. *Res. Policy* 47, 462–473. https://doi.org/10.1016/j.respol.2017.12.007.

Tickell, A., Peck, J.A., 1995. Social regulation after Fordism: regulation theory, neo-liberalism and the global-local nexus. *Econ. Soc.* 24, 357–386. https://doi.org/10.1080/03085149500000015.

Vadén, T., Lähde, V., Majava, A., Järvensivu, P., Toivanen, T., Hakala, E., Eronen, J.T., 2020. Decoupling for ecological sustainability: a categorisation and review of research literature. *Environ. Sci. Policy* 112, 236–244. https://doi.org/10.1016/j.envsci.2020.06.016.

Vink, E.T.H., Rábago, K.R., Glassner, D.A., Gruber, P.R., 2003. Applications of life cycle assessment to NatureWorks^{TM} polylactide (PLA) production. *Polym. Degrad. Stab.* 80, 403–419. https://doi.org/10.1016/S0141-3910(02)00372–00375.

Vivien, F.-D., Nieddu, M., Befort, N., Debref, R., Giampietro, M., 2019. The hijacking of the bioeconomy. *Ecol. Econ.* 159, 189–197. https://doi.org/10.1016/j.ecolecon.2019.01.027.

Wiedenhofer, D., Virág, D., Kalt, G., Plank, B., Streeck, J., Pichler, M., Mayer, A., Krausmann, F., Brockway, P., Schaffartzik, A., Fishman, T., Hausknost, D., Leon-Gruchalski, B., Sousa, T., Creutzig, F., Haberl, H., 2020. A systematic review of the evidence on decoupling of GDP, resource use and GHG emissions, part I: bibliometric and conceptual mapping. *Environ. Res. Lett.* 15, 063002. https://doi.org/10.1088/1748-9326/ab8429.

2 A political economy of the ecological transition towards a post-fossil economy

Chapter 1 proposes to approach the ecological transition from a mesoeconomic point of view in keeping with the various systemic approaches stemming from evolutionary economics (Dopfer, 2012; Dopfer et al., 2004; Malerba, 2002) but also from transition studies. Mesoeconomics, according to evolutionary authors, aims at studying the way in which groups of limited size are formed (Elsner et al., 2015) as a condition for the deployment of economic cooperation. In political economy, it seeks to study in contemporary societies the forms of differentiation of global space into spaces that make the tensions in capital accumulation sustainable. Cooperation is only one of the forms to make these tensions acceptable. They can be combined with other forms, competition and institutionalized domination, coopetition, etc. To account for these phenomena, it is necessary to have an analytical tool that is not *ex-post*, but that takes into account the intentions of the actors at the time of their actions (for example, following a strategy of substitution or incremental improvement). These intentions are structured by technological, economic or environmental expectations, based on the promises that are offered by new or old products or processes.

Moreover, these studies show that these meso-spaces are formed through differentiation either by the way a specific socio-economic problem is solved or by the use of a specific technology. Nevertheless, these spaces are populated by heterogeneous actors linked together either horizontally (Cohendet et al., 2020, 2014) or vertically in global value chains (Gereffi et al., 2005; Ponte, 2019). As a result, these spaces harbor various forms of business models, product types, etc. that actors seek to control. Finally, as indicated in the introduction, it is necessary that this analytical framework should be able to link past/present/future.

From these elements come the following questions, which this chapter aims to answer:

- What are the foundations of these spaces?
- What are the elements that contribute to the differentiation of these spaces?

DOI: 10.4324/9781003103011-2

- How can we account for and explain the decisions of actors in the present by linking their long-term trajectories and the formation of their expectations?

In order to answer these questions, this chapter puts forward the notion of ecological transition regimes defined as "semi-stable hierarchical configurations of material and immaterial relations between actors and artifacts" (Befort, 2020). The objective of this concept is to provide an analytical tool capable of identifying the regularities in the behavior of actors in this new phase of capitalism that is the ecological transition. This concept, at the crossroads of a discussion between evolutionary economics and transition studies, follows Spash's (Spash, 2020) call to develop a political economy of transition rooted in reality.

The first section discusses the epistemic foundations of ecological transition regimes by combining Multi-Level Perspective (MLP) and political economy. The second section highlights that these regimes rely on an infrastructure of common resources inherited from the past and projected by actors into the future. The third section outlines how these resources and regimes are framed by a dedicated institutional architecture. To do so, this study draws on regulationist research in terms of social blocks (Amable and Palombarini, 2009) and Beckert's micro sociology of capitalism (2016, 2013). The last section puts a particular focus on the place of innovation in ecological transition regimes.

1. Regimes at the heart of the transition

1.1 The relations between sustainability transition studies and the political economy

Sustainability transition studies emerged in the late 1990s, with strong support from the Dutch government, with the analytical and policy goal of examining and guiding the transition to sustainability (Köhler et al., 2019; Langeveld et al., 2012). This research stream is divided into sub-streams: technological innovation systems, niche strategic management and MLP. Despite the internal interest of the first two streams, MLP is the most interesting for our perspective.

The MLP model analyzes the multi-level transitions of socio-technical systems, formed by the dynamic interactions of a landscape level, a regime level and a niche level (Geels, 2020, 2014a, 2011; Geels and Schot, 2007; Smith et al., 2005, 2010). In this model, the niches are the locus of radical innovations. Socio-technical regimes are the level of established practices and rules constraining actors. Regimes are semi-stable hierarchical configurations of material and immaterial relations between actors and artifacts in which stakeholders compete to take control of these configurations by defining the boundaries of the regime (Befort, 2020). These two levels are embedded into an exogeneous socio-technical landscape.

The main characteristics of this research stream fit with political economy principles. First, MLP is partly rooted in evolutionary economics by sharing the key role of innovation institutions and organizations in the shaping of lock-ins on long-term trajectories. Second, although the question of the characterization of capitalism is not a structuring one, capitalism acts as an accepted background for the model (Feola, 2020). From this perspective, each component of the model (landscape, regime, niche) draws from the capitalist background in focusing the analysis on the regime level. This makes it the locus of capital accumulation and reproduction of the growth-oriented model (Vandeventer et al., 2019). The interest of the regime concept developed in MLP is to be much more flexible than sectors, especially pointing out the recomposition of sectoral frontiers in the transition process and the formation of new economics spaces which are not sectors. Thus, the notion of regime does not assume *ex-ante* a specific shape of the regime. The configuration of the regime may take the shape of a sector (the automotive sector), value chains (green gas production by farms for example) or exploration strategies by incumbent firms (Geels, 2011). Hence, the meso level is partially autonomous.

From a political economy perspective (Tickell and Peck, 1995) this evolution of the shape of regimes is illustrated by the evolution of innovation policies and their scope regarding their focus in the frame of capitalism stages (Schot and Steinmueller, 2018). Whereas linear innovation policies were typical of the Fordist period which focused on sectoral development, the post-Fordist era focused on networks and global value chains (Grabs and Ponte, 2019; Mondliwa et al., 2021). They aimed at networking regions, industries and public research in order to increase the competitive advantage of the firms. The emerging innovation policy generation now aims at transforming productive systems while assuming it has a mission to fulfill through mission-oriented policies. Nevertheless, there is a debate about the content of such policies regarding their mission, if they should target or not (green) growth and the role of innovations in such "transformative policies" (Foray, 2018; Giampietro et al., 2019).

Transitions occur under pressure coming from the landscape, destabilizing the socio-technical regime and open windows of opportunities for innovation niches that form transition paths whose challenge lies in their strategic positioning vis-à-vis the regime (Smith and Raven, 2012). The MLP has been used in a mechanical way which depicts the regime essentially as a monolithic barrier (Geels, 2014b). This conception leads to the denial of the role of actors and power relations in the functioning of regimes (Meadowcroft, 2011; Smith et al., 2005).

Outside periods of transition, regimes are dynamically stable, which does not mean that tensions disappear, but that they are stabilized by networks of institutions taking shape in both material and immaterial devices. During a period of transition, actors seek to position themselves in a new configuration in order to define its boundaries. To do so they produce narratives which translate expectations into promises to define and take control of material elements (calls for projects, programs, subsidies, obtaining monopolies, etc.) (Bauer, 2018; Franceschini and Pansera, 2015; Giurca, 2018). Since the regime is partially autonomous from the overall system, the question arises as to the extent to which the regime is autonomous.

The MLP model considers, in line with a neo-Schumpeterian interpretation of innovation, that innovation niches compete and pressure the regime. The regime acts as a selection environment towards innovation niches through the conjunction of actors' strategies to preserve their dominant position and the regime's institutions (Geels and Penna, 2015; Penna and Geels, 2012). The MLP researchers hypothesize that niches follow various transition paths ranging from conformity with the regime to its complete replacement. This view is supported by a second hypothesis that competition between niches will give rise to a dominant technological design that will eliminate diversity among niches, but also within the regime. It should be noted, however, that this hypothesis is coming under discussion. On the one hand, it has been shown that a regime can be characterized by the existence of sub-regimes (Befort, 2020). On the other hand, concerning the dynamics of transition, several transition pathways can follow one another in a transition period (Geels et al., 2016; Levidow and Upham, 2017).

1.2 Strategic behaviors in the ecological transition

The MLP has been criticized, both internally and by other currents in transition studies (notably by proponents of technological innovation systems), because of a supposedly mechanistic interpretation of transition processes, both on the side of the incumbents who would allow themselves to compete without reacting and on the side of the niches which are considered as necessarily sustainable since they are niches, as well as the supposedly automatic stability of the regime (Geels, 2011). This is where the role of agency, understood as the capacity of actors to impose and control the selection environment in order to maintain their hegemony, comes into play (Geels, 2014a, b; Kuokkanen et al., 2018). This hegemony manifests itself in particular through the imposition of shared and unquestioned expectations on other agents, with the exception of periods of crisis or transition (Geels and Schot, 2010; Hess, 2013; Smith et al., 2010). This struggle takes the form of heterogeneous coalitions bringing together firms, public actors and R&D. These coalitions draw on material and immaterial resources to structure the shape of the regime (Kuokkanen et al., 2018).

The relative freedom of action of actors leads to the emergence of a variety of possible responses that depend on the strategic positioning of actors and their knowledge base (Penna and Geels, 2012). While the structure of the regime resulting from the transition phase is the issue at stake in the mobilization of actors, those actors also mobilize innovation niches, either to promote innovations that are favorable to their vision of the transformation of the regime, for example through integration strategies, or by investing in a variety of competing niches, or by establishing themselves as multi-level actors who constitute niches themselves (Berggren et al., 2015; Jørgensen, 2012).

This strategy of constituting themselves as multi-level actors also leads these actors to form coalitions aimed at steering visions of the "macro" future in a direction that is compatible with their vision of regimes. (Bakker, 2014; Geels and Raven, 2006; Ruef and Markard, 2010; van Lente and Bakker, 2010). Thus, major actors of contemporary capitalism regularly participate in greenwashing sessions at international summits during which they present their vision of the transition. These actors, although criticized for their greenwashing, are very much involved in structuring the shape of the ecological transition. Therefore, the process of ecological transition can be understood as a dialectical process between change and reproduction (Sorrell, 2018; Svensson and Nikoleris, 2018). Actors must arbitrate between opportunities for change and their capacity to change, under the constraint of their institutional environment but also of the material and immaterial resources available to firms (Musiolik et al., 2020). Thus, the MLP shows that actors are caught up in three types of activities constituting the transition process: the production of visions of the future intended to orient the shape of the regime, the development of institutions aimed at structuring the mode of operation of the regime, and innovation activities aimed at adapting the firm's activity to the emerging regime.

1.3 A political economy analysis of the multi-level perspective

The MLP proposes a vision of transition processes centered on the recomposition of coalitions around a variety of technologies that structure a regime. From a political economy perspective, the regime is thus the level at which the renewal of forms of capital accumulation is at stake in the transition. The question then arises as to the form that the regime will take and the relations that this regime has with the landscape, the niches and other regimes. Regarding the form of the regime, the MLP is silent on how visions of the future are articulated with the economic models of the actors. Similarly, these visions of the future are not linked to specific institutional forms. Namely, in the MLP, visions of the future are not the product of a materiality of actors' interests, contrary to what has been argued elsewhere. (Beckert, 2016; Vivien et al., 2019). Thus, the MLP is lacking a theory of how actors (1) actually try to control and achieve defined visions of the future, (2) how these visions compete, and (3) how they are implemented in institutions.

This is because MLP overlooks the conflictual dimension of the relations between actors, unlike political economy which makes it a catalyst for change. This dimension is mentioned as one of the elements of the dynamics of transition. Thus, the emergence of institutions is analyzed, under the inspiration of neo-institutional theory, from the angle of the morphogenetic evolution of networks in the transition process (Fuenfschilling and Truffer, 2014; Geels, 2020). Denying the conflictual dimension of the dynamics of transition leads to the hypothesis that the coalitions of actors are monolithic and are not themselves subjected to conflicts of interest. Moreover, the MLP does not provide any appreciation of the hierarchy of institutions or the form of their articulation with existing or emerging economic forms, either within or outside the regime, or with past trajectories.

Finally, the MLP hypothesizes the emergence of a *dominant design* that signals the end of the transition process. This assumption is problematic from theoretical, empirical and political points of view. From the theoretical point of view, it means that the transition movement is in reality a movement of destruction which dismantles the variety that is constitutive of the transition period. Consequently, a stabilized regime, i.e. one that is not in transition, would have seen its questioning disappear entirely. However, analyzing the transition in terms of a search for hegemony points out a dialectic relation, hence a conflictual one, and not a monolithic structure (Bourdieu, 2005). Such a hypothesis is therefore contradictory with the idea, which is adopted here, of regimes that are dynamically stable but dominated by a coalition of actors. Empirically, the case of agriculture shows that despite the hegemonic pressure of the dominant coalition, diversity is maintained. Thus, the development of organic agriculture from the 1960s onwards is consubstantial with the development of productivist agriculture (Allaire and Daviron, 2019). The contemporary debate over the appropriation of the "organic" label by productivist agriculture illustrates this struggle between dominant and dominated actors to control the form of the regime and ensure the sustainable maintenance of a diversity that is constitutive of the contemporary agricultural regime. (Allen and Kovach, 2000; Desquilbet et al., 2018; Guthman, 2004). From the point of view of public policy, asserting that a dominant design is necessary implies selecting the best technology (Langeveld et al., 2012). This is problematic because (1) it poses the problem of the selection criterion, and it is impossible to calculate *a priori* the increasing returns to adoption, and (2) Jevons' paradox points to the risks of the rebound effects of a technology (Giampietro and Mayumi, 2008).

Thus, the transition can be described as a multi-dimensional conflict (Douai and Montalban, 2012) between coalitions of actors aiming to take control of a socio-technical regime, the form of which is one of the issues of this conflict. This conflict is driven by coalitions that draw on a variety of material and immaterial resources to impose their interests on the regime. As the regime acts as a selection environment, the actors also compete to impose their selection criteria. This conflict is partially autonomous from the overall structure of the mode of production and the dominant forms of accumulation in the sense that the form of the regime (sector, value chain, local systems of production, etc.) is influenced by the overall dynamics of capitalism.

Consequently, the political economy of the ecological transition must analyze the transition by taking into account (1) the form of the division of labor, (2) the coordination of this division of labor, and (3) the resources mobilized by the actors. From a temporal point of view, this perspective is threefold, since it must take into account the past trajectories of the actors, their present situation and the way in which they form expectations about their future. Thus, this study replaces the hypothesis of the emergence of a dominant design by the force of markets with the following dynamic. The transition is a dynamic of exploration of technological variety framed by institutional arrangements that the actors seek to control. The eventual reduction of this variety is then the product of the struggle.

Therefore, the transition phase, at the meso level, can be characterized as the conjunction between a phase of institutional change and transformation of production and innovation, carried out by actors from heterogeneous spaces. These spaces can be geographical, as shown by the research that seeks to apply a spatial perspective to transition processes (Hansen and Coenen, 2015). These spaces are also localized spaces in the division of labor, whether they are value chains (Birch, 2008), sectors or systems of innovation (Antonelli, 2008; Gawer, 2014) or innovation ecosystems (Cohendet et al., 2020). Thus, actors deploy transition strategies at these different levels. The discussion between the political economy of capitalism and the MLP raises three questions:

- What is the nature of the material and immaterial resources that actors mobilize to build their economic space in the ecological transition?
- How do visions of the future and economic models fit into the ecological transition?
- What are the dynamics of the emergence of institutions situated in the ecological transition?

2. From productive heritages to common-pool resources as a support for capitalist accumulation

The previous section aimed to highlight the key role of the notion of regime in capturing the dynamics of the emergence of new economic spaces at the meso level, through a discussion between the political economy of capitalism and MLP. In this framework, not only do actors not act solely at the level of the firm, but it is in their interest to seek to act on the organization of change to ensure their reproduction. The dynamics of change are thus constituted by a dialectic of reproduction and the production of novelty. From then on, this dynamic involves the identities of the actors (White, 2008). Indeed, it is possible to trace the evolution of a certain number of old companies that have sought to reinvent themselves during their long existence. For example, in the case of energy, it is likely that current oil companies will replace their majority activity of oil production with the production of renewable energies. These companies will then have maintained themselves as such (British Petroleum will continue to exist, for example), but the core of their activity will have been transformed from the production of fossil energy to the production of renewable energy. As evolutionary work shows, innovation is structured by the body of knowledge accumulated in the past. From a political economy point of view, as well as from a modern evolutionary economy point of view (Nelson et al., 2018) it is a set of resources that will guide the production of novelties.

2.1 From productive heritages to common-pool resources as a support for accumulation

To account for this work of selecting ancient resources structuring the production of novelties, I propose to mobilize the notion of *productive heritages*. Modernity had kept us away from the idea of heritages (and for researchers from the interest of working on them), because it was a paradigm in which progress made a certain number of objects and production *processes* obsolete, where there was no need to preserve them (for instance, the Formica table replacing the old oak table of our grandparents). The scientific and technical progress acted in modernity by invalidating heritages. The notion of heritage is ambivalent. It designates the transmission of both individual property and objects, which constitute an inheritance from the past, that tradition has sought to remove from market relations, for they are part of the common good. It is this duality that is fruitful because productive heritages can be defined as a set of resources attached to an individual or a group translating its identity, which is constituted by an instituted set of assets, transmitted by the past, and selected in the present as the actors believe that they have a value for the future (Barrère, 2007; Calvo-Mendieta et al., 2017; Nieddu, 2007).

Productive heritages are resources that are sought after for their collective value, which must be shared in order to exist, and that are considered a legacy to justify the effort to preserve them in phases of uncertainty regarding their ability to produce new objects at acceptable market conditions (Nieddu et al., 2010). Then, these heritages take the form of common pool resources in the sense of Potts (2019). From this point of view, innovation niches constitute common pool resources since, by definition, they are preserved from the market calculation because of their inability to pass the validation tests imposed by the regime.

These common pool resources are carried out by communities and allow them to project themselves into the future in a dynamic of reproduction through the production of novelties. These resources can be intangible resources that allow for learning between users and producers, shared coordination tools as well as qualification and recognition mechanisms (Antonelli, 2006; Antonelli and Patrucco, 2016; Cowan and Foray, 1997; Hess and Ostrom, 2011; Ostrom, 1990). These resources are also material, such as technological infrastructures or natural resources (Boisvert and Vivien, 2012). Thus, the regimes are carried by conflicting communities whose existence is based on the (re)production of common-pool resources structuring productive heritages transmitted to the future.

2.2 Natural resources, division of labor and institutionalization of regimes

From an ecological economics perspective inspired by Georgescu-Roegen, Giampietro (2019) questions the issue of circularity in the bioeconomy. The author stresses that economic systems are inscribed in natural systems with which they maintain relations in the form of flows of matter and energy circulating:

- from the biosphere to social systems (in the form of natural resources in particular)
- within social systems (in the form of products, capital, etc.)
- from social systems to the biosphere (e.g. in the form of effluents and waste).

From the point of view of the economics of ecological transition, the organization of these flows of matter is the result of a process of emergence and structuring. These flows are instituted and the division of labor is organized along these material flows. From the point of view of oil value chains, offshore platforms are infrastructures for the transformation of material flows extracted and then transformed within global value chains. Thus, in the context of growth-driven capitalism, firms are constrained to expand and intensify their capacity to extract natural resources, while at the same time facing (1) their potential depletion, and (2) social contestation over the possibility of these flows. The mechanisms of resistance to change described by Penna and Geels (2012) show that these infrastructures of transformation of material, the related techniques and the natural resources constitute common-pool resources.

Therefore, the regimes can be understood as being stabilized by a set of infrastructures, production techniques and forms of relationship with nature that guide the organization of innovation and production. The articulation of all these resources constituted as such by the actors then forms instituted productive heritages. Thus, there emerges standards of treatment of the material, organization of the production, norms of productivity, etc. (Beckert, 2019; Boisvert and Vivien, 2012; Ponte, 2016; Salais and Storper, 1992).

3. Institutions and ecological transition

3.1 Institutions as rules of the game

The political economy of capitalism shares with MLP the recognition of the role of institutions in the structuring and functioning of regimes of innovation and production. In these streams, the identification of institutions coupled with the socio-economic practices of actors makes it possible to determine the form and functioning of regimes. Political economy defines institutions as "the rules of the game", that is, the formal and informal rules that apply to actors in a space (Amable and Palombarini, 2009). From this perspective, institutions are seen as (1) expressing the interests of a dominant social group, and (2) the result of a compromise between the dominant and the dominated social group. Thus, in defining the rules to be followed, institutions also participate in transcribing visions of the future. The articulation of institutions takes the form of an institutional architecture characterized by a hierarchy between institutions and a complementarity between these institutions (Amable, 2016; Boyer, 2005; Crouch et al., 2005). Some institutions are considered by the dominant actors to be of greater importance because they are the ones that most guarantee the preservation of their interests. Furthermore, complementarity indicates that the presence of several institutions produces reinforcing positive effects that would not have existed if these institutions had not been present together. These institutions participate in defining shared norms, expectations and rules that make it possible to confront the two uncertainties of capitalism – uncertainty about production and uncertainty about market opportunities (Boyer and

Freyssenet, 2005; Jullien and Smith, 2011). In the context of the ecological transition, it is necessary to add a third uncertainty about the nature, size and legitimacy of material flows.

These institutions are the product of political work by allied social groups who, in order to define the boundaries of their space, engage in a political work of meaning-making that Jullien and Smith (2011) call *problematization*. The actors define a productive problem to be solved and provide answers to it, thus helping to generate shared imaginaries. The actors respond to these problems with technical devices that help legitimize the problem. Therefore, these responses establish rules that constrain the actors but also open up opportunities outside these rules. These rules are set out and defended by social groups structured by alliances (Jørgensen, 2012; Jullien and Smith, 2008). These alliances can act at different levels but also at different scales. Therefore, alliances can vary according to the arenas observed.

3.2 Five building blocks to analyze the emergence and evolution of ecological transition regimes

To analyze the processes by which the ecological transition is structured, the analytical framework developed here is based on the four building blocks that make up the micro-foundations of capitalism (commoditization, innovation, competition, access to capital), to which I add that of the relationship to nature (Beckert, 2016, 2013).

Commoditization describes the process by which goods and services become commodities, i.e. goods that can be traded on a market. From this perspective, products are defined as a set of attributes that actors must combine to respond to external (regulatory, demand, etc.) and internal (mark-ups, productivity objectives, etc.) pressures within the framework partially determined by the regime. In this process, it is necessary that the functionalities of the products should be socially recognized. To achieve this, the *market devices*, which are "material and discursive assemblages that intervene in the construction of *markets*", intervene in the process (Muniesa et al., 2007). They translate actors' subjectivity into materiality and calculable devices. Thus, accounting or even labels and life cycle analyses of products participate in creating markets (Gregson et al., 2013; Miller and O'Leary, 2007). In return, consumers are waiting for an expected use value.

Competition, in the process of ecological transition, goes through a double process. On the one hand, it is traditionally a confrontation between actors to capture demand to increase profits. To do this, firms use a variety of strategies such as price reduction, innovation, differentiation or entry barriers (Mondliwa et al., 2021). On the other hand, as pointed out by socio-economists, competitive strategies can be construed as strategies for mastering niches inside a market, within which narratives relating to the "functionalities" of products are developed (Beckert, 2019). Thus, within a niche, the dominant actors manage to impose a combination of functionalities linking product quality and productivity, technologies used and marketing methods expressed by narratives that translate the convention of this niche, leading to situations of oligopoly. As a result, competition between actors is expressed both in the attempt to control a niche and in the attempt to control a market – the niche may or may not cover the whole market.

Innovation is now a key dimension of corporate strategy in capitalism. Indeed, the production of novelties allows the organization of differentiation strategies enabling the continuation of growth. Technical and organizational change is localized and relies on the partial knowledge of heterogeneous actors (Antonelli, 2008; Langlois, 2003). In the perspective of the formation of new spaces, the actors are inscribed in heterogeneous knowledge bases. To innovate, actors must therefore be able to appropriate external knowledge that must be hybridized with their knowledge. Innovations for the ecological transition can be analyzed as innovations whose promoters promise that they will have a positive environmental impact. Nevertheless, work on eco-innovation proposes to question the way products fit or not into the dominant paradigm, which introduces the distinction between drop-in innovations and functional innovations. The former aims to maintain the existing paradigm, while the latter aims to fulfill equivalent functionalities favoring low-tech and degrowth options, instead of promising sustainability without changes thanks to technological change. The question raised here is to determine whether innovations that claim to allow the ecological transition are actually substituting polluting products, or whether they are managed as complementary products in business strategies.

The fourth building block is access to capital, particularly through credit. This can take different forms: it can be credit and capital obtained on the financial markets or through investment funds. For example, large investment funds are now turning significantly to agricultural markets. Similarly, the financing of biotechnologies illustrates the formation of a *finance-led* innovation regime based on the raising of funds by knowledge-based start-ups structured on the basis of technico-economic promises of technological disruption (Coriat et al., 2003). Access to capital can also be the result of alliance strategies between incumbents and start-ups (participation of incumbents in start-ups, joint ventures, etc.) (Festel, 2010; Festel et al., 2012; Potts, 2019). Finally, actors also find sources of funding in regional, national or international calls for projects. The logic of calls for projects helps to guide access to capital under the condition that innovation projects are in line with the visions of the future transcribed in these calls for projects (Kenis et al., 2009).

The last constitutive dimension of ecological transition regimes is that of access to natural resources. The economics of ecological transition, following ecological economics, considers that economic systems are embedded in social systems, which themselves interact with the biosphere. Consequently, access to natural resources must be mediated by specific institutions that organize the conditions of ownership, access and reproduction or not of natural resources (Vatn, 2005). These institutions result from conflicts between actors organized on a continuum between free access that can lead to the depletion of resources and the strict prohibition of access (Douai and Montalban, 2012; Ostrom, 1990). It is in this context that rules which are supported by private actors, NGOs and public authorities are emerging. However, these rules of access to natural resources are based on evaluation systems that reflect contradictory values. In addition, actors must manage the use of new resources, the creation of new flows (incoming or outgoing in the case of recycling) and also the possible disappearance of traditional material flows.

4. Innovation and ecological transition[1]

Often neglected in political economy research, the issue of innovation is nevertheless a key factor in contemporary capitalism as shown by evolutionary studies (Nelson et al., 2018). Therefore, this section aims to put forward a political economy reading of the ecological transition of innovation strategies.

4.1 Drop-in vs. functional innovations

Eco-innovations are considered a key solution to climate change since they are supposed to increase efficiency and stimulate green growth while having a positive impact on the environment (Barbieri et al., 2016; Cecere et al., 2014; de Jesus and Mendonça, 2018; Faucheux and Nicolaï, 2011; Markard et al., 2012; Popp et al., 2011). However, ecological economics is divided between two positions on eco-innovation.

On the one hand, the technology-enthusiastic view considers eco-innovation mainly from the standpoint of innovation economics. It considers eco-innovation development in different but not exclusive ways, namely, as a driver (Triguero et al., 2013), a diffusion (Gilli et al., 2014), a consumer-awareness problem (Coad et al., 2009), or a policy issue (Bergek and Berggren, 2014; Ghisetti and Pontoni, 2015). On the other hand, a stream of ecological economists who adopt a strong, systemic sustainability perspective have developed critical arguments regarding innovation or eco-innovation, which they understand as substitutes in a world of relative, as opposed to pure, scarcity (Daly, 1991). They doubt that eco-innovations exist, will be enough to achieve sustainability or could be properly defined (Kallis et al., 2013; Kemp, 2010; van den Bergh, 2011). Inspired by Illich, they criticize technology (Martinez-Alier et al., 2010) and consider eco-innovation as a way of instrumentalizing a technological myth to escape the reality of planetary boundaries while risking rebound effects (Giampietro and Mayumi, 2015; Spash, 2020).

One way to move beyond this debate has been to try and find the "right definition" of eco-innovation in order to be able to choose which innovations to support (Belis-Bergouignan et al., 2004; Cecere et al., 2014; Faucheux and Nicolaï, 2011; Rennings, 2000; Rennings et al., 2013). Four criticisms may be leveled at these attempts to find the "right definition". First, there are no eco-innovations *per se*, because there aren't any technologies with no impact on the environment (Daly,

1991; Kemp, 2010). Second, classifications of "eco-innovations" done by institutions such as OECD or WIPO (Barbieri et al., 2020) include technologies acknowledged as loosely sustainable such as biofuels or carbon capture and storage. Third, even if technologies may be sustainable, they may generate rebound effects (Font Vivanco et al., 2016; Giampietro and Mayumi, 2008). Fourth, one could argue that technologies should be compared regarding sustainability indicators. This leads to new problems since (1) the sustainability argument is a part of the promise, and (2) indicators such as life cycle analysis are loosely comparable and depend on the technologies and choices of criteria (Vatn, 2005).

Consequently, the definition of eco-innovations is an institutional construction carried out by actors seeking to give meaning to a type of innovation that they wish to see accepted as "sustainable". From this viewpoint, eco-innovations are a part of the contemporary evolution of capitalism being at the forefront of dominant political agendas because of the expectation that they will achieve ecological transition (EIO, 2013; OECD, 2019, 2017, 2010). If there can be no "good definition" of eco-innovation, the need to identify innovation policy principles for sustainability transition towards a post-growth economy subsists. To overcome this issue, innovation may be analyzed as "drop-in innovations" and "functional innovations". The former are innovations aiming to maintain the existing paradigm. If the notion of "drop-in" innovation was initially used in green chemistry to designate chemicals of bio-based origin with a chemical structure identical to that of oil-based products (Bozell and Petersen, 2010), I propose to interpret it as an innovation presented as sustainable and whose objective is the reproduction of the dominant paradigm. The latter are innovations aiming to fulfill equivalent functionalities, from a systemic perspective, favoring low-tech and degrowth options, instead of promising *status quo* sustainability, thanks to technological change.

4.2 Techno-economic promises and their properties

"Techno-economic promises" are expectations set into motion through resource allocation in order to reach a specific vision of the future regarding the socio-economic benefits of technological development. They help to "guide activities and define roles, provide legitimization, and attract interest and credit" (Joly, 2010, p.205). Actors use promises to spread their expectations, and frame both public policy and their competitors (Geels and Verhees, 2011). As such, promises are not just rhetorical devices; they lead to economic activities such as R&D and innovation.

Promises have three properties: legitimacy, credibility, and irreversibility (Joly, 2010). First, promises need to create legitimacy for technology, through positive expectations linked to technological change. This legitimacy should be accompanied by a feeling of urgency. In the case of eco-innovations, promises are about their ability to solve the ecological transition through the stimulation of growth (OECD, 2019, 2017).

Second, a promise needs to be credible. It requires the recognition of various actors: laboratories, governments, research programs and funders. To obtain this recognition, actors produce market devices (see above for a definition of market devices) (Muniesa et al., 2007). They translate actors' subjectivity into materiality and calculable devices. In the case of techno-economic promises, they may take the form of publications in top journals, property rights, such as patents, or prestigious research grants giving credibility to the promise.

Third, promises create irreversibility. Their translation into market devices allows actors to attract material and immaterial resources making the object of the promises exist (as demonstration objects for example), and actors act *as if* the outcomes of the promises already existed (Beckert, 2016). The exhaustion of such attracted resources can then generate lock-ins on specific technological trajectories (David, 1985). Promises in turn become coordination devices imposing norms on the technological trajectories to follow. If techno-economic promises are material and rhetorical devices about future outcomes, they are also embedded into existing past trajectories (Arthur, 1989; Liebowitz and Margolis, 1995; Rosenberg, 1976). Hence, promises involve the past, the present and the future.

4.3 The promises and functionalities of eco-innovations

The previous section addressed techno-economic promises from an economization view inspired by economic sociology and political economy adopting an *ex-ante* view (Beckert, 2016; Borup et al., 2006; Muniesa et al., 2007). This approach considers that actors have to articulate existing trajectories, mostly those into which they are embedded, as well as their strategies, and they must cope with the materiality of their products (Georgescu-Roegen, 1971).

Authors from eco-innovation literature share commonalities with this position (Arfaoui et al., 2014; Belis-Bergouignan et al., 2004; Oltra and Saint Jean, 2009). In this framework, an eco-innovation is defined in relation to its break with the unsustainable paradigm. Following Lancaster (1966), products are considered as a set of attributes. Firms have to combine these attributes to answer external (regulatory, demand, etc.) and internal (mark-ups, productivity objectives, etc.) pressures (Cecere et al., 2014). In the case of eco-innovation, if the product is to be developed and adopted, a positive environmental impact is expected, in addition to productivity or product performances. Firms may choose to embed their product in the dominant paradigm through incremental innovation, or to move outside the dominant paradigm, producing radical innovations (Dosi, 1988).

This has three consequences for the economics of promises. First, there are two types of functionalities. On the one hand, there are product functionalities, which are the techno-economic attributes of the product. It means that actors choose, under the constraint of their available knowledge, between various possible combinations of attributes. On the other hand, there are expected functionalities. These are functionalities that the consumer (whether an intermediary or a final customer) expects to experience as they consume the product, i.e., an expected use value. Promises are about the ability of product attributes to satisfy expected functionalities. Eco-innovation promises pertain to product functionalities, and to the way the product is consumed. Hence, products will be evaluated by consumers (whether intermediate or end users) with respect to these expected functionalities.

Second, in the dynamics of R&D, actors choose to break lock-ins on specific functionalities, within the limits of their bounded rationality. Promises are about their ability to unlock, and the outcome of such unlocking, which will consequently be evaluated. But promises, by pointing out desirable outcomes, highlight lock-ins that need to be addressed. Thus, innovation processes are oriented toward the lock-ins blocking the development of the product as it is promised.

Third, innovation studies consider lock-ins as emergent outcomes of a set of interacting systemic features resulting from past historical incidents, and which are mostly an *ex-post* and exogenous explanation of lock-ins (Arthur, 2011, 1989). The economization analysis of promises departs from this analysis advancing an *ex-ante* explanation. On the one hand, actors choose between possible techno-economic combinations depending on the trajectories they belong to. This influences the knowledge they can use and the type of demand expectations actors can address with their products (Gebauer et al., 2012). In other words, actors have the lock-ins of their trajectory. On the other hand, actors produce narratives promising to unlock their lock-ins to satisfy an expected functionality in their attempt to impose framings. This creates systemic barriers to alternatives. Lock-ins are not just technological, they also lock in a paradigm (Unruh, 2002, 2000). Hence, the development of promises is about the development of credibility and legitimacy of unlocking lock-ins which are both social and technological, i.e., participating in ecological transition, along with localized technological progress (Antonelli, 2009).

4.4 Functionalities and the cycle of eco-innovation promises

Promises follow a dynamic cycle called the "hype cycle" (Fenn and Raskino, 2008), during which actors develop and try to maintain their promises. This cycle follows several phases (see Figure 2.1).

The first period is a (re)discovery period, during which knowledge is developed, technological developments are anticipated, and positive expectations may be formed (Markard and Truffer, 2008). The period of promise formulation follows the initial period of discovery and formation of the knowledge base. During this second promise formulation phase, actors get involved at three interconnected levels in "coalitions for innovation" (Antonelli, 2009; Truffer et al., 2008). First, they seize and problematize a social issue at the global level framing lower levels, and acting as a fictional imaginary producing a shared mind-set, values and visions for the future. Thus, it explains why most eco-innovation promises share a common narrative on their ability to solve climate issues. Second, these expectations are translated at the meso level into agendas with foresight exercises (van Lente and Bakker, 2010). These agendas act as a selection environment, producing techno-economic requirements

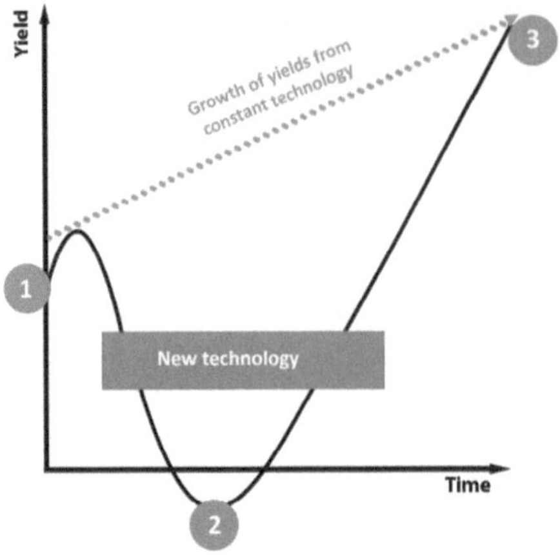

1. **Imitation**: laboratory yields close to industrial yields

2. **Experiment**: "hopeful monstrosities" (Ravent and Geels, 2010); strong expectation (and so promises) of growing yield of adoption; the commitment to the trajectory leads to its maintenance while the results do not reach the initial objectives

3. **Exploitation**: growth of yields and organization of the diffusion of innovation, especially through the formation of agreements aimed at organizing the coordination of the division of labor

Figure 2.1 A stylized representation of early promises cycles

regarding products' functionalities (types of uses, expected production costs, etc.), which orient local R&D (firms or research laboratories) towards specific promised functions. Third, at the local R&D level, actors develop their products based on the knowledge they have access to, the product functionalities they can manage, and the expected functionality they want to deliver.

After the hype, a disappointment phase occurs, where initial promises are unsatisfied (Ruef and Markard, 2010). More specifically, actors identify hurdles on commercialization, design, demand and technical specifications. Nevertheless, this phase is temporary, and is followed by the formulation of new promises, which are potentially embedded into new frames and new ways of considering the technology (Borup et al., 2006).

The theoretical framework depicts promises as an economization process of actors formulating promises about their ability to unlock lock-ins, based on the attempt to fulfill expected functionalities with the product functionalities they control, under techno-economic constraints (the knowledge they master, existing production infrastructures, etc.). This mechanism of fulfilling expectations is hypothesized as the core explanation to understanding turning points, and how actors rebuild their credibility in the cycle of promises. Thus, actors need to draw into their existing resources in order to rebuild their credibility in the disappointment phase.

5. Conclusion

This chapter lays the foundations of a political economy of ecological transition around the central concept of ecological transition regimes. These regimes are formed by the conjunction of an architecture of rules and a set of economic practices. These regimes express the multiple boundaries of the emerging economic spaces in which the actors operate. Therefore, actors are located in a topology of rules, geographically and in time. In order to exist, these regimes are structured by productive heritages that are qualified by the actors as resources to be preserved for their future value. The resources constituting these productive heritages are common immaterial resources (knowledge, know-how, etc.) and material resources. The regimes thus express complex forms of institutionalization/de-institutionalization of relations to natural resource flows between ecosystems and socio-economic systems. Consequently, these regimes also emphasize relationships to nature which are inherited from the past and challenged in these regimes. These resources are translated into assets and RPCs through the organization of the division of labor, the forms of which can be innovation systems, value chain segments, etc. These regimes, because they express regularities in a conflict of institutionalization and de-institutionalization of relations, are thus contested, and it is this contestation that makes them dynamic.

Note

1 This section is reprinted from Befort, The promises of drop-in vs. functional innovations: The case of bioplastics, *Ecological Economics 181*, p.106886, Copyright 2021, with permission from Elsevier.

Bibliography

Allaire, G., Daviron, B. (Eds.), 2019. *Ecology, capitalism and the new agricultural economy: the second great transformation*, Critical food studies. Routledge.

Allen, P., Kovach, M., 2000. The capitalist composition of organic: the potential of markets in fulfilling the promise of organic agriculture. *Agric. Hum. Values* 17, 221–232.

Amable, B., 2016. Institutional complementarities in the dynamic comparative analysis of capitalism. *J. Institutional Econ.* 12, 79–103. https://doi.org/10.1017/S1744137415000211.

Amable, B., Palombarini, S., 2009. A neorealist approach to institutional change and the diversity of capitalism. *Socio-Econ. Rev.* 7, 123–143. https://doi.org/10.1093/ser/mwn018.

Antonelli, C., 2009. The economics of innovation: from the classical legacies to the economics of complexity. *Econ. Innov. New Technol.* 18, 611–646. https://doi.org/10.1080/10438590802564543.

Antonelli, C., 2008. *Localised technological change: towards the economics of complexity*. Routledge.

Antonelli, C., 2006. The business governance of localized knowledge: an information economics approach for the economics of knowledge. *Ind. Innov.* 13, 227–261. https://doi.org/10.1080/13662710600858118.

Antonelli, C., Patrucco, P.P., 2016. Organizational innovations, ICTs and knowledge governance: the case of platforms, in: Bauer, J.M., Latzer, M. (Eds.), *Handbook on the economics of the internet*. Edward Elgar Publishing, pp.323–343.

Arfaoui, N., Brouillat, E., Saint Jean, M., 2014. Policy design and technological substitution: investigating the REACH regulation in an agent-based model. *Ecol. Econ.* 107, 347–365. https://doi.org/10.1016/j.ecolecon.2014.08.013.

Arthur, W.B., 2011. *The nature of technology: what it is and how it evolves.* Free Press.

Arthur, W.B., 1989. Competing technologies, increasing returns, and lock-in by historical events. *Econ. J.* 99, 116–131. https://doi.org/10.2307/2234208.

Bakker, S., 2014. Actor rationales in sustainability transitions: interests and expectations regarding electric vehicle recharging. *Environ. Innov. Soc. Transit.* 13, 60–74. https://doi.org/10.1016/j.eist.2014.08.002.

Barbieri, N., Ghisetti, C., Gilli, M., Marin, G., Nicolli, F., 2016. A survey of the literature on environmental innovation based on main path analysis: a survey of the literature on environmental innovation. *J. Econ. Surv.* 30, 596–623. https://doi.org/10.1111/joes.12149.

Barbieri, N., Marzucchi, A., Rizzo, U., 2020. Knowledge sources and impacts on subsequent inventions: do green technologies differ from non-green ones? *Res. Policy* 49, 103901. https://doi.org/10.1016/j.respol.2019.103901.

Barrère, C., 2007. Vers une théorie économique substantiviste du patrimoine. *Econ. Appliquée* LX, 7–30.

Bauer, F., 2018. Narratives of biorefinery innovation for the bioeconomy: conflict, consensus, or confusion? *Environ. Innov. Soc. Transit.* 28, 96–107. https://doi.org/10.1016/j.eist.2018.01.005.

Beckert, J., 2019. Markets from meaning: quality uncertainty and the intersubjective construction of value. *Camb. J. Econ.* https://doi.org/10.1093/cje/bez035.

Beckert, J., 2016. *Imagined futures: fictional expectations and capitalist dynamics.* Harvard University Press.

Beckert, J., 2013. Capitalism as a system of expectations: toward a sociological microfoundation of political economy. *Polit. Soc.* 41, 323–350. https://doi.org/10.1177/0032329213493750.

Befort, N., 2020. Going beyond definitions to understand tensions within the bioeconomy: the contribution of sociotechnical regimes to contested fields. *Technol. Forecast. Soc. Change* 153, 119923. https://doi.org/10.1016/j.techfore.2020.119923.

Belis-Bergouignan, M.-C., Oltra, V., Saint Jean, M., 2004. Trajectories towards clean technology: example of volatile organic compound emission reductions. *Ecol. Econ.* 48, 201–220. https://doi.org/10.1016/j.ecolecon.2003.09.010.

Bergek, A., Berggren, C., 2014. The impact of environmental policy instruments on innovation: a review of energy and automotive industry studies. *Ecol. Econ.* 106, 112–123. https://doi.org/10.1016/j.ecolecon.2014.07.016.

Berggren, C., Magnusson, T., Sushandoyo, D., 2015. Transition pathways revisited: established firms as multi-level actors in the heavy vehicle industry. *Res. Policy* 44, 1017–1028. https://doi.org/10.1016/j.respol.2014.11.009.

Birch, K., 2008. Alliance-driven governance: applying a global commodity chains approach to the UK biotechnology industry. *Econ. Geogr.* 84, 83–103.

Boisvert, V., Vivien, F.-D., 2012. Towards a political economy approach to the convention on biological diversity. *Camb. J. Econ.* 36, 1163–1179. https://doi.org/10.1093/cje/bes047.

Borup, M., Brown, N., Konrad, K., Van Lente, H., 2006. The sociology of expectations in science and technology. *Technol. Anal. Strateg. Manag.* 18, 285–298. https://doi.org/10.1080/09537320600777002.

Bourdieu, P., 2005. *The social structures of the economy.* Polity.

Boyer, R., 2005. Coherence, diversity, and the evolution of capitalisms: the institutional complementarity hypothesis. *Evol. Institutional Econ. Rev.* 2, 43–80. https://doi.org/10.14441/eier.2.43.

Boyer, R., Freyssenet, M., 2005. *Les modèles productifs*. La Découverte (version française actualisée).

Bozell, J., Petersen, G., 2010. Technology development for the production of biobased products from biorefinery carbohydrates: the US Department of Energy's "Top 10" revisited. *Green Chem.* 12, 539–554.

Calvo-Mendieta, I., Petit, O., Vivien, F.-D., 2017. Common patrimony: a concept to analyze collective natural resource management: the case of water management in France. *Ecol. Econ.* 137, 126–132. https://doi.org/10.1016/j.ecolecon.2017.02.028.

Cecere, G., Corrocher, N., Gossart, C., Ozman, M., 2014. Lock-in and path dependence: an evolutionary approach to eco-innovations. *J. Evol. Econ.* 24, 1037–1065. https://doi.org/10.1007/s00191-014-0381-5.

Coad, A., de Haan, P., Woersdorfer, J.S., 2009. Consumer support for environmental policies: an application to purchases of green cars. *Ecol. Econ.* 68, 2078–2086. https://doi.org/10.1016/j.ecolecon.2009.01.015.

Cohendet, P., Grandadam, D., Simon, L., Capdevila, I., 2014. Epistemic communities, localization and the dynamics of knowledge creation. *J. Econ. Geogr.* 14, 929–954. https://doi.org/10.1093/jeg/lbu018.

Cohendet, P., Simon, L., Mehouachi, C., 2020. From business ecosystems to ecosystems of innovation: the case of the video game industry in Montréal. *Ind. Innov.* 28, 1–31. https://doi.org/10.1080/13662716.2020.1793737.

Coriat, B., Orsi, F., Weinstein, O., 2003. Does biotech reflect a new science-based innovation regime? *Ind. Innov.* 10, 231–253. https://doi.org/10.1080/1366271032000141634.

Cowan, R., Foray, D., 1997. The economics of codification and the diffusion of knowledge. *Ind. Corp. Change* 6, 595–622. https://doi.org/10.1093/icc/6.3.595.

Crouch, C., Streeck, W., Boyer, R., Amable, B., Hall, P.A., Jackson, G., 2005. Dialogue on "institutional complementarity and political economy". *Socio-Econ. Rev.* 3, 359–382. https://doi.org/10.1093/SER/mwi015.

Daly, H.E., 1991. *Steady-state economics*. Island Press.

David, P., 1985. Clio and the economics of QWERTY. *Am. Econ. Rev.* 75, 332–337.

de Jesus, A., Mendonça, S., 2018. Lost in transition? Drivers and barriers in the eco-innovation road to the circular economy. *Ecol. Econ.* 145, 75–89. https://doi.org/10.1016/j.ecolecon.2017.08.001.

Desquilbet, M., Maigné, E., Monier-Dilhan, S., 2018. Organic food retailing and the conventionalisation debate. *Ecol. Econ.* 150, 194–203. https://doi.org/10.1016/j.ecolecon.2018.04.025.

Dopfer, K., 2012. The origins of meso economics: Schumpeter's legacy and beyond. *J. Evol. Econ.* 22, 133–160. https://doi.org/10.1007/s00191-011-0218-4.

Dopfer, K., Foster, J., Potts, J., 2004. Micro-meso-macro. *J. Evol. Econ.* 14, 263–279. https://doi.org/10.1007/s00191-004-0193-0.

Dosi, G., 1988. Sources, procedures, and microeconomic effects of innovation. *J. Econ. Lit.* 26, 1120–1171.

Douai, A., Montalban, M., 2012. Institutions and the environment: the case for a political socio-economy of environmental conflicts. *Camb. J. Econ.* 36, 1199–1220. https://doi.org/10.1093/cje/bes046.

EIO, 2013. *Policies and practices for eco-innovation uptake and circular economy transition*. Eco-Innovation Observatory, Funded by the European Commission.

Elsner, W., Heinrich, T., Schwardt, H., 2015. The size dimension of complex economies: towards a meso-economics, in: *The Microeconomics of Complex Economies*. Elsevier, pp.419–447. https://doi.org/10.1016/B978-0-12-411585-9.00014-2.

Faucheux, S., Nicolaï, I., 2011. IT for green and green IT: A proposed typology of eco-innovation. *Ecol. Econ.* 70, 2020–2027. https://doi.org/10.1016/j.ecolecon.2011.05.019.

Fenn, J., Raskino, M., 2008. *Mastering the hype cycle: how to choose the right innovation at the right time.* Harvard Business Press.

Feola, G., 2020. Capitalism in sustainability transitions research: time for a critical turn? *Environ. Innov. Soc. Transit.* 35, 241–250. https://doi.org/10.1016/j.eist.2019.02.005.

Festel, G., 2010. Industrial biotechnology: market size, company types, business models, and growth strategies. *Ind. Biotechnol.* 6, 88–94. https://doi.org/10.1089/ind.2010.0006.

Festel, G., Detzel, C., Maas, R., 2012. Industrial biotechnology: markets and industry structure. *J. Commer. Biotechnol.* 18, 11–21.

Font Vivanco, D., McDowall, W., Freire-González, J., Kemp, R., van der Voet, E., 2016. The foundations of the environmental rebound effect and its contribution towards a general framework. *Ecol. Econ.* 125, 60–69. https://doi.org/10.1016/j.ecolecon.2016.02.006.

Foray, D., 2018. Smart specialisation strategies and industrial modernisation in European regions: theory and practice. *Camb. J. Econ.* https://doi.org/10.1093/cje/bey022.

Franceschini, S., Pansera, M., 2015. Beyond unsustainable eco-innovation: the role of narratives in the evolution of the lighting sector. *Technol. Forecast. Soc. Change* 92, 69–83. https://doi.org/10.1016/j.techfore.2014.11.007.

Fuenfschilling, L., Truffer, B., 2014. The structuration of socio-technical regimes: conceptual foundations from institutional theory. *Res. Policy* 43, 772–791. https://doi.org/10.1016/j.respol.2013.10.010.

Gawer, A., 2014. Bridging differing perspectives on technological platforms: toward an integrative framework. *Res. Policy* 43, 1239–1249. https://doi.org/10.1016/j.respol.2014.03.006.

Gebauer, H., Worch, H., Truffer, B., 2012. Absorptive capacity, learning processes and combinative capabilities as determinants of strategic innovation. *Eur. Manag. J.* 30, 57–73. https://doi.org/10.1016/j.emj.2011.10.004.

Geels, F.W., 2020. Micro-foundations of the multi-level perspective on socio-technical transitions: developing a multi-dimensional model of agency through crossovers between social constructivism, evolutionary economics and neo-institutional theory. *Technol. Forecast. Soc. Change* 152, 119894. https://doi.org/10.1016/j.techfore.2019.119894.

Geels, F.W., 2014a. Reconceptualising the co-evolution of firms-in-industries and their environments: developing an inter-disciplinary triple embeddedness framework. *Res. Policy* 43, 261–277. https://doi.org/10.1016/j.respol.2013.10.006.

Geels, F.W., 2014b. Regime resistance against low-carbon transitions: introducing politics and power into the multi-level perspective. *Theory Cult. Soc.* 31, 21–40. https://doi.org/10.1177/0263276414531627.

Geels, F.W., 2011. The multi-level perspective on sustainability transitions: responses to seven criticisms. *Environ. Innov. Soc. Transit.* 1, 24–40. https://doi.org/10.1016/j.eist.2011.02.002.

Geels, F.W., Kern, F., Fuchs, G., Hinderer, N., Kungl, G., Mylan, J., Neukirch, M., Wassermann, S., 2016. The enactment of socio-technical transition pathways: a reformulated typology and a comparative multi-level analysis of the German and UK low-carbon electricity transitions (1990–2014). *Res. Policy* 45, 896–913. https://doi.org/10.1016/j.respol.2016.01.015.

Geels, F.W., Penna, C.C.R., 2015. Societal problems and industry reorientation: elaborating the Dialectic Issue Life Cycle (DILC) model and a case study of car safety in the USA (1900–1995). *Res. Policy* 44, 67–82. https://doi.org/10.1016/j.respol.2014.09.006.

Geels, F.W., Raven, R., 2006. Non-linearity and expectations in niche-development trajectories: ups and downs in Dutch biogas development (1973–2003). *Technol. Anal. Strateg. Manag.* 18, 375–392. https://doi.org/10.1080/09537320600777143.

Geels, F.W., Schot, J., 2010. The dynamics of socio-technical transitions: a socio-technical perspective, in: Grin, J., Rotmans, J., Schot, J. (Eds.), *Transitions to sustainable development: new directions in the study of long term trans-formative change*. Routledge.

Geels, F.W., Schot, J., 2007. Typology of sociotechnical transition pathways. *Res. Policy* 36, 399–417. https://doi.org/10.1016/j.respol.2007.01.003.

Geels, F.W., Verhees, B., 2011. Cultural legitimacy and framing struggles in innovation journeys: a cultural-performative perspective and a case study of Dutch nuclear energy (1945–1986). *Technol. Forecast. Soc. Change* 78, 910–930. https://doi.org/10.1016/j.techfore.2010.12.004.

Georgescu-Roegen, N., 1971. *The entropy law and the economic process*. Harvard University Press.

Gereffi, G., Humphrey, J., Sturgeon, T., 2005. The governance of global value chains. *Rev. Int. Polit. Econ.* 12, 78–104. https://doi.org/10.1080/09692290500049805.

Ghisetti, C., Pontoni, F., 2015. Investigating policy and R&D effects on environmental innovation: a meta-analysis. *Ecol. Econ.* 118, 57–66. https://doi.org/10.1016/j.ecolecon.2015.07.009.

Giampietro, M., 2019. On the circular bioeconomy and decoupling: implications for sustainable growth. *Ecol. Econ.* 162, 143–156. https://doi.org/10.1016/j.ecolecon.2019.05.001.

Giampietro, M., Kovacic, Z., Strand, R., Völker, T., 2019. *Report on narratives behind the circular economy concept*. No. MAGIC (H2020–GA 689669. Project Deliverable 5.7. European Union's Horizon 2020.

Giampietro, M., Mayumi, K., 2015. *The biofuel delusion: the fallacy of large-scale agro-biofuels production*. Earthscan.

Giampietro, M., Mayumi, K., 2008. Efficiency, Jevons' paradox and the evolution of complex adaptive systems, in: Polimeni, J.M., Mayumi, K., Giampietro, M., Alcott, B. (Eds.), *The Jevons Paradox and the myth of resource efficiency improvements*. Routledge, pp.79–140.

Gilli, M., Mancinelli, S., Mazzanti, M., 2014. Innovation complementarity and environmental productivity effects: Reality or delusion? Evidence from the EU. *Ecol. Econ.* 103, 56–67. https://doi.org/10.1016/j.ecolecon.2014.04.004.

Giurca, A., 2018. Unpacking the network discourse: actors and storylines in Germany's wood-based bioeconomy. *For. Policy Econ.* https://doi.org/10.1016/j.forpol.2018.05.009.

Grabs, J., Ponte, S., 2019. The evolution of power in the global coffee value chain and production network. *J. Econ. Geogr.* 19, 803–828. https://doi.org/10.1093/jeg/lbz008.

Gregson, N., Watkins, H., Calestani, M., 2013. Political markets: recycling, economization and marketization. *Econ. Soc.* 42, 1–25. https://doi.org/10.1080/03085147.2012.661625.

Guthman, J., 2004. The trouble with "organic lite" in California: a rejoinder to the "conventionalization" debate. *Sociol. Rural.* 44, 301–316.

Hansen, T., Coenen, L., 2015. The geography of sustainability transitions: review, synthesis and reflections on an emergent research field. *Environ. Innov. Soc. Transit.* 17, 92–109. https://doi.org/10.1016/j.eist.2014.11.001.

Hess, C., Ostrom, E., 2011. *Understanding knowledge as a commons: from theory to practice.* MIT Press.

Hess, D.J., 2013. Industrial fields and countervailing power: the transformation of distributed solar energy in the United States. *Glob. Environ. Change* 23, 847–855. https://doi.org/10.1016/j.gloenvcha.2013.01.002.

Joly, P.-B., 2010. On the economics of techno-scientific promises, in: *Débordements: Mélanges offerts à Michel Callon* (version électronique). Presse des Mines.

Jørgensen, U., 2012. Mapping and navigating transitions: the multi-level perspective compared with arenas of development. *Res. Policy* 41, 996–1010. https://doi.org/10.1016/j.respol.2012.03.001.

Jullien, B., Smith, A., 2011. Conceptualizing the role of politics in the economy: industries and their institutionalizations. *Rev. Int. Polit. Econ.* 18, 358–383. https://doi.org/10.1080/09692291003723615.

Jullien, B., Smith, A. (Eds.), 2008. *Industries and globalization: the political causality of difference, globalization and governance.* Palgrave Macmillan.

Kallis, G., Gómez-Baggethun, E., Zografos, C., 2013. To value or not to value? That is not the question. *Ecol. Econ.* 94, 97–105. https://doi.org/10.1016/j.ecolecon.2013.07.002.

Kemp, R., 2010. Sustainable technologies do not exist. *Ekonomiaz*, 2–17.

Kenis, P., Janowicz-Panjaitan, M., Cambré, B., 2009. *Temporary organizations.* Edward Elgar Publishing. https://doi.org/10.4337/9781849802154.

Köhler, J., Geels, F.W., Kern, F., Markard, J., Onsongo, E., Wieczorek, A., Alkemade, F., Avelino, F., Bergek, A., Boons, F., Fünfschilling, L., Hess, D., Holtz, G., Hyysalo, S., Jenkins, K., Kivimaa, P., Martiskainen, M., McMeekin, A., Mühlemeier, M.S., Nykvist, B., Pel, B., Raven, R., Rohracher, H., Sandén, B., Schot, J., Sovacool, B., Turnheim, B., Welch, D., Wells, P., 2019. An agenda for sustainability transitions research: state of the art and future directions. *Environ. Innov. Soc. Transit.* 31, 1–32. https://doi.org/10.1016/j.eist.2019.01.004.

Kuokkanen, A., Nurmi, A., Mikkilä, M., Kuisma, M., Kahiluoto, H., Linnanen, L., 2018. Agency in regime destabilization through the selection environment: the Finnish food system's sustainability transition. *Res. Policy* 47, 1513–1522. https://doi.org/10.1016/j.respol.2018.05.006.

Lancaster, K.J., 1966. A new approach to consumer theory. *J. Polit. Econ.* 74, 132–157. https://doi.org/10.1086/259131.

Langeveld, H., Sanders, J., Meeusen, M. (Eds.), 2012. *The biobased economy: biofuels, materials, and chemicals in the post-oil era.* Earthscan.

Langlois, R.N., 2003. The vanishing hand: the changing dynamics of industrial capitalism. *Ind. Corp. Change* 12, 351–385. https://doi.org/10.1093/icc/12.2.351.

Levidow, L., Upham, P., 2017. Linking the multi-level perspective with social representations theory: gasifiers as a niche innovation reinforcing the energy-from-waste (EfW) regime. *Technol. Forecast. Soc. Change* 120, 1–13. https://doi.org/10.1016/j.techfore.2017.03.028.

Liebowitz, S.J., Margolis, S.E., 1995. Path dependence, lock-in, and history. *J. Law Econ. Organ.* 11, 205–226.

Malerba, F., 2002. Sectoral systems of innovation and production. *Res. Policy* 31, 247–264.

Markard, J., Raven, R., Truffer, B., 2012. Sustainability transitions: an emerging field of research and its prospects. *Res. Policy* 41, 955–967. https://doi.org/10.1016/j.respol.2012.02.013.

Markard, J., Truffer, B., 2008. Technological innovation systems and the multi-level perspective: towards an integrated framework. *Res. Policy* 37, 596–615. https://doi.org/10.1016/j.respol.2008.01.004.

Martinez-Alier, J., Kallis, G., Veuthey, S., Walter, M., Temper, L., 2010. Social metabolism, ecological distribution conflicts, and valuation languages. *Ecol. Econ.* 70, 153–158. https://doi.org/10.1016/j.ecolecon.2010.09.024.

Meadowcroft, J., 2011. Engaging with the politics of sustainability transitions. *Environ. Innov. Soc. Transit.* 1, 70–75. https://doi.org/10.1016/j.eist.2011.02.003.

Miller, P., O'Leary, T., 2007. Mediating instruments and making markets: capital budgeting, science and the economy. *Account. Organ. Soc.* 32, 701–734. https://doi.org/10.1016/j.aos.2007.02.003.

Mondliwa, P., Roberts, S., Ponte, S., 2021. Competition and power in global value chains. *Compet. Change* 25, 328–349. https://doi.org/10.1177/1024529420975154.

Muniesa, F., Millo, Y., Callon, M., 2007. An introduction to market devices. *Sociol. Rev.* 55, 1–12. https://doi.org/10.1111/j.1467-954X.2007.00727.x.

Musiolik, J., Markard, J., Hekkert, M., Furrer, B., 2020. Creating innovation systems: how resource constellations affect the strategies of system builders. *Technol. Forecast. Soc. Change* 153, 119209. https://doi.org/10.1016/j.techfore.2018.02.002.

Nelson, R.R., Dosi, G., Helfat, C.E., Pyka, A., Saviotti, P.P., Lee, K., Dopfer, K., Malerba, F., Winter, S.G., 2018. *Modern evolutionary economics: an overview.* Cambridge University Press. https://doi.org/10.1017/9781108661928.

Nieddu, M., 2007. Le patrimoine comme relation économique. *Econ. Appliquée* 60, 87–104.

Nieddu, M., Garnier, E., Bliard, C., 2010. L'émergence d'une chimie doublement verte. *Rev. Econ. Ind.* 4, 53–84.

OECD, 2019. *Innovation and business/market opportunities associated with energy transitions and a cleaner global environment.* OECD.

OECD, 2017. *Investing in climate, investing in growth.* OECD. https://doi.org/10.1787/9789264273528-en.

OECD, 2010. *Eco-innovation in industry: enabling green growth.* OECD. https://doi.org/10.1787/9789264077225-en.

Oltra, V., Saint Jean, M., 2009. Sectoral systems of environmental innovation: an application to the French automotive industry. *Technol. Forecast. Soc. Change* 76, 567–583. https://doi.org/10.1016/j.techfore.2008.03.025.

Ostrom, E., 1990. *Governing the commons: the evolution of institutions for collective action.* Cambridge University Press.

Penna, C.C.R., Geels, F.W., 2012. Multi-dimensional struggles in the greening of industry: a dialectic issue lifecycle model and case study. *Technol. Forecast. Soc. Change* 79, 999–1020. https://doi.org/10.1016/j.techfore.2011.09.006.

Ponte, S., 2019. *Business, power and sustainability in a world of global value chains.* Zed.

Ponte, S., 2016. Convention theory in the Anglophone agro-food literature: past, present and future. *J. Rural Stud.* 44, 12–23. https://doi.org/10.1016/j.jrurstud.2015.12.019.

Popp, D., Hafner, T., Johnstone, N., 2011. Environmental policy vs. public pressure: innovation and diffusion of alternative bleaching technologies in the pulp industry. *Res. Policy* 40, 1253–1268. https://doi.org/10.1016/j.respol.2011.05.018.

Potts, J., 2019. *Innovation commons: the origin of economic growth.* Oxford University Press.

Rennings, K., 2000. Redefining innovation: eco-innovation research and the contribution from ecological economics. *Ecol. Econ.* 32, 319–332. https://doi.org/10.1016/S0921-8009(99)00112–00113.

Rennings, K., Markewitz, P., Vögele, S., 2013. How clean is clean? Incremental versus radical technological change in coal-fired power plants. *J. Evol. Econ.* 23, 331–355. https://doi.org/10.1007/s00191-010-0198-9.

Rosenberg, N., 1976. On technological expectations. *Econ. J.* 86, 523. https://doi.org/10.2307/2230797.

Ruef, A., Markard, J., 2010. What happens after a hype? How changing expectations affected innovation activities in the case of stationary fuel cells. *Technol. Anal. Strateg. Manag.* 22, 317–338. https://doi.org/10.1080/09537321003647354.

Salais, R., Storper, M., 1992. The four "worlds" of contemporary industry. *Camb. J. Econ.* 16, 169–193.

Schot, J., Steinmueller, W.E., 2018. Three frames for innovation policy: R&D, systems of innovation and transformative change. *Res. Policy* 47, 1554–1567. https://doi.org/10.1016/j.respol.2018.08.011.

Smith, A., Raven, R., 2012. What is protective space? Reconsidering niches in transitions to sustainability. *Res. Policy* 41, 1025–1036. https://doi.org/10.1016/j.respol.2011.12.012.

Smith, A., Stirling, A., Berkhout, F., 2005. The governance of sustainable socio-technical transitions. *Res. Policy* 34, 1491–1510. https://doi.org/10.1016/j.respol.2005.07.005.

Smith, A., Voß, J.-P., Grin, J., 2010. Innovation studies and sustainability transitions: the allure of the multi-level perspective and its challenges. *Res. Policy* 39, 435–448. https://doi.org/10.1016/j.respol.2010.01.023.

Sorrell, S., 2018. Explaining sociotechnical transitions: a critical realist perspective. *Res. Policy* 47, 1267–1282. https://doi.org/10.1016/j.respol.2018.04.008.

Spash, C.L., 2020. A tale of three paradigms: realising the revolutionary potential of ecological economics. *Ecol. Econ.* 169, 106518. https://doi.org/10.1016/j.ecolecon.2019.106518.

Svensson, O., Nikoleris, A., 2018. Structure reconsidered: towards new foundations of explanatory transitions theory. *Res. Policy* 47, 462–473. https://doi.org/10.1016/j.respol.2017.12.007.

Tickell, A., Peck, J.A., 1995. Social regulation after Fordism: regulation theory, neoliberalism and the global-local nexus. *Econ. Soc.* 24, 357–386. https://doi.org/10.1080/03085149500000015.

Triguero, A., Moreno-Mondéjar, L., Davia, M.A., 2013. Drivers of different types of eco-innovation in European SMEs. *Ecol. Econ.* 92, 25–33. https://doi.org/10.1016/j.ecolecon.2013.04.009.

Truffer, B., Voß, J.-P., Konrad, K., 2008. Mapping expectations for system transformations. *Technol. Forecast. Soc. Change* 75, 1360–1372. https://doi.org/10.1016/j.techfore.2008.04.001.

Unruh, G.C., 2002. Escaping carbon lock-in. *Energy Policy* 30, 317–325. https://doi.org/10.1016/S0301-4215(01)00098–00092.

Unruh, G.C., 2000. Understanding carbon lock-in. *Energy Policy* 28, 817–830. https://doi.org/10.1016/S0301-4215(00)00070–00077.

van den Bergh, J.C.J.M., 2011. Environment versus growth: a criticism of "degrowth" and a plea for "a-growth". *Ecol. Econ.* 70, 881–890. https://doi.org/10.1016/j.ecolecon.2010.09.035.

van Lente, H., Bakker, S., 2010. Competing expectations: the case of hydrogen storage technologies. *Technol. Anal. Strateg. Manag.* 22, 693–709. https://doi.org/10.1080/09537325.2010.496283.

Vandeventer, J.S., Cattaneo, C., Zografos, C., 2019. A degrowth transition: pathways for the degrowth niche to replace the capitalist-growth regime. *Ecol. Econ.* 156, 272–286. https://doi.org/10.1016/j.ecolecon.2018.10.002.

Vatn, A., 2005. *Institutions and the environment*. Edward Elgar.

Vivien, F.-D., Nieddu, M., Befort, N., Debref, R., Giampietro, M., 2019. The hijacking of the bioeconomy. *Ecol. Econ.* 159, 189–197. https://doi.org/10.1016/j.ecolecon.2019.01.027.

White, H.C., 2008. *Identity and control: how social formations emerge*, 2nd ed. Princeton University Press.

3 From the development of industrial chemistry to the emergence of the bioeconomy

As indicated in the introduction, the bioeconomy is presented by its proponents as a broad transition to the use of renewable resources in substitution for fossil resources. While the bioeconomy is a contested field, the use of biomass is perhaps the lowest common denominator among the various visions of the bioeconomy. Chapter 2 highlights the need to understand the principles guiding and structuring the way actors think as they develop their production and innovation activities. As Antonelli (2014) shows, actors are able to identify only knowledge available in their surroundings. To do so, especially in a context of complex knowledge and reassembling, they must develop principles and tools of coordination. Moreover, the exploration strategies of actors are the product of a long history that helps guide change.

Consequently, this chapter aims to link the development of the bioeconomy to the long history of industrial chemistry, which, from its origins, has developed from a perspective of substitution of traditional resources by new resources. From the perspective of the economics of ecological transition developed in this chapter, it is therefore necessary to consider this issue from the angle of the institutionalization of new material flows and the de-institutionalization of old flows, or their re-legitimization. This also raises the question of the possible complementarities of these new and old flows, possibly allowing an increase in the sphere of production. Consequently, these reflections in terms of new flows must also be interpreted within the general movement of expansion of capital accumulation: do these new flows aim to inscribe the socio-economic activities of production, exchange and consumption within natural limits, or do they institutionalize new flows in order to expand production, possibly with an environmental argument?

The first section of this chapter outlines this substitution hypothesis as a guiding principle from the early developments in industrial chemistry. Then the second section explains how biomass, after having been substituted by oil, has returned to the center of the debate. Finally, the third section shows the role of biorefineries as a coordinating device.

1. Chemistry as a substitution discipline

Chemistry emerges and structures itself simultaneously as a science and as an economic activity in situations of resolution of concrete problems. This

DOI: 10.4324/9781003103011-3

symbiotic birth of a scientific discipline and an industry can be dated to the middle of the 18th century, in the world of the French encyclopedists and the Enlightenment, and it can be shown that it is intrinsically linked to the economic question of substitution.

For example, until the 18th century, the French production of soda used for soap factories, glass factories, etc. was largely dependent on the import of foreign raw materials (Bensaude-Vincent and Stengers, 1996). To ease this constraint, the Royal Academy of Sciences launched a competition in 1781 to produce soda from sea salt. N. Leblanc won this competition in 1789 with a process that now bears his name. In 1791, he obtained one of the first patents resulting from the industrial property law adopted by the Constituent Assembly. Bensaude-Vincent and Stengers (*Ibid.*, p.209) analyze this invention as marking the beginning of the substitution era, since soda was not extracted but produced from reactions.

This invites an understanding of chemistry as a "discipline" of substitution. A discipline, not only in the academic sense of the term, but also as a disciplinary effort oriented towards the search for substitutions. The work of Bensaude-Vincent and Stengers provides two examples that allow us to grasp the extent to which the substitution orientation structures chemistry, in particular with regard to coloring agents and rubbers.

1.1 Dyes as an example of the implementation of a programmed search by a substitution logic

The history of the emergence of synthetic dyes in the mid-19th century is of twofold interest here. First, they were produced from the valorization of co-products that constituted waste (coal tars) in the context of the expansion of the coal gas industry for the supply of public lighting. It is estimated that about 20% of the distilled coal was transformed into gas, thus leaving large quantities of co-products. On the other hand, these gave rise to the development of close ties between research and business. Based on the knowledge inherited from Berthollet's seminal 1791 book *Elements de l'art de la teinture*, and by trial and error, Perkin succeeded in 1858 in producing an aniline-based mixture that could be used to dye silk, and later also cotton and wool. The deployment of aniline technology led to the discovery of a large number of dyes, numbering in the hundreds at the time, and formed the basis for the development of the synthetic dye industry, which was used to produce a large quantity of blues, violets, mauves and reds, and some blacks, browns and greens. In the second half of the 19th century, there was a great movement to replace dyes of natural origin by products derived from coal chemistry. It is this movement that I term, following the expression of Bensaude-Vincent and Stengers, the emergence of an era of "programmed research" through "programmed synthesis". This differentiates it from the preceding period, which was punctuated by inventions that could be described as aleatory, as in the case of Perkin's mauve. All in all, the production of synthetic indigo required 30 years of research before it could be commercialized.

1.2 Rubber, between colonial control of territories and natural resources and substitution

Rubber, whose use dates back to the Mayas, has been widely diffused, thanks to the invention of the vulcanization process, through the development of transport. It is thus an example of a chemical process of treating a natural resource which brings expected functionalities to it. Its development made the control of rubber-producing territories a central element of the geostrategy of nations, such as the English smuggling seeds out of Amazonia and replanting them with rubber tree stumps in Asia. Research on synthetic substitutes was essentially driven by the desire to escape the variations in the price of raw materials from before World War I. The Germans, deprived of access to the colonial territories, had developed a particularly active research effort, which led to the use of an abundant and cheap gas in carbochemistry and petrochemistry, and became one of the current stars of substitution research by synthetic biology means: butadiene. In the meantime, DuPont provided their researcher W.H. Carothers with considerable resources (which also led to the creation of nylon) to achieve these synthetic substitutes. World War II was a tremendous impetus for "programmed research". While the Germans could deal with blockades thanks to their production of synthetic rubber, the Americans were forced, because of the territories lost by the Allies in the Far East, to carry out a formidable mobilization to find substitutes. They endowed a "rubber czar" with wide-ranging powers and mobilized all the research departments of the university faculties and private companies:

> The butadiene and styrene they needed could be extracted not only from petroleum, but also from alcohol; a large part of the grain, potato, molasses and other carbohydrate crops was allocated to this use. (…) The problem posed at the beginning of the war by the shortage of rubber was solved with billions.
>
> (Mark, 1970, pp.139–140)[1]

However, this example is quite relevant to the subject of this chapter, namely the transition to the use of renewable resources: a certain number of products in chemistry can be obtained indiscriminately from carbonaceous resources of fossil or natural origin, and this has been the case for a very long time. The rest is a question of relative prices in the substitution games, with of course an advantage for products of fossil origin – possibly taking into account the fact that certain functionalities cannot be achieved by fossil sources at acceptable prices, and therefore that in a certain number of cases the natural origin remains. But in both cases, the carbon chains are transformed by synthetic chemistry, whether it is fossil carbon or "bio" carbon.

It is necessary to emphasize the importance of this point. Natural rubber is a polymer that is not disappearing and still accounts for 20% of rubber uses (compared to 75% in 1950), because synthetic and natural rubbers are different in their chemical structure and do not offer the same functionality, at least at acceptable prices. On the other hand, there are ways of substituting natural rubbers with "biosourced" products through synthetic chemistry. These routes consist of producing the precursor in the synthetic chemistry of rubber, butadiene, and then building the polymer structure through synthetic chemistry. We must therefore differentiate between natural polymers and "bio-based" products, which are derived from chemical reconstruction and are, in fact, synthetic polymers in the same way as polymers derived from fossil raw materials.

1.3 Hypercompetition of raw materials and processes

While there is now a renewed interest in natural rubbers due to the predicted shortage of butadiene resulting from the disruption caused by the emergence of shale gas, there is also interest in obtaining precursor monomers from chemical and tire companies: Goodyear and Genencor are working on obtaining isoprene to obtain butadiene (as are Lanxess and Gevo). Michelin has an agreement with Amyris on isoprene, but the Clermont-Ferrand (France) firm is also developing a project on butadiene. But the company has also developed a joint venture with Barito Pacific to acquire three rubber concessions in Sumatra and Borneo to combat "uncontrolled deforestation". Various firms have an agreement with Global Bioenergies, one of the most advanced biotechnology firms in synthetic biology today, to produce bio-based butadiene. For these products, the use of fillers or plasticizers of biosourced origin (such as vegetable oils or isosorbide to replace the phthalates used in certain rubbers) is also being considered by companies such as Roquette or Novamont.

Four substitution trajectories can therefore be identified: the first is the replacement of a natural product (in the sense of a natural polymer that was functionalized to meet a need) by a synthetic product with equivalent economic functionalities. The second is "biomimicry", which involves copying the structure of the natural product by assembling its polymeric structure from precursors of fossil origin. The third is the attempt to copy products often of fossil origin, but not always, by synthetic products made from biosourced precursors. The fourth consists in extracting, but preserving in their original form, macromolecules or major components of the plant (starch or cellulose), to functionalize them in order to compete with synthetic products of fossil or even biosourced origin – as can be seen today with functionalized starches competing with PVCs that can be made by biosourced or fossil means (Befort, 2020).

It is important to recognize the need to analyze the trajectories in terms of ecological transition regimes, as well as to identify the actors who take hold of them, and eventually to understand the reasons for their actions. Indeed, the logic of substitution in given directions implies the production of oriented knowledge and the exploration of the transition to the industrialization of reactions allowing substitution in the laboratory. However, these directions are not given randomly (by scientific advances that are the result of serendipity, for example), but they result from the strategies of actors present in the field, whose logic must be understood (seeking to sell a surplus raw material, to come to dominate a market through a monopoly position, to satisfy a need, etc.).

2. How did biomass return to the heart of chemistry?

The phrase "green chemistry" must be seen as a specific institutional construction, which was imported from the United States and spread throughout the academic and industrial worlds, and every chemist in a corporate or university laboratory can be expected to know the 12 principles of green chemistry.

In order to understand this institutional construction, we must remember that chemistry has long been the embodiment of modernity. Chemistry is consubstantial with the idea of continuous progress. However, this idea of modernity has undergone, since the last quarter of the 20th century, a violent crisis fueled by a series of disasters and incidents of pollution caused by chemical activity. In spite of its extraordinary achievements, chemistry has been pointed at to such an extent that the founding work on the contestation of the paradigm of progress carried out by the science-industry complex, namely *Silent spring* by R. Carson (2002 [1962]), which confronts the chemical giant Dupont de Nemours on DDT, has aroused, and still does, deep hatred, as can be seen for example on the blog of the libertarian think-tank the Competitive Enterprise Institute. In order to contain the controversy, Nixon created the Environmental Protection Agency in 1970, thus opening up another controversy over the public policy tools best able to contain accidents and pollution. Businesses advocated "soft-law" solutions rather than regulatory constraints, through voluntary initiatives such as Responsible Care, an initiative of the Canadian chemical industry that was recognized worldwide and adopted in a United Nations charter. They criticized regulations that blocked innovation and, according to them, promoted end-of-pipe adaptations. It is in this context that several conceptions of chemistry reducing pollution at source are confronting each other on the semantic field. The semantic field has also been invaded by different names and designations: environmental chemistry, eco-compatible chemistry, sustainable chemistry, soft chemistry, etc. preceded the use of the term green chemistry. This institutional response came with the adoption of the Pollution Prevention Act in 1990 and the adoption by the US Environmental Protection Agency of a methodology setting out 12 principles of green chemistry (Anastas and Warner, 1998).

These 12 principles appear like the Ten Commandments: they reveal a messianic logic, intended to convince actors to use this cognitive framework. But like the Ten Commandments, certain principles are more applied than others and each actor can choose those that they think are attainable, those that they must respect absolutely ("thou shalt not kill"), and those with which they can make accommodations. It should be noted that the seventh principle is that of the substitution, as far as possible, of fossil resources by renewable resources.

The phrase "as far as possible" is therefore based on the technical and economic capacities of the actors, but also on their degree of proximity to these resources.

It was at the turn of the millennium that this seventh principle became dominant in scientific publications or in the prizes awarded to companies for green chemistry actions, including a prize awarded to Monsanto in 1999 for the improvement of its "round-up" production process according to the principle of saving atoms. Nevertheless, the imposition of the theme of the vegetal in the green chemistry movement must be read, not in the light of a hypothetical lack of oil – a recurrent theme throughout the 20th century about its probable disappearance – but as the result of the substitution strategy of the agro-industries. It is clear that it is not for environmental reasons but because of structural surpluses in agricultural production that agribusinesses view oil shocks as opportunities to re-explore past substitution logics. There are two reasons for this surge (Nieddu et al., 2010). The first is that agro-industries have mastered the transformation of the use of plants and have retained the "memory" of non-food uses of plants from the two world wars, such as the production of liquid fuels of plant origin. The second reason is that agribusinesses know how to develop segments of value chains that are capable of carrying out the first transformation of biomass and delivering these products to agribusinesses or paper industries.

3. Coordinating the transition thanks to a technical artifact: the biorefinery

At the turn of the millennium, the two dynamics described above (the dispute over chemistry and the search for new outlets for agro-industries) came together in a certain number of collective projects gathering actors from the chemical and agro-industry sectors as well as new entrants: actors from biotechnologies. The conjunction of these major movements has given rise to a problem that is not just that of green chemistry (how to succeed in producing a sustainable chemistry?) or the transition to the use of renewable resources. The issue for the actors is to question the way in which they can make the substitution operations that they are concerned about economically sustainable – and secondly, if possible, to make plant-based chemistry ecologically sustainable. Nevertheless, it should be emphasized that the biorefinery as a technical object, but also as a cognitive object intended to think about substitution, appeared *before* these three major trends met. For this reason, the actors problematize their construction of the biorefinery by trying to articulate (raw materials/processes/products) in a sustainable way.

The literature in chemistry that seeks to define the concept of the biorefinery (Clark and Deswarte, 2008; Kamm et al., 2006) proposes a linear vision, more pedagogical than corresponding to a field reality, in three generations of biorefineries. The first generation of biorefineries was developed in the early 1990s for the sole production of liquid fuels, based on the idea that a single raw material should produce a single product. But this strategy overlooks the fact that production generates co-products among which important quantities of furfural were obtained, in addition to ethanol or glycerol in the case of biodiesels. Furfural is used as a solvent in petrochemicals or as a flavoring for chocolate, butter, cinnamon, etc. in the food industry. If glycerol is a "natural" fat, it is also obtained petrochemically from propylene. This opens the way to a return to bio-based products and to the development of its use in pharmaceuticals, in cosmetics (moisturizing agent, solvent, lubricant; in toothpastes, moisturizing creams, Marseille soaps), as a plasticizer in paper, as a lubricant in fibers or in electronic cigarette liquids. The development of biofuel production has led to an explosion in the production of glycerol, which has quite naturally replaced glycerol of fossil origin (Bauer and Hulteberg, 2013). The second generation of biorefineries is likely to be based on a single raw material, but also on the exploitation of all the co-products resulting from this production. The idea being that the economic situation of biofuels depends on the price of oil: in periods of falling oil prices, it may be more profitable to produce molecules with higher added value, due to the high production costs of biofuels. It has been observed that actors use this price argument in their speeches to justify abandoning the exploration of a technological pathway in their portfolio or to make new technico-economic promises on molecules. As a result, actors are seeking to make the production of liquid fuels profitable by using co-products. They therefore conduct real inventories: chemical molecules that also hold technical and economic promise, such as 1.3-propanediol (for polyurethanes), epichlorohydrin, ethanol and animal feed (see de Jong et al., 2012). This second generation was expected to take place quickly following the first, but the experts I interviewed reported that some of these production units are only at the demonstration stage. The third generation of biorefineries may be able to use a variety of products with a variety of processing technologies on the same site. Depending on relative price variations, production pathways would be modified, leading to a reversal of the hierarchy between products and co-products. This would enable the most profitable combination of raw materials and processes to be selected almost instantaneously according to market conditions. The authors go on to interpret this narrative not as a historical reality, but rather as a proposal to structure thinking around a starting point: the oil shocks of the 1970s. In this sense, this representation shows that two sources of variety emerge: the origins of biomass (dedicated plantations such as cereals, palm oil or beet), raw materials from the agri-food or food industry (chicken waste, milk, cooking oils) or agricultural by-products (straw, bagasse); the processes can be, in these representations, either thermochemical or biological. In other words, they are both based on ways of conceiving the chemistry inherited from petrochemistry, consisting of a first step of fractionation into a series of molecules which will then be reformed into molecules of interest. This point is therefore the core of the problem, as shown by the need for actors to theorize their entry into the biorefinery issue.

4. Conclusion: towards a circular bioeconomy?

This chapter points to the dynamics of institutionalization and de-institutionalization of material flows in the bioeconomy and in the extension of the development of the bioeconomy. Here, it is the notion of *substitution* that organizes the way actors think and conduct technical and economic learning. The development of "today's" bioeconomy, through the intermediary of the biorefinery, is organized around a double issue. On the one hand, actors have to identify the coherent combinations (raw materials/processes/products) relevant to their business model. On the other hand, they have to arbitrate between the substitution of a material flow by another one aiming at the same product (*drop-in substitution*) or aiming at a product offering identical or new functionalities (*functional* substitution). The first case introduces a very strong constraint on the innovation process since the characteristics of the competition on the market will strongly determine the possible choices. Similarly, agro-industry chose to preserve its specialization on a particular biomass when it could choose to diversify its production, and thereby participate in the transformation of material flows for the development of a post-fossil economy.

Recent developments in the bioeconomy aim to integrate it within the circular economy as stated in the 2018 European strategy: "the scopes of the Circular Economy and the Bioeconomy intersect in their common aim to add value to biological waste and residues" (European Commission Directorate-General for Research and Innovation, 2018, p.50). While circularity was not explicitly mentioned in the 2012 strategy, several strategies anticipated its development: the cascading use of biomass, the use of bio-waste as biomass or the synergy between different types of bioeconomy. The OECD (2017; Philp, 2018) adopts a much narrower vision which considers that the circular bioeconomy corresponds to the biorefinery of waste. In this perspective, the notion of the cascade mentioned above plays a key role. The idea of the cascade, inspired by the development of petrochemicals at the turn of the 1930s (Galambos et al., 2007) is to organize production according to the added value of the materials produced. For example, this principle aimed to organize the profitability of the second-generation biorefinery by targeting high-value-added applications in pharmaceuticals and cosmetics, then producing energy with the remaining fractions (Carus et al., 2015, 2011). In this perspective, the aim was to ensure the economic sustainability of the biorefinery. It is therefore essentially a strategy of developing new flows of complementary materials rather than a strategy of substitution of functionalities.

However, a holistic vision of the circular bioeconomy can be contemplated whereby the principles guiding this bioeconomy would certainly take up the cascading use but would be constrained by the limited availability of biomass (D'Amato et al., 2019, 2018; Morone and D'Amato, 2019). From this perspective, the goal of the bioeconomy is to transform production and consumer systems using biomass, i.e. to act as a transition lever. The development of this circular bioeconomy is based on two complementary strategies. On the one hand, it is necessary to develop strategies of creative destruction and niche support aimed at destabilizing economic activities recognized as unsustainable (Kivimaa and Kern, 2016). On the other hand, support for niches must be based on support for functional innovations.

Note

1 Author's translation.

Bibliography

Anastas, P.T., Warner, J.C., 1998. *Green chemistry: theory and practice*. Oxford University Press.

Antonelli, C., 2014. *Localised technological change: towards the economics of complexity*, Routledge studies in global competition. Routledge.

Bauer, F., Hulteberg, C., 2013. Is there a future in glycerol as a feedstock in the production of biofuels and biochemicals? *Biofuels Bioprod. Biorefining* 7, 43–51. https://doi.org/10.1002/bbb.1370.

Befort, N., 2020. Going beyond definitions to understand tensions within the bioeconomy: The contribution of sociotechnical regimes to contested fields. *Technol. Forecast. Soc. Change* 153, 119923. https://doi.org/10.1016/j.techfore.2020.119923.

Bensaude-Vincent, B., Stengers, I., 1996. *A history of chemistry*. Harvard University Press.

Carson, R., 2002. *Silent spring*, 40th anniversary ed. Houghton Mifflin.

Carus, M., Carrez, D., Kaeb, H., Ravenstijn, J., Venus, J., 2011. Level playing field for bio-based chemistry and materials. Nova Paper 1. https://renewable-carbon.eu/publications/product/nova-paper-1-on-bio-based-economy-level-playing-field-for-bio-based-chemistry-and-materials-−-full-version/, accessed on 10/17/2022.

Carus, M., Dammer, L., Essel, R., 2015. Options for designing the political framework of the European bio-based economy. Nova Paper 6. https://renewable-carbon.eu/publications/product/nova-paper-6-on-bio-based-economy-options-for-designing-the-political-framework-of-the-european-bio-based-economy-%E2%88%92-full-version/, accessed on 10/17/2022.

Clark, J.H., Deswarte, F.E.I. (Eds.), 2008. *Introduction to chemicals from biomass*, Wiley series in renewable resources. Wiley.

D'Amato, D., Korhonen, J., Toppinen, A., 2019. Circular, green, and bio economy: how do companies in land-use intensive sectors align with sustainability concepts? *Ecol. Econ.* 158, 116–133. https://doi.org/10.1016/j.ecolecon.2018.12.026.

D'Amato, D., Veijonaho, S., Toppinen, A., 2018. Towards sustainability? Forest-based circular bioeconomy business models in Finnish SMEs. *For. Policy Econ.* 101848. https://doi.org/10.1016/j.forpol.2018.12.004.

CSL_BIBLIOGRAPHY de Jong, E., Higson, A., Walsh, P., Wellisch, M., 2012. Product developments in the bio-based chemicals arena. *Biofuels, Bioproducts and Biorefining 6*, 606–624. https://doi.org/10.1002/bbb.1360.

European Commission, Directorate-General for Research and Innovation, 2018. *A sustainable bioeconomy for Europe: strengthening the connection between economy, society and the environment: updated bioeconomy strategy*. European Commission.

Galambos, L., Hikino, T., Zamagni, V. (Eds.), 2007. *The global chemical industry in the age of the petrochemical revolution*. Cambridge University Press.

Kamm, B., Gruber, P.R., Kamm, M. (Eds.), 2006. *Biorefineries: industrial processes and products: status quo and future directions*. Wiley-VCH.

Kivimaa, P., Kern, F., 2016. Creative destruction or mere niche support? Innovation policy mixes for sustainability transitions. *Res. Policy* 45, 205–217. https://doi.org/10.1016/j.respol.2015.09.008.

Mark, H.F., 1970. *Les polymères*. Robert Laffont Science.

Morone, P., D'Amato, D., 2019. The role of sustainability standards in the uptake of bio-based chemicals. *Curr. Opin. Green Sustain. Chem.* 19, 45–49. https://doi.org/10.1016/j.cogsc.2019.05.003.

Nieddu, M., Garnier, E., Bliard, C., 2010. L'émergence d'une chimie doublement verte. *Rev. Econ. Ind.* 4, 53–84.

OECD, 2017. *Biorefineries models and policy*. No. DSTI/STP/BNCT(2016)16/FINAL. OECD.

Philp, J., 2018. The bioeconomy, the challenge of the century for policy makers. *New Biotechnol.* 40, 11–19. https://doi.org/10.1016/j.nbt.2017.04.004.

4 The institutional architecture of the bioeconomy

The theoretical framework developed here invites us to connect production and innovation activities to the institutional architecture of emerging economic spaces. The previous chapter, through a historicized reading of the emergence of the bioeconomy as the product of a history of raw material substitution, articulates the conjunction between institutional architecture and innovation diachronically. The purpose of this chapter is to highlight the institutional architecture structuring the contemporary development of the bioeconomy. To do this, this chapter proposes to study the three main tools for structuring the boundaries of the bioeconomy. In other words, the objective of the mechanisms studied here is to define what is part of the bioeconomy and what is not.

If the debates around the definition of the bioeconomy (cf. Chapter 1) have participated in structuring visions and imaginaries of what the bioeconomy should be, these debates do not explain with which devices, nor by which processes, material realities are imposed. In other words, we need to understand how visions are translated into economic activities, and conversely, how these material realities (business models, inherited knowledge, production infrastructures, etc.) structure the imaginaries of the bioeconomy. To do this, this chapter mobilizes an approach in terms of development arenas (Jørgensen, 2012). These arenas are spaces that bring together heterogeneous actors where socio-material activities and institutions organizing the functioning of transitional spaces are constructed (Jullien and Smith, 2008). More specifically, the spaces are the place where the actors *problematize* the future. That is, they construct the problem to which the development of their productions must respond.

The first section, based on the study of three structuring projects (Eurobioref, Biocore and Suprabio), explains the role played by these projects in structuring a reflection in terms of value chains. The second section focuses on the emergence of the European public–private partnership BioBased Industry (BBI), which emerged from these projects to structure value chain models. The third section points to the role of standards aimed at labeling bio-based products. The fourth section is dedicated to the analysis of the emergence of the bioeconomy in several countries.

DOI: 10.4324/9781003103011-4

1. The development of industrialization projects as a tool for structuring the economic space

As the documents produced by the European Commission (COM 2014/2), by researchers at European Union research centers (Scarlat et al., 2015) and by analyses of the state of the bioeconomy (McCormick and Kautto, 2013) remind us, the European Union's strategy involves the financing of structuring research projects for the bioeconomy, with three of them (Eurobioref, Biocore and Suprabio) emerging as fundamental in the development because of the funding they attract and their reception.

The challenge of these projects, as shown by the feedback symposium of the three projects held in February 2014 in Brussels, was to demonstrate the interest of financing "flagships" projects. That is, to build "life-size" *success stories* whose role would be to instigate a movement of transition towards the use of plants. The statements made by the European Commission's Bioeconomy Directors General during the restitution symposium are particularly enlightening from this point of view. From now on, the European Commission declared that it wished to finance processes (1) that could be industrialized, i.e. evaluated according to a sufficiently high Technology Readiness Level (TRL) criterion, (2) that would no longer be biofuel projects based on the use of agricultural resources dedicated to food, and (3) to support projects that could not be relocated outside of Europe. The hypothesis of this study, following the observation of the closing conference and the interviews conducted, is that the primary objective of these projects is to produce not the results of scientific research, but "value chain models" composed by the actors within these projects. These are therefore markers of the development arena.

1.1 The Eurobioref project: a response from specialty chemicals to the economic models of biofuels – co-products

In the summary book of the Eurobioref project published in 2012 (Aresta et al., 2012), Dubois (2012), research manager at Arkema, writes in the conclusion of the second chapter: "there is currently a tremendous interest in bio-based products, but at the same time all the conditions are met to build a bio-economy bubble, with projects without enough economic background" (Dubois, 2012, p.47). This conclusion is supported by a simulation of the CAPEX required to build a biorefinery and a presentation of the major biorefinery models which the author believes are profitable.

The concept of CAPEX refers to the evaluation of the capital cost of an industrial project. The chemical industry, a highly optimized industry, has "turnkey" models like Turton (2012). Dubois (2012) therefore mobilizes a model of this type in order to evaluate the capital investments required for existing biorefineries. According to the author, it is the priority production of products with higher added value, then the valorization of co-products towards less profitable applications, that should guide the development of these production units:

> a way to reach the targets (…) is certainly to combine the production of high-value chemicals and materials and to use the residues of the biorefinery to produce fuels. In this case, the fuels do not need to support most of the capital cost and can have access to lower-value feedstock.
>
> (*Ibid.*, p.47)

Arkema (through its original company Ato Chimie) has been working since the early 1960s with a plant resource that has been well known to chemists since the early 20th century: castor oil, from which a polyamide is derived that was nicknamed at that time the "French nylon". Given the characteristics of this polyamide, rather than offering commodity intermediates,[1] the firm has always offered sophisticated applications within specific markets, and this is exactly what Dubois is trying to replicate by relying on Arkema's refinery in Marseille where it produces its polyamide[2]: "in this type of biorefinery, it is important to identify the key product" (*Ibid.*, p.25).

Dubois thus develops an economic model of a value chain segment in which the firm would develop a specialty molecule on which it would have a monopoly. The products derived from the high value-added molecule are used to amortize the capital cost of the installation, which, because of its orientation towards higher value-added products, does not need to reach the levels of economy of scale of ethylene or biofuel plants, for example.

The productive legacies of the main firms involved in the project can be recognized here. (Borregaard, Novozymes, Arkema and Novance). Indeed, in 2012 members of Borregaard (Rodsrud et al., 2012) published in the same book as Dubois a contribution telling the *success story* of the Norwegian "wood biorefinery", starting from the production of wood, to the production of low value-added products related to sugar as a chemical platform, and eventually to the search for higher value-added products. During one of the round tables at the 2014 Eurobioref conference, the exchanges between Arkema and Booregaard focused precisely on the need to ensure the profitability of production units through the production of higher value-added products. However, the article by Rodsrud et al. (2012) mentions biofuel production, which is also present in the Eurobioref business model diagram. If we look at the value chain models submitted at the end of the project, we can identify six models, but in reality, only four correspond to tested models, the others having been abandoned or corresponding to the test of the integration of the chain models in existing units. Among the four selected models, the first two refer to the production of polyamides, i.e. the heart of Arkema's assets, whose pre-processing of co-products make it possible to supply raw materials (short chains of fatty acids) to the other chains dedicated to the production of biofuels and butanol, i.e. products with low added value.

We can therefore see Arkema's influence in defining the shape of the economic model of the value chain, which it has imposed by conceptualizing its *business model*. By positioning itself in this way, Arkema is seeking to dominate the upstream part of its value chain by testing raw materials and imposing transformation processes, on which actors such as Borregaard or Novance (for oil refining) are positioned. The Eurobioref model is therefore a compromise dominated by Arkema, which is trying to hold together a variety of technological trajectories that are necessary for Arkema's model to be sustainable.

1.2 The Biocore project: a value chain business model around CIMV's Organosolv process

CIMV is a French firm, a spin-off of public–private funded research, founded in 1998, which established itself for its test on the site of the biorefinery of Pomacle-Bazancourt (one of the most important biorefineries in Europe). The *process* of the biorefinery of Pomacle-Bazancourt involves the biotechnological fractionation of plants to obtain lignin, cellulose and hemicellulose, which are the three major components of biomass from which biotechnological processes are thought to be possible. The upstream part of the value chain is again, like Eurobioref, dominated by CIMV which imposes its raw material transformation process to supply such companies as DSM or Tarkett. In collaboration with DSM, the production of second-generation ethanol from cellulose obtained by the CIMV process was announced in 2011. Nevertheless, it should be kept in mind that CIMV proposes a compromise of products in which lignin is the dominant product of the process, in order to obtain lignins with particular qualities. The process is therefore not a standard ethanol production process. The challenge of this strategy here lies in the "extension of the biomass feedstock base" (Biocore, 2014, p.6), which is a major issue in the development of biorefineries: the value proposition built within the project is therefore to provide a unique process, applicable to a variety of biomass types available in Europe, for a variety of applications (O'Donohue, 2014). Here, the core of the matter lies in lignin, for which CIMV holds patents. The next step is to valorize the co-products of lignin production. To achieve this, the valuations go through biotechnological processes. This necessity to demonstrate the variety of possible uses of a raw material demonstrates the intensity of competition on raw materials. CIMV's process is a response similar to that of Arkema, which, in order to respond to potentially higher prices, offers products with higher added value, but from a different productive heritage. CIMV proposes a conceptualization whereby the process would be widely diffused, turning CIMV into a supplier of transformed materials for biotechnologies, but also of intellectual property, having the possibility of licensing its process.

This rather unusual positioning (as regards a process of primary transformation of raw materials) can be explained by CIMV's competition with paper manufacturers in the wood industries in the Nordic countries, and more particularly with Borregaard, as shown by the development of a pulp production process in 2008 and a lengthy intervention by Borregaard on the conversion of cellulose and hemicellulose during a research school organized within the framework of Eurobioref. This brings us back to the problem of designing the value chain in which the firms will take a position. Although they try to maintain their position in very specific segments of the value chain (in this case, the fractionation of a variety of biomass), they may be forced to enter into agreements with other firms in order to secure outlets for their products. Thus, the trade-off that forms the "commodity chain economic model" is dominated in Biocore by CIMV. Conversely, it forces it to make room for a variety of outlets and processing for its raw material.

1.3 The Suprabio project: towards profitable biofuels?

The latest project from the European Union FP7, whose aim was to develop a value chain model, is the Suprabio project. In the presentation of the project, the promoters claim the possibility, from thermochemical and biotechnological processes, to produce molecules with high added value. However, the main issue retained in the project is the problem of reducing the production costs of biofuels, which would be produced from lignin or cellulose (Bhattacharya, 2014).

As in Eurobioref, Borregaard has developed a wood pre-treatment process to reach the cellulose and use it in one of the many technological paths explored in the project. Since Borregaard is involved in this project, it comes as no surprise that the feedstock being tested is first wood and then wood residues. The model developed here is therefore a commodity chemistry model dedicated to biofuels which can be installed in Borregaard's production unit.

1.4 Lessons learned from the analysis of the three European projects

The previous subsection has shown that the definition of "value chain business models" was at stake in all three projects. These models are constructed as compromises that take place within development arenas in which actors compete, thus producing internal and external dynamics. The resulting compromises contribute to the problematization of space, whose variety of projects, even in their competitiveness, participates in giving rise to a space that concentrates institutional efforts towards the emergence of the use of biomass. This space therefore consists of an arena of development, which is in fact composed of multiple arenas, giving rise to and crystallizing conflicts between actors. All of this therefore proceeds to highlight the dynamics at work.

The first conflicts that we have identified concern the competition for the financing that allows the organization of the passage to the demonstrative stage. It is therefore the need for capital that is revealed not only by the position held by Arkema, but also by the modeling carried out within the Biocore project or by Borregaard's rationale. The second level of competition, which takes place within the arenas this time, concerns the definition of the sector segment on which the project's efforts will be concentrated. The project involves the domination of a sector by one or more actors. It is in this regard that, despite the hypercompetition that was confirmed to me by participants in the different projects, the actors are forced to cooperate in order to collectively construct the supply and outlets for the controlled commodity chain segments.

The last level of competition is the supply of raw materials. This issue was addressed in each of the projects. In the case of Eurobioref, Arkema conducted tests in Madagascar, for instance. At the same time, it is asking for stable or even lower agricultural prices in Europe to maintain its production there – thereby also justifying its choice for higher value-added products to compensate for the cost of capital and raw materials. In the case of CIMV and Borregaard, this means using local raw materials. From the point of view of projects and the emergence of the bioeconomy, I identify several logics. The first is the construction of industrial success stories. For both Arkema and CIMV, their goal is to demonstrate the feasibility of existing or quasi-existing production – a logic of "qualification" of bioeconomy activities. The second logic identified here is a form of injunction to bring together a variety of actors, who, until the end of the project, were trying to link the actors of the chemical, agro-industrial, biotechnological and wood and pulp industries.

2. Taking control of the development arena by forming a public–private partnership

2.1 The PPP as the dominant form of compromise on industry governance

It is in the context of the intense competition described above that the BBI Public–Private Partnership (PPP) between the European Union and the Bioindustry Consortium (BIC) was set up.

The initial objective, in line with the FP7 projects described above, is to organize the transition from the pilot stage to the industrialization of processes. As early as 2013, it was established that the European Commission would finance the PPP up to the amount of €975 million and that the actors wishing to participate would finance the rest (with a ratio of about €1 public for €3 private) for a total budget of €3.7 billion. It was, therefore, from the beginning of the PPP, a question of including it in existing and dominant collective productive assets, given the sums required to apply for the calls for projects launched within the framework of the PPP, but also as an extension of the European funding already granted. It seems that there has been intense lobbying by the actors to win the subsidies, as the PPP funding accounts for most of the funding granted for the bioeconomy under Horizon 2020 (from 2014 to 2020). The second objective was to be able to involve SMEs in the PPP. In this respect, they benefit from a lower entry fee than for large firms or competitiveness clusters. These different elements make it possible to put forward the idea that, despite the competition between the actors, it is indeed a question of constituting a community of bioeconomy actors. For example, Dirk Carrez, the Director General of the PPP, also happens to be the former Director of Europabio, a biotechnology *lobby* in Brussels. It is therefore from this point of view that I wish to analyze the formation of the PPP. To do so, I will study the business models of pathways developed within the PPP and then within the first projects that were funded in the first call for projects (results made public on June 24, 2015).

2.2 The economic models of the sectors defined in the PPP

In its 2012 report, BIC defined the outline of the PPP arena. Among the list of founding members, and the list of current members, the chemical industry is absent with the notable exception of Solvay, which has biotechnology activities in Brazil, and Clariant, which mobilizes biotechnology in the production of coatings for wood or plastics. The founding members are large agricultural cooperatives (Cristal Union, SüdZucker), agro-industry firms (Cargill, Roquette), energy producers (such as Abengoa Bioenergia), biotechnologies (Novozymes), bioplastics (Novamont), cardboard (Smurfit Kappa Group) and paper manufacturers (Metsä, for example), competitiveness clusters (IAR, the Dutch Biorefinery Cluster, etc.) and collective organizations (Susa, the Dutch Biorefinery Cluster, Suschem, Europabio, Cefic, etc.). A takeover of power is thus becoming apparent, which is confirmed in the intentions of the project, but also in the goals defined by the actors.

The goals announced in the 2012 report were as follows (Bio-Based Industries Consortium, 2012):

1 "diversify farmer's income and provide them with additional margins by up to 40% by using available residues" (*Ibid.*, p.10)
2 "Enable 30% of overall chemical production to become bio-based" (*Ibid.*, p.12)
3 "supply 25% of Europe's transport energy needs by sustainable advanced biofuels" (*Ibid.*, p.14)
4 "support the European market for bio-based fibre and polymers such as viscose, carbon fibres, nano-cellulose derivatives and bioplastics to grow rapidly" (*Ibid.*, p.18)
5 "reindustrialise Europe by creating a new rural infrastructure of biorefineries" (*Ibid.*, p.25)
6 "realise a new generation of bio-based materials and composites" (*Ibid.*, p.30).

Each of these objectives indicates that the construction of an alliance between agro-industries, wood producers and biotechnologies in the structuring of a bioeconomy is at stake, with the aim of appropriating part of the value created by the chemical industry (see objective 2).

The project is based on five demonstrative value chains that have been defined in the PPP's Strategic Innovation and Research Agenda (SIRA). For each of these value chain models, research axes have also been selected, which makes it possible to draft a typology of the different Value-Chains Models (VCMs) outlined in the PPP research agenda (Table 4.1).

This synoptic table provides us with a synthetic representation of the VCMs that the BBI PPP is building. The right-hand column includes not only the descriptions of the expected demonstrations for each of the economic models,

Table 4.1 The five commodity chain economic models supported by the PPP (from SIRA, 2013)

VCM 1: agro-industrial biorefinery Examples of companies: SüdZucker, ARD, Solvay, Cargill, NordZucker, KLM, Novozymes	Increase of agricultural yields (cultivation techniques, GMOs…) and use of residues; integration in farms or storage place for pretreatment; main use of locally available biomass; decomposition of lignocellulose by biotechnological processes; oil chemistry (PH2 and 3); biofuels, platform molecules and materials (from low to high added value) and packaging; large size units; construction of new markets and term-to-term substitution; segments of more or less integrated chains.
VCM 2: wood biorefinery Examples of companies: Metsä, UPM, Borregaard, Sappi, KLM, Novozymes	Intensification of the use of locally available wood (new species and residues); (thermo) chemical and biotechnological wood fractionation processes; chemical molecules, biofuels, packaging; upstream positioning in relation to CV1 to provide fibers for materials.
VCM 3: new products oriented by the sustainable development issue – biorefinery and biofuels not mentioned, or in a very minor way Example of a firm: Novamont, but also Fertiberia, supplier of fertilizers for agriculture, indicating on its website no appetence for sustainable development	• Insists on the objective of achieving high added value in terms of sustainability, not only economic. • Circular economy logic: use of residues + use of plants not used until now for their complexity capable of providing new materials, alternatives to products of fossil origin; emphasis on bioproducts that could be provided in return to agriculture (e.g. biocides). • Ecodesign and end-of-life issues of the product presented.
VCM 4: waste biorefinery company example: Novozymes	Collection and sorting of waste (organic or from the exploitation of wood such as bark); biotechnological and thermochemical *processes*; exclusively technological vision dedicated to the production of biofuels; ensures coherence with the overall circular economy scheme.
VCM 5: addition of material production *processes* in existing energy units	Pre-treatment in farms or storage places; orientation of thermochemical processes towards the production of chemical molecules (aromatic in particular), with lignin for example, before producing energy; use of residual ashes; essentially thermochemical or even biotechnological processes.

but also makes these requests consistent with the research fields that are open for each model.

In VCM 1, it is clearly about the biorefinery as it has been imposed in the agricultural world: a biorefinery model based on the use of local resources, collected by the regional agricultural cooperatives, but which, in order to increase the quantities produced, need to increase the radius of collection and thus decrease the weight of agricultural raw materials, hence the requests for research on dehydration.

VCM 2 corresponds to the wood biorefinery. In this case, it is a question of maintaining both biotechnological and thermochemical techniques (the Fischer-Tropsch process) mastered by the wood and pulp industries. The introduction of the waste recovery issue refers to a debate on the availability of lignin as a co-product of paper production, which is sometimes used as a reference for a fully bio-based product. Currently, and this is causing disputes between the pulp industry and the wood industry, the main suppliers of lignin are the paper producers, while the wood producers seek to move downstream in the value chains by carrying out primary wood processing. However, as the case of CIMV has shown, lignin producers need to demonstrate the efficiency of their products and may be forced to move down the value chains as well.

VCM 3 is essentially driven by Novamont in its strategy of problematizing the industry as a non-biofuel biorefinery, around products on longer value chain segments than those of lignin production for biofuels or platform molecules for example. In this case, it seems that the reference to the use of plants not yet used was a result of Novamont's intense activity in defining the PPP to obtain financing for the launching of its production unit using thistles in Sardinia. Novamont has been developing a discourse around this material for several years with the idea that its exploitation does not disrupt local agriculture and that it allows the reindustrialization of a territory by buying, in *joint venture* with Versalis, a former ethylene factory located in Porto Torres.

The VCM 4 is in line with Europe's resolve, also reflected in various national roadmaps, to revalue organic waste coming from households from the perspective of the circular bioeconomy. The representative of Europabio with whom I spoke confirmed that this is a "compromise that the private actors have made with the European Commission". In other words, the actors had no choice but to integrate this dimension to obtain European funding. For example, Novozymes offers enzymes capable of purifying water, and thus recovering waste that can then be reprocessed. Finally, VCM 5 is a value chain segment that aims to transform bio-based energy production units (e.g. heating) into small refining units for the production of biofuels, by thermochemical means. Here, rather little information is brought forward as regards the origin of the raw materials and so on, except that they should be dehydrated before arriving at the refinery. It could thus correspond to two types of already existing production units. On the one hand, it could be a question of converting energy production units (heat for example) that can be installed in rural areas to dedicate them to the production of biofuels – with the well-known problem of the profitability of these productions. On the other hand, it could also be a question of converting existing refinery units (as in the port of Ghent) into biofuel production units, in which the raw materials would be imported and transformed (or burned by thermochemical processes) and the choice of these raw materials would be made according to world prices in agriculture.

From the beginning of the project, the funds allocated to each of the VCMs were planned (Table 4.2).

Table 4.2 Projected funds for each of the MEFs (from SIRA, 2013)

	Funds for demonstration projects (in € millions)	*Flagship projects (in € millions)*	*Total (in € millions)*
VCM 1	292.5	1313.0	1605.0
VCM 2	142.5	281.4	423.9
VCM 3	150.0	234.5	384.5
VCM 4	112.5	351.8	464.3
VCM 5	52.5	164.2	216.7

The announced funding clearly positions VCM 1 (the agro-industry VCM) in a dominant position, with €1.6 billion, which is almost half of the planned funding. Apart from VCM 5, whose status, as mentioned above, is unstable, VCMs 3 and 4 are supported in more or less equal shares: this clearly shows that sectors that are not based on the production of biofuels are being developed at the European level, some of which refuse to use it altogether. Thus, Novamont obtained during the first call for projects about €25 million for the FIRST2RUN project (flagship project) to develop its plant devoted to the treatment of thistle in Sardinia.

The two demonstration projects that have been funded are led by UPM (with €18 million) and the Dutch cooperative Cosun (about €11 million). The first project aims to implement in Finnish production units the processes for transforming wood into lignin and to contribute to its recovery into biofuels (with the Swedish Sekkab process) and into 1.2-propanediol with the Metabolic Explorer process. The second project aims to further develop biosourced plastics for packaging from beet sugar, the first steps of which were launched at Wageningen University with Cosun, but also Refresco, who are members of the project. Finally, five research and development projects have been financed (each with a budget of between €2 and €3 million), two of which focus on fertilizer production or fertilization and the other three on the use of lignin.

3. Institutionalizing standards to define bio-based products: product identity as a market-building tool

The problem relating to the definition of products also raises the issue of the type of substitution (term-to-term vs. new functionalities) that is being tackled by the actors. But the actors are also competing over the definition of technical standards. In the European debate, the American program on bio-based products is regularly mentioned. The analysis of the Biopreferred program indicates that the issue of the definition of products is addressed by the public authorities, but that the choice of the certification standard is not neutral. The choice of the ASTM D6866 standard by the US government is being debated, particularly with regard to the implications on production methods.

3.1 The American Biopreferred program

The Biopreferred program was created under the 2002 Farm Bill. The purpose of the Farm Bill was essentially to institute massive subsidies to US agriculture, particularly with regard to wheat. This program was confirmed in 2014 in a new Farm Bill. The program is based on two pillars. First, the US administration promotes the purchase of bio-based products based on the categories of established products. Second, firms conduct a voluntary labeling process. To be included in the list, threshold levels of bio-based content have been set. For example, fuel additives must have a minimum of 92% bio-based content or two-stroke engine oils must have 34% bio-based content. Except for those categories where minimum bio-based content is already defined, the minimum bio-based content is 25%. In order to be certified, a product "had to be new and emerging" (Buckhalt, 2014) in order to encourage the development of new bio-based products and avoid labeling products that are already marketed.

The method chosen by the US government is the ASTM D6866 standard which calculates the ratio between the amount of plant-based carbon, measured thanks to carbon 14, and the total content in carbon. This method is therefore above all part of a drop-in substitution approach in the sense that products are reduced to their carbon content, while products of plant origin are rich in other components (which is not the case with products of fossil origin). Despite this program, the US policy on biosourced product development has been criticized for its lack of ambition. The author explains that there are no real US policies to support the development of bio-based products, since they are developed under the Farm Bills and there are no goals defined with specific numbers or real constraints on purchases made by the different administrations. The first explanation put forward by the author is that "bio-based products industries" are too small compared to the petrochemical industry, which can impose its views thanks to the financing of American electoral campaigns. As an example, the author writes that it was the implementation of legislation on methyl tert-butyl ether emissions in fuels, in addition to public support for ethanol, that led to its widespread use in the United States. The criticism from the Sustainable Biomaterials Collaborative directly targets the standard adopted in the Biopreferred program. The criticism is based on the idea that "not all bio-based products are created equal" (Platt, 2011). That is, a bio-based product is not necessarily biodegradable, it may be produced from GMOs, it may rely on an intensive use of pesticides, etc.

However, the ASTM D6866 standard erases all these differences by presenting the bio-based content only, which results in misleading consumers by not valuing sufficiently sustainable products. The institute therefore offers an alternative standard that aims to take into account the production of raw materials (no GMOs or pesticides, protection of soils and workers, etc.), the production process (reduced energy consumption, recyclable products, avoiding toxic mixtures, etc.) and the end of life (recycling or degradation, use of relevant labels). The solution adopted for labels (Working Landscape Certificate;

WSL) is to provide a gradation on the products (bronze/silver/gold) and which is declined according to the types of products. The certification is therefore based on the use of the products, but also on the labels obtained elsewhere. In the case of plastic tableware, it is expected that it can be biodegradable or recyclable, that it should have the "Ok compost" label from Vinçotte or the European standard on degradation, but also that the biosourced content should be over 90%, contain no GMOs, etc.

3.2 The reflection on standards in Europe

As the European Union began to launch its 2020 programs, the question of public support for biofuels arose. At the 2014 Eurobioref conference in Brussels, representatives of the European Commission reported that the Commission no longer wished to support the production of biofuels based on biomass that is used in food. Yet, Carus et al. (2015) support the idea that the Renewable Energy Directive, through the subsidies and exemptions granted, guides investments towards biofuels and not towards bio-based products. In this case, biofuels are not regarded as "bio-based products" (in the sense of plastics, chemical intermediates, fibers, etc.), but as pertaining to the field of energy and support for biofuels as a competition between materials and energy.

In this context, the European Commission has defined, through a European technical committee, a bio-based product as follows: "this standard defines a bio-based product as a product which is wholly or partly derived from biomass. (...) The bio-based product is normally characterized by the bio-based carbon content or the bio-based content" (Carus et al., 2015, p.5). The definition produced by the European Commission and taken up by the actors shows that a bio-based product is defined by a technical standard, and that there are two standards. On the one hand, the product can be defined by its bio-based carbon content and, on the other hand, it can be defined by its bio-based material content. This debate is fundamental, because transition policies work by issuing quotas that help create demand.

To address this issue, several steps have been taken. The first was to launch two research projects (KBBPPS and Open-Bio) aimed at building a compromise on standards for assessing the bio-based content of products. The first project, Knowledge Based Bio-based Products' Pre-Standardization (KBBPS), aimed to build an inventory of methodologies (in technical terms) on content assessment to feed into the work of the Technical Committee on standardization. This project was led by NEN, the Dutch Standards Institute. In this project, all members, with the notable exception of Novamont, are either a standards institute or a research organization.

The second project, Open-Bio, was broader and did not only aim at standardization. The aim was to develop "market pulls", in particular by developing communication tools for bio-based products. To do so, a study was carried out to determine the functionalities on which it could be important to communicate. This study shows that the actors believe that what is important is to be able to certify the renewable origin of raw materials, as well as the additive functionalities that will affect the final consumer (mainly biodegradable or recyclable), the CO_2 emissions and the type of raw materials used.

Participants in the project, particularly those responsible for organizing the drafting of meeting minutes or reports, explained to me that the project was a place of confrontation between several groups of actors. The first group of actors, essentially supporters of biofuel production, sought to impose the ASTM D6866 standard for assessing the carbon content of renewable sources. A second group, bringing together agribusinesses (such as Roquette and ACDV) and Novamont, defended the idea that biomass content could not be reduced to carbon alone, at the risk of neglecting the hydrogen or oxygen present in biomass. The third type of actor is BASF, which has developed its own label that establishes an average presence of biomass over an entire production cycle. The compromise that emerged, based on the interviews conducted and the reports I had access to, is that the biomass content can be assessed either by the presence of carbon or by bio-based content or by interval. The consultation of the certification guide established by the ACDV makes it possible to determine that this is a victory for its members given that in 2013 the organization was proposing a method of this type (ACDV, 2013). The outcome of the project enabled NEN to offer to certify products according to the European standard that was adopted in late 2015. The last objective of the project is to establish a list that is similar to the Biopreferred list of bio-based products available in Europe. At the moment, this project is still ongoing and is expected to be published at the end of 2016. This project adds an additional constraint to the certification. It must be "transversal", i.e., it must be able to be used in different sectors/fields/areas/branches.

The issue is then in the choice of standard: should there be one standard for all products, or should there be (as is the case today) a variety of standards (which could possibly be assessed by another standard such as the WSL)? The current position in Europe on this point would tend to allow private standards to emerge and for these standards to remain and be applied by the actors, even to the extent of constituting certification portfolios.

4. The development of the bioeconomy in national spaces: the case of the United States

The final element involved in developing the boundaries of the economic space formed by the bioeconomy is that of backcasting which is used to establish national roadmaps for the development of the bioeconomy. This method is inspired by organization management and energy production planning (Robinson, 1982; Vergragt and Quist, 2011). Starting from possible futures, backcasting defines pathways to reach them, identifying technological lock-ins to solve using innovations nurtured in niches. Hence, they produce strategies and then contribute to a vision of the future and to navigation governance (Geels and Raven, 2006; Langeveld et al., 2012; van Lente, 2012).

This method has been used in particular to define the concept of biorefinery or what a circular bioeconomy could correspond to. Nevertheless, the use of baskcasting and roadmaps has also been used at the national level, and not only at the cross-sectoral level. If national roadmaps have been used before, it was with a view to identifying competing visions of the bioeconomy. The hypothesis of this chapter is that it is possible to link these roadmaps to national productive legacies. Thus, the behavior of actors is interpreted as a strategy of reproduction of their common pool resources.

To understand the origins and effects of these roadmaps, the case of the United States will be mobilized here. Following the results of the previous chapters, this chapter analyzes the US bioeconomy roadmaps in terms of the diversity of technological trajectories, value chain product development, substitution strategies and industrialization.

The United States has a long history of valorization of plants through the chemurgy movement. It has been shown that, as is still the case nowadays, this movement was driven by industrialists, agribusinesses and researchers and that they defended the non-food use of plants as a vector of independence for the United States. In addition, the United States was the first country to develop a roadmap for the bioeconomy. The bioeconomy was not yet called as such, as it was called "carbohydrate economy". The change came about as a result of the importation of the roadmap method from the management of companies such as Motorola to public management. It mentioned a will to bring out bio-based productions, from a diversity of raw materials and technologies.

4.1 An ancient history of non-food uses of plants

The issue of transition to the use of renewable resources is not new to American society. Indeed, Finlay (2003) explains that the "chemurgy" movement started to develop in the 1920s. This movement, which was mainly driven by either actors aiming for social progress through chemistry, or industrialists (such as H. Ford or members of Dow Chemicals), or journalists, already had three objectives (which varied from one actor to another): to develop non-food uses for agricultural products, to develop new commodities that would be useful for industry, and to use all parts of the plant and agricultural waste. This movement prevailed in the post-World War I context. At the end of the war, chemistry was praised for its participation in the war effort (production of fertilizers, pesticides, explosives, etc.). However, this participation in the war effort and the intensification of agricultural production caused a crisis of overproduction in the agricultural world during the 1920s. At the international level, the period was marked by international tensions over trade, which resulted in a strong interest in certain resources available in the United States. Thus, England increased the tariffs for rubber which it produced in Asia, or the price of vegetable oils used for industrial greases. In addition, it should be noted that at that time of discovery of large oil fields, there were already concerns about possible resource shortages. Thus, Ford engineers developed paints, lubricants and plastic parts for automobiles.

This period also saw the development of intermediates such as levulinic acid, which is today presented as one of the key molecules for the transition. The discourse on chemurgy emphasizes an anchoring of production on US-grown agricultural resources, both as a source of economic prosperity, but also as a means of securing the country's energy independence. Finlay (2003) points out that members of the chemurgy movement continued their work around the latter issue by publishing a 900-page report devoted to the use of agriculture during the war (USDA, 1951). Nonetheless, the post-World War II period marked the decline of the movement, particularly following the development of petroleum chemistry. It should be noted that the development of this type of chemistry is linked to what made chemistry successful during and after World War I: the rationalization of its production and the thinking based on the periodic table of elements and polymer chemistry (cf. Chapter 3). What can be retained from the chemurgy movement is the political positioning around the question of energy independence for the United States and the depletion of oil resources. But the chemurgy movement also formalizes a problematization of agro-industries (opposing a dominant vision in terms of a "food and fiber system"):

> an emergent chemurgic revolution meant that farmers should discard the cultivation of old-fashioned crops with "time-worn nicknames" like corn and wheat and instead view their job as the cultivation of products with real meaning: cellulose, starch, lignin, levulose, and the like. A farm's value, Hale believed, should be measured in terms of its organic compounds, rather than its capability to produce food and fiber.
>
> (Finlay, 2003, p.37)

Farms must be dedicated to producing raw materials that can be used for both food (e.g. starch) and non-food purposes. Therefore, it is their ability to produce feedstocks, not biomass, that must be evaluated.

4.2 Towards a "carbohydrate economy"? The American vision in 1998

The United States published in 1998 the first roadmap dedicated to the emergence of a "carbohydrate economy". It identifies the carbon chains of agricultural origin as sources of carbon and identifies an unresolved problem of articulation between agriculture and chemistry, which will be the core of the roadmap's problematization with regard to the current "hydrocarbon economy".

For example, the document begins with the following observation: "Use of plant/crop resources for energy, or as basic building blocks for industrial production, has been limited because of a poor fit with the hydrocarbon processing system that has been successfully developed to utilize fossil fuels" (US Department of Energy, 1998, p.2). Yet biomass supply is described as strategic for the United States:

> The vision is to provide continued economic growth, healthy standards of living, and strong national security through the development of plant/crop-based renewable resources that are a viable alternative to current dependence on non-renewable, diminishing fossil fuels. (…) Plant/crop-based renewable resources are a strategic option to meet the growing need for industrial building blocks, and to maintain the leadership position for the US into the next century.
>
> (*Ibid.*, p.2)

Thus, part of the problematization of the chemurgy is found in terms of the role of agriculture both as a means of additional growth for the US economy, but also of energy independence. However, the contribution of the use of renewable resources was only estimated at 10% in 2020: "Note that the vision for 2020 assumes fossil fuels will still contribute 90% of the base inputs. The addition of plant-based renewables is not an either/or situation, it is a necessary contribution to meet future demands" (*Ibid.*, p.8). Hence, a reflection on the articulation between an economy based on the use of renewable resources and another economy based on fossil resources can be found in other American roadmaps.

4.3 *The formation of value chains for a carbohydrate economy*

4.3.1 Identify the raw material / technology pairing

The identification endeavor of the technologies and raw materials needed is based on the hope of a merger between the raw materials already available (waste and co-products, existing crops, dedicated crops and GMOs) and the processes that can be used: existing chemistry, modified chemistry, biotechnological processes and the production of new molecules. The research front from which the development effort must be made is therefore at the crossroads of these two approaches. This opportunity assessment tool is used to structure the foresight work and assign a role to raw materials or processes: "In the shorter term, modified processes will allow economic use of plant/crop-based resources, while longer-term opportunities exist via the application of recent biotechnology advances" (*Ibid.*, p.3). In this narrative, it is a question of hybridizing the productive heritage of traditional chemistry with biotechnology developments, rather than establishing competition between these two industries. The report goes on to highlight the diversity of articulations between raw materials and processes, their different levels of productivity and the different levels of productivity of agricultural regions (Table 4.3).

The study in the report of these different types of diversity serves in fact to identify what are called "hot spots", i.e. "promising" raw material/technology combinations.

The document is considered by the actors in the field as foundational. Regarded as such, it underlines the fact that it is the basis of a way of thinking

Table 4.3 The different types of diversity in the plant/crop-based renewable resources 2020 (developed by author)

Type of diversity	*Quote from the roadmap*
Diversity of articulations (raw materials/processes)	"Plant-based inputs may take several forms (wood, cellulose, lignin, starch, amino acids, etc.), and may be sourced from different places (biomass, crop residues, dedicated crops, crop processing by-products, etc.)" (p.21). "In many cases, major sources of plant materials are not even geographically suited to be the locations of petrochemical processing facilities. The use of plant/crop-based resources requires the development of concepts around 'alternative processing' *rather than* just 'alternative sources' for existing processes" (p.3).
Diversity of productivity levels in agricultural regions	"Some proponents of increased use of plant-based renewables point to the many acres of so-called marginal land (low unit biomass production), and suggest that those acres should be the source of materials for feedstocks. Marginal land is called marginal for a reason. If economic comparisons are to be made using plant production levels from marginal land, *it is difficult to envision why such a system alone would be economically* viable" (p.11). "Plant-based inputs may take several forms (wood, cellulose, lignn, starch, amino acids, etc.), and may be sourced from different places (biomass, crop residues, dedicated crops, crop processing by-products, etc.)" (p.21).
Diversity of process productivity levels in the (raw material/process) pair	"A major issue to be addressed in supply relates to the intent of the original production and how that is to be managed. Today, trees are grown for wood and pulp, crops are grown for food, feed, or fiber, *and have not been well optimized for multiple uses.* Evaluation of input costs have been based on plant/crop inputs from non-optimized (as raw materials) plant production systems, and thus carry an up-front economic penalty" (p.10).

about the development of economic activities in terms of couples (raw materials/processes), but also on the basis of existing raw materials and technologies. From the point of view of the United States in particular, we can see that this roadmap crystallizes both positions inherited from the chemurgy movement and the emergence of biotechnologies in the United States.

4.3.2 Marketing of products in a carbohydrate economy

Regarding the issue of commercialization, the roadmap highlights the fact that a number of products (from a variety of raw materials) are already being produced:

> Although the total quantity consumed is low, plant-based materials are currently used for a wide variety of chemicals, ranging from paints to adhesives to lubricants. Soybeans have been a traditional source of vegetable oils, and more recent genetic advances have allowed the production of specialty oils for particular lubricant markets. Also, in recent years the use of soybean-derived ink has become relatively common.
>
> (*Ibid.*, p.9)

However, the issue of the development of bio-based product production discussed throughout the report dealt with productivity levels. This issue, at the level of the commercial report, is addressed as follows:

> Plant materials, such as lignin or starch, can also be high-volume, low-cost materials *and could compete on a commodity basis if the appropriate systems were developed.* The types of cost comparisons that have been done historically showed that plant-based materials were not particularly well-suited to the economics of the petrochemical industry, but in cases where cost was similar, the portion of material derived from plants increased significantly (...). The real issue is perhaps one of cost of conversion to "force fit" plant-derived materials into a manufacturing system that requires a different chemical strategy. (...) *There is a need to avoid the conflict of "either/or" and explore what opportunities can be developed to use the best of both sources of raw materials.*
>
> (*Ibid.*, p.12; emphasis added)

Thus, the mode of product development must be based on the articulation between raw materials/processes/exploitable opportunities.

4.4 Two competing bioeconomies

Regarding the definition of the bioeconomy, we can observe here the distinction between the bioeconomy of biotechnologies, promoted by the *National bioeconomy blueprint* of 2012 (The White House, 2012), and the *Why biobased?* Roadmap (Golden and Handfield, 2014), which is more in line with that of the chemurgy.

4.4.1 *The* National bioeconomy blueprint

This document was published with the support of the White House in 2012, as evidenced by B. Obama's signature at the conclusion of the document. It defines the bioeconomy as follows: "the growth of today's US bioeconomy is due in large part to the development of three foundational technologies: genetic engineering, DNA sequencing, and automated high-throughput manipulations of biomolecules" (The White House, 2012, p.1). That is, the bioeconomy is driven by biotechnology. Therefore, what is part of the bioeconomy is anything within the scope of biotechnology: "The US bioeconomy is all around us: new drugs and diagnostics for improved human health, higher-yielding food crops, emerging biofuels to reduce dependency on oil, and bio-based chemical intermediates, to name just a few" (*Ibid.*, p.7). The definition is thus aligned with that of the OECD, unless it is actually the other way around, with the major fields being health, energy, agriculture and the environment.

The bioeconomy could be favored, according to the roadmap, by facilitating patent filings and removing a number of regulations on biotechnology control, but also by providing preferred access for US-developed processes and products to government procurement through federal procurement programs. These recommendations, presented in the definition of the bioeconomy, were also incorporated from the perspective of industrialization in the *Industrialization of biology* roadmap (National Research Council of the National Academies, 2015).

4.4.2 The Why biobased? *bioeconomy: a biorefinery bioeconomy*

As the title implies, the paper is more about feedstocks than technologies. Therefore, the bioeconomy is defined as:

> The Bioeconomy is characterized by a new generation of environmentally-friendly materials and products and economic opportunities for US-based agriculture, chemical, and manufacturing sectors and their value chains, with far-reaching potential impacts on socioeconomic development and the resurgence of production in the US (...) *The Bioeconomy is the global industrial transition of sustainability utilizing renewable aquatic and terrestrial resources in energy, intermediate, and final products for economic, environmental, social, and national security benefits.*
>
> (Golden and Handfield, 2014, p.1; emphasis added)

We thus find here the idea of a great transition towards the use of renewable resources, while taking up the discourse around the relocalization of industrial production in the United States, but also by redeveloping the "rural areas" (to use the expression used):

> The emerging bioeconomy has the potential to create unprecedented growth in the rural economy and create a higher level of self-sufficiency for farming and rural communities. (...) The conversion of lignocellulosic biomass is considered to provide maximum benefits to the rural economy.
>
> (*Ibid.*, p.2)

After describing the development of biotechnologies in the first section of this chapter, the discussion on chemurgy has made it possible to show two lines supporting the emergence of a bioeconomy, but with different visions. I will show below that these two lines help to structure the American roadmaps. The preceding analyses have shown the influences structuring the definition of the bioeconomy and its overall functioning. There is a tension between a vision of a bioeconomy based on biotechnologies and a second vision based on the diversity of technological trajectories. The first American roadmap posed the problem of the industrialization of processes. It is therefore necessary to determine how this issue is dealt with in the roadmaps.

4.5 Industrializing biotechnologies to support the development of the bioeconomy

4.5.1 Process industrialization in the National bioeconomy blueprint

In the *National bioeconomy blueprint*, industrialization is first addressed from the drivers' points of view. These concern first of all public support for scale-up, i. e. the problem of shifting from the laboratory stage to the industrial demonstrator, then to the pilot and finally to the production unit. In the case of the production of tannin foams, I attended "live" discussions on these problems. Tackled by technical questions (choice of machines, etc.), these problems also refer to the problem of uncertainty linked to product demand (who will consume tannin foams because they are formaldehyde-free?) and thus to the problem of what the actors call the *valley of death* (Ellwood et al., 2022). That is to say, beyond the uncertainty that is inherent in the investment, it is reinforced by the fact that the demand is not identified. The definition of this standard is one of the drivers highlighted in the roadmap, based on the ASTM Method 6866 standard in the framework of the biopreferred program. Launched in 2002, it aims to force the choice of bio-based products in public procurement. Initially confidential, it is from 2012 that we see a strengthening of this program with the extension of the list of products approved by the USDA. For example, Biosuccinum produced by Reverdia, which is a joint venture between DSM and Roquette, has obtained the biopreferred label. Similarly, some of the materials used on American military bases (such as soap, towels, etc.) are of plant origin. The American report also insists on building *pools of* resources to face the "valley of death" (expression used in the report): "strategic objectives: Identify and support opportunities for the development of *public–private partnerships and pre-competitive collaborations – where competitors pool resources, knowledge, and expertise* to learn from successes and failures" (The White House, 2012, p.38; emphasis added). To this end, a certain number of means have been identified to support the constitution of collective resources, such as "open-source initiatives", the formation of public-private partnerships or even prizes to reward processes or products.

4.5.2 The Industrialization of biology *report, which extends the* National bioeconomy blueprint *on industrialization*

This roadmap aims to "create a roadmap for accelerating the advanced manufacturing of chemicals using biological systems" (National Research Council of the National Academies, 2015, p.1). To that end, the roadmap aims to address the change in scale for production:

> Lower costs, increases in production speed, flexibility of manufacturing plants, and increased production capacity are among the many potential benefits that *the increased industrialization of biology may bring to producers and consumers of chemical products that have not previously been available at scale.*
>
> (*Ibid.*, p.2; emphasis added)

The answer to the availability of bio-based chemical molecules thus lies in the industrialization of biology and "the convergence of biology with chemistry and engineering in transformative new ways" (*Ibid.*, p.30). Thus, in the industrialization model, chemistry is mobilized as a discipline and economic sector that has key processes in the industrialization of biology.

The triptych (raw materials/processes/products) developed here is based on the articulation between technologies derived from biotechnologies towards products then produced by the chemical industry:

> Biological engineering seeks to take advantage of the tools of recombinant DNA technology while applying systems and network analyses to the challenge of engineering more productive host organisms. (…) These principles have already been successfully applied to generate highly efficient and productive germentation processes for a number of products. Early successes include, for example, the production of industrial enzymes, artemisin, lactic acid, 1.3-propanediol, isoproneids, and alcohol-based biofuels.
>
> (*Ibid.*, p.4)

The key technologies for this are synthetic biology, DNA sequencing, bioinformatics, and complementary technologies from chemistry for product design. The chemical industry is thus relegated to the rank of supplier of supplementary technologies. Concerning raw materials, the roadmap states that currently, it is essentially sugar extracted from starch that is used, but that this will have to be complemented by cellulose, whose uses are to be developed, just as for methane or CO_2:

> Cellulosic biomass holds great promise as a feedstock, but there are still many challenges associated with using recalcitrant cellulosic material in industrial biotechnology. (…) There is also significant active work in facilitating the use of syngas, methane, and carbon dioxide in manufacturing.
>
> (*Ibid.*, p.5)

However, the production will face the problem of the production of organisms used in fermentation. This requires knowledge of the target molecule, otherwise the production target of the bioorganisms cannot be refined. Then it is necessary to identify prices and volumes as well as a specific quality according to the type of product. Thus, it is necessary to develop technical-economic studies to achieve this. The roadmap addresses this issue through the definition of a series of models. The first is the "vertically integrated development" firm. In this model, all activities, from the production of raw materials to the sale of the final product, are undertaken by the firm. The second model is that of "horizontal stratification", which refers to fragmented value chains. The next two models actually refer to production units. The third model is that of the large biorefinery copying the petrochemical industry. The last model, "distributed production", describes small production units using locally available resources.

The issue that was discussed previously was mainly that of raw materials and processes. Indeed, the question of products was certainly mentioned in connection with the other two dimensions, but it is noteworthy that strategies for replacing products should be theorized.

The first approach is term-to-term substitution: "one approach is the direct replacement of existing monomers derived from petrochemical sources with the same structure made by microbial fermentation" (*Ibid.*, p.60). The problem related to this model is that it directly induces price competition and targets mainly commodity products, inducing important capital mobilizations. The second model is described as the production of "new polymers" with two functions, for example biosourced or biodegradable, in addition to the chemical functions. In this respect, PDO is a molecule of interest, as it is no longer simply derived from ethylene, but also biosourced. The last strategy is the production of polymers from polypeptides, i.e. amino acids. While here it is essentially a question of thinking about how products are transformed, the report notes the anchoring in the way of thinking about products in chemistry: a distinction is made between commodity and specialty chemistry. On the one hand, commodity chemistry must aim at products that can be produced from widely available raw materials. On the other hand, specialty products could make it possible to take advantage of the fact that chemical production processes do not necessarily exist to develop products with high added value.

5. Conclusion

This chapter has examined the definition of the institutional architecture of the bioeconomy. It is based on major devices that aim to define what is and is not part of the bioeconomy. The first of these is the import of a logic of projects (Kenis et al., 2009; Tukiainen and Granqvist, 2016) as a tool for identifying the technologies that can be mobilized and developed to structure the development of a bioeconomy.

The second device is that of economic models, whether they are models of firms (start-ups vs. incumbents for example; cf. Chapters 5 and 6) or of value chains. Therefore, the demonstration projects have made it possible to test the articulation between a company at the heart of a project, which must have access to raw materials (imported or available on the scale of its territory, as is the case with Novamont), and outlets, on a "life-size" basis in flagship projects.

The third mechanism is that of product qualification. Indeed, in the hypothesis of a drop-in substitution strategy, which is dominant today, it is impossible to easily distinguish a biosourced product from a petroleum-based product. It is therefore to meet this need to distinguish the biosourced functionality that these labels have been developed. Besides, still in this logic of distinction of the products between them, other labels can be used such as those which certify the organic character of certain chemical products. If the usefulness of labels has been demonstrated in the literature, their practical utility in the development of a bioeconomy seems to be worthy of discussion. Indeed, it is necessary to distinguish between bio-based products and petroleum-based products, because for the time being both types of products remain on the market. The joint forecasts concerning the increase in the quantities of petroleum-based plastics and biosourced plastics (see intern report) do not allow us to predict a complete substitution. Consequently, the development of these products could be used either for a strategy of "greening" of the standard ranges, or as tools to deepen the differentiation of the products between them.

Finally, this chapter highlights the behavior of actors in the structuring of an emerging economic space. This consists in taking a stance by theorizing economic models that these actors could master. Henceforth, their relative weight in relation to other actors enables them to gain a foothold in this new space.

Notes

1 i.e. intermediates produced in very large quantities in basic chemistry for sale to fine chemistry according to a traditional division of labor in petroleum chemistry.

2 Incidentally, Dubois uses the word "biorefinery" to refer to this production unit, which is a traditional unit of chemistry.

Bibliography

ACDV, 2013. *ACDV approbation guidelines: voluntary labeling system for the bio-based content of products and materials*. ACDV.

Aresta, M., Dibenedetto, A., Dumeignil, F. (Eds.), 2012. *Biorefinery: from biomass to chemicals and fuels*. de Gruyter.

Bhattacharya, A.K., 2014. Suprabio project: an overview. Presented at the Tomorrow's biorefinery, Brussels.

Bio-Based Industries Consortium, 2012. *The bio-based industries vision: accelerating innovation and market uptake of bio-based products*. Bio-Based Industries Consortium.

Biocore, 2014. *Building tomorrow's biorefineries: findings from case studies performed in the framework of FP7 project Biocore*. Biocore.

Buckhalt, R., 2014. *Biobased products: creating new markets in the US and around the world*.

Carus, M., Dammer, L., Essel, R., 2015. Options for designing the political framework of the European bio-based economy. Nova Paper 6. https://renewable-carbon.eu/publications/product/nova-paper-6-on-bio-based-economy-options-for-designing-the-political-framework-of-the-european-bio-based-economy-%E2%88%92-full-version/, accessed on 10/17/2022.

Dubois, J.-L., 2012. Refinery of the future: feedstock, processes, products, in: Aresta, M., Dibenedetto, A., Dumeignil, F. (Eds.), *Biorefinery: from biomass to chemicals and fuels*. De Gruyer, pp.20–47.

Ellwood, P., Williams, C., Egan, J., 2022. Crossing the valley of death: five underlying innovation processes. *Technovation* 109, 102162. https://doi.org/10.1016/j.technovation.2020.102162.

Finlay, M.R., 2003. Old efforts at new uses: a brief history of chemurgy and the American search for biobased materials. *J. Ind. Ecol.* 7, 33–46. https://doi.org/10.1162/108819803323059389.

Geels, F., Raven, R., 2006. Non-linearity and expectations in niche-development trajectories: ups and downs in Dutch biogas development (1973–2003). *Technol. Anal. Strateg. Manag.* 18, 375–392. https://doi.org/10.1080/09537320600777143.

Golden, J.S., Handfield, B., 2014. *Why biobased? Opportunities in the emerging bioeconomy*. US Department of Agriculture.

Jørgensen, U., 2012. Mapping and navigating transitions: the multi-level perspective compared with arenas of development. *Res. Policy* 41, 996–1010. https://doi.org/10.1016/j.respol.2012.03.001.

Jullien, B., Smith, A. (Eds.), 2008. *Industries and globalization: the political causality of difference, globalization and governance*. Palgrave Macmillan.

Kenis, P., Janowicz-Panjaitan, M., Cambré, B., 2009. *Temporary organizations*. Edward Elgar Publishing. https://doi.org/10.4337/9781849802154.

Langeveld, H., Sanders, J., Meeusen, M. (Eds.), 2012. *The biobased economy: biofuels, materials, and chemicals in the post-oil era*. Earthscan.

McCormick, K., Kautto, N., 2013. The bioeconomy in Europe: an overview. *Sustainability* 5, 2589–2608. https://doi.org/10.3390/su5062589.

National Research Council of the National Academies, 2015. *Industrialization of biology: a roadmap to accelerate the advanced manufacturing of chemicals*. National Research Council.

O'Donohue, M., 2014. *Insight into Biocore's results*. Presented at the Tomorrow's biorefineries in Europe, Brussels.

Platt, B., 2011. *What makes a sustainable biomaterial? Criteria and market-based tools*.

Porter, M.E., 1990. *The competitive advantage of nations*, 10th ed. Palgrave.

Robinson, J.B., 1982. Energy backcasting: a proposed method of policy analysis. *Energy Policy* 10, 337–344. https://doi.org/10.1016/0301-4215(82)90048–90049.

Rodsrud, G., Frölander, A., Sjöde, A., Lersch, M., 2012. Conversion of cellulose, hemicellulose, and lignin into platform molecules: biotechnological approach, in: Aresta, M., Dibenedetto, A., Dumeignil, F. (Eds.), *Biorefinery: from biomass to chemicals and fuels*. De Gruyer, pp.141–166.

Scarlat, N., Dallemand, J.-F., Monforti-Ferrario, F., Nita, V., 2015. The role of biomass and bioenergy in a future bioeconomy: policies and facts. *Environ. Dev.* 15, 3–34. https://doi.org/10.1016/j.envdev.2015.03.006.

SIRA, 2013. *Bio-based and renewable industries for development and growth in Europe*. European Commission.

Tukiainen, S., Granqvist, N., 2016. Temporary organizing and institutional change. *Organ. Stud.* 37, 1819–1840. https://doi.org/10.1177/0170840616662683.

Turton, R. (Ed.), 2012. *Analysis, synthesis, and design of chemical processes*, 4th ed. Prentice Hall.

US Department of Energy, 1998. *Plant/crop-based renewable resources 2020. A vision to enhance US economic security through renewable plant/crop-based resource use*. US Department of Energy.

USDA, 1951. *Crops in peace and war: The yearbook of agriculture, 1950–1951*. USDA.

van Lente, H., 2012. Navigating foresight in a sea of expectations: lessons from the sociology of expectations. *Technol. Anal. Strateg. Manag.* 24, 769–782. https://doi.org/10.1080/09537325.2012.715478.

Vergragt, P.J., Quist, J., 2011. Backcasting for sustainability: introduction to the special issue. *Technol. Forecast. Soc. Change* 78, 747–755. https://doi.org/10.1016/j.techfore.2011.03.010.

The White House, 2012. *National bioeconomy blueprint*. The White House.

5 Alliance-driven governance and the relationship of firms to territories in the bioeconomy

The territorial anchoring of the bioeconomy is seen as a means of ensuring its sustainability, particularly in view of the development of a "circular bioeconomy" (Carus and Dammer, 2018; Stegmann et al., 2020). The latter is seen as a means of redeveloping rural activity through sustainable production, supporting innovation through the development of bioeconomy clusters and reducing the transport of goods. The territory is then perceived as a space for making available, within a cluster or a "biohub", biomass that is already used or under-used (new plants, organic waste, etc.), on which it would be sufficient for economic actors to come and set up (IEA Bioenergy, 2020; OECD, 2017a). In this vision, the development of the bioeconomy is then simply a problem of availability of resources and production infrastructures.

The social sciences literature on the bioeconomy has focused on the structures and networks of the bioeconomy as exposed in the previous chapters (Bauer, 2018; Bauer et al., 2017; Befort, 2020; Bugge et al., 2016; de Besi and McCormick, 2015; Giurca, 2018; Leipold and Petit-Boix, 2018; Purkus et al., 2018; Schmidt et al., 2012; Vivien et al., 2019) or key technologies for the bioeconomy (Bell et al., 2018; Bröring et al., 2020; Cherubini et al., 2009; Strøm-Andersen, 2020). The emergence of the bioeconomy can be seen from all these studies as a demonstration of strategies for alliances between firms, but also with other types of organizations such as research organizations, public authorities, etc. (Morone et al., 2019; Morone and D'Amato, 2019). Moreover, the emergence of a knowledge economy and the fragmentation of knowledge make it necessary to identify and adopt dispersed knowledge for actors wishing to innovate (Antonelli, 2008; Patrucco, 2014). In addition to this problem of knowledge combination, actors in the bioeconomy are faced with the problem of identifying one or more new raw materials that would substitute the use of oil resources.

Consequently, strategies for the development of a bioeconomy must be seen as the result of a triple constraint (Figure 5.1).

The development of a bioeconomy is therefore much more complex than simply the problem of making sufficient resources available on a territorial scale that can be easily exploited by companies. The previous chapters show that it is necessary for actors to develop value chain segments into which they can fit.

DOI: 10.4324/9781003103011-5

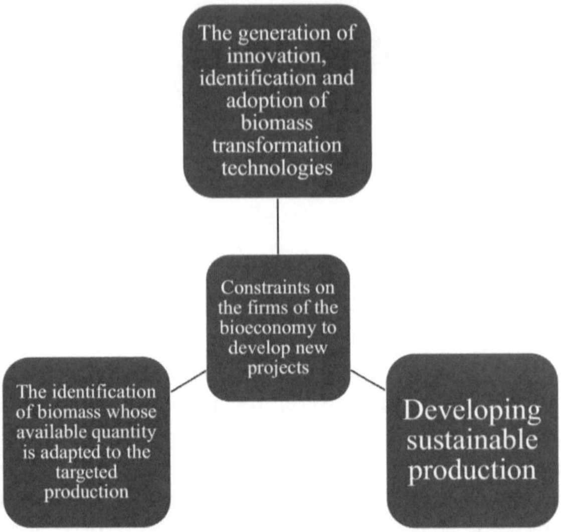

Figure 5.1 Constraints on the firms of the bioeconomy to develop new projects

This chapter aims to open the debate on the behavior of firms in the transition to a bioeconomy with the objective of highlighting the complexity of this issue. Thus, if actors must mobilize material and immaterial resources within alliances in order to develop innovation and production activities in the bioeconomy, these alliances and the relation of firms with the territories must be analyzed. To achieve this goal, this chapter adopts a perspective in terms of *alliance-driven governance* (Birch, 2017). In the case of emerging economic spaces, actors must be able to tie together varied material and immaterial resources located in specific territories, in a multi-scalar logic (MacKinnon et al., 2019). In order to address the formation of these alliances, this chapter focuses more specifically on the territorial anchoring strategies of firms that are emblematic of the bioeconomy.

The first section develops an analytical framework in terms of *alliance-driven governance*. The second section presents the case study approach adopted in this study. The third section is devoted to the presentation of the results of the types of alliances and the relationships to territories maintained by the four firms under study. The fourth section discusses the results of the analysis, showing that actors in the bioeconomy must manage multi-level and multi-scalar alliances to develop their activities. Finally, the conclusion identifies avenues for developing the research outlined in this chapter.

1. An alliance perspective on the bioeconomy

1.1 Clusters and their limits

The relationship of the bioeconomy with its territory has been studied mainly from a structural perspective, on the assumption that clusters would be able to support the development of the bioeconomy (Hermans, 2018). This study considers bioclusters as "*à la Porter*" clusters, i.e. the performance of an economic activity is linked to the conditions of its local environment (Porter, 1990). This approach met with great success in innovation policies from the 1990s onwards with a view to stimulating the emergence of regional innovation systems (Schot and Steinmueller, 2018). The underlying assumption was that the concentration of different parts of a system in a single region would lead to the formation of global leaders (Birch, 2008; Coenen et al., 2004; Cooke, 2004; Cooke and Leydesdorff, 2006). Thus, research on proximity has gained traction in identifying factors fostering regional cooperation and innovation (Balland et al., 2015; Boschma, 2005).

Nevertheless, the evolution of the large vertically integrated firm in an environment of deepened division of labor and complexified fragmented knowledge increased the need for dedicated coordination activities to generate complementarities (Antonelli, 2009, 2008; Brusoni, 2005; Campagnolo and Camuffo, 2009; Consoli and Patrucco, 2008; Langlois, 2003). Therefore, clusters are supposed to play this coordination role with the development of knowledge production and dissemination coordination organizations (Bathelt and Cohendet, 2014; Patrucco, 2005). However, despite the concentration in geographical areas of interlinked activities, it has been shown that firms had no more contact with each other than if they had not belonged to the cluster (Birch, 2009; Malmberg and Power, 2005). As knowledge has become hyper-specialized and very fragmented, the probability that the knowledge available in the territory will be of interest to all actors is then very low. Nevertheless, the cluster has a role in the appropriation of knowledge produced externally, which an actor who is a member of the community formed by the cluster is able to appropriate and disseminate at the cluster level (Beaudry and Breschi, 2003; Orsenigo, 2001).

1.2 Clusters as parts of global knowledge-based commodity chains

The fact that firms are able to disseminate external knowledge throughout their cluster reminds us that these firms belong to global knowledge-based commodity chains (Birch and Cumbers, 2010). That is to say that cluster actors belong to globalized value chains located in specific spaces. Consequently, the actors are linked together by "different processes all of which necessitate access to, as well as the purchase and absorption of, different types of knowledge from scientific discoveries through to marketing reports" (Birch, 2017, p.28). It should be added that these value chains involve not only innovation but also production. Actors must (1) find knowledge that complements the knowledge they possess, and (2) source, process and exchange raw materials. Actors in these chains must then build alliances with suppliers of knowledge, raw materials, etc. that are located in specific spaces and contexts.

The activity of actors in these global knowledge-based commodity chains is therefore multi-level and multi-scalar (Coenen et al., 2012; Truffer and

Coenen, 2012). Thus, actors must compose their strategies in the bioeconomy both in a globalized perspective and in specific spaces holding resources and must be able to capture external resources thanks to the institutional environment of the territory (Cohendet et al., 2014). The choices of anchoring and alliances are therefore multiple coordinations between heterogeneous actors who tie together various resources (knowledge, natural resources, etc.). At the scale of a given territory, a firm may behave as if it were a niche actor, whereas at a global scale, it is an incumbent (Berggren et al., 2015). Consequently, a choice of territorial anchoring of an actor must be analyzed within the framework of its alliances, the institutional context in which it evolves and the exchanges maintained by the actors within the cluster and with the outside of the cluster.

2. Methodology

To analyze the territorial anchoring choices of bioeconomy firms in terms of their alliances and the institutional context in which they operate, this chapter draws on four case studies of firms that are emblematic of the bioeconomy for their territorial anchoring models. The case study method is particularly recognized when conducting exploratory studies aimed at reconstructing the long-term trajectories and richness of the contexts in which the actors operate (Flyvbjerg, 2006; Piore, 2006; Yin, 2014). Similarly, the case studies make it possible to transcribe the empirical richness of the cases studied.

The four firms were selected for the following reasons.

Sofiproteol (April Group since 2015) can be considered as the archetype of the bioeconomy's incumbent and of an alliance logic to control its entire value chain. Linked to one of the most powerful agricultural unions in France, the National Federation of Farmers' Unions, it is a financial structure that was created in 1983 in order to integrate the transformation tools of the French oilseed and protein crop value chain existing at the time, and to be its "armed arm" in terms of industrial valorization. However, from the 1990s onwards, it became one of the leading chemical companies in France through its turnover in biodiesel and derived products. Today, it relies on an institute of excellence (ITE Pivert) created in 2012 as part of public investment program "The investments for the future", responsible for leading public–private research collaboration in the bioeconomy.

Novamont is the product of the history of the Italian chemical crisis. When Montedison was taken over by Feruzzi, Italy's leading food company, Feruzzi's CEO Raul Gardini had the intuition that the future of agribusiness would lie in green chemistry (Vandebroucke and Prost, 1987), and offered the possibility within the group for a research business unit to develop work to produce less harmful chemicals and biosourced plastics. The firm is thus probably the first in Europe to have theorized a model of transition to a post-oil bioeconomy. When the group went bankrupt in the early 1990s, the business unit's researchers decided to maintain it and give it its current independent form as a knowledge-based company.

Created in 2004, Arkema is the product of one of the many restructurings of the French chemical industry which took over assets formerly owned by Elf-Atochem then Atofina. This restructuring led the company to refocus on its expertise in specialty chemicals. Its most important competitive advantage was a type of bio-based polymer, polyamides, developed in France in the 1940s under the name Rilsan. According to an interview with Arkema's Director of Research, in the 1970s and 1990s, the company's chemists avoided communicating the biological origin of its products. Today, on the contrary, this feature has (re)become central. Indeed, the company prides itself on having won a series of Pottier awards (prizes awarded to major innovations in chemistry for sustainable development) between 2006 and the present day, highlighting this origin, which gives it a lead in the bioeconomy over many of its competitors. Arkema is also involved in many European projects.

Finally, we can observe the intensity of the emergence of start-ups in the sector. In transition studies (Langeveld et al., 2010), start-ups are considered as the companies which make change happen. The dissemination of their innovations would then produce an innovation trajectory that would reshape the socio-technical regime in place. The case of Metabolic Explorer, created in 1999, was chosen for our research. It is a knowledge-based company, based on the advances resulting from the scientific revolution in genetic engineering in the academic world; and it is one of the very first in France to claim to specifically mobilize these advances in the field of agro-industries explicitly seeking to supplant oil-based chemistry. Compared to many more recent firms of this type, Metabolic Explorer gives us a relatively long observation perspective.

In order to tackle the question, the study relies on the firms' narratives. Narratives not only have a structuring effect on the actors, but they also express their visions and make it possible to identify the strategies developed by the firms (Brown and Michael, 2003; Franceschini and Pansera, 2015; Renner and Giampietro, 2020; Saltelli et al., 2020).

Following the stage of reconstructing the firms' storytelling, these narratives were confronted with a variety of heterogeneous empirical material: interviews with key actors, scientific publications related to the firms, patents, reports, announcements of joint ventures, investment declarations, etc. The narratives were then presented to the public. The cross-checking between the storytelling of the firms, heterogeneous empirical material and the context to which the firms belong make it possible to reconstruct the development trajectory of the actors and their strategic choices.

3. Results

3.1 Sofiproteol (April Group since 2015): dominant actors of a value-chain and construction of a localized cluster

Sofiproteol was founded in 1983 in response to the crisis that revealed France's dependence on imported soybean meal used in animal feed (Diry, 1987).

Created by the inter-branch organizations of oilseed producers, this organization therefore has a double facet. Firstly, it is the centerpiece of the value chain. It is the tool for integrating all the functions that the agricultural world delegates to its collective organizations (integration of the upstream and downstream parts of the value chain, with food product brands present in supermarkets in Europe, a tool for financing new industrial facilities, lobbying the European Commission, etc.). But Sofiproteol (April) is also deploying a multinational firm strategy described in its 2013 strategic plan, with international acquisitions (Belgium, Romania, Morocco, Algeria, Malaysia). In addition, we can identify a scenario of territorial anchoring of the firm on a regional territory (Picardy, Northern France), and a movement of mutual specialization, with strong interactions with the latter in the co-construction of a cluster which is taking shape today with the PIVERT Energy Transition Institute.

3.1.1 A major actor in oilseeds trying to replicate this dominant position in chemistry

The "soybean crisis" has its source in the compromise between European countries and the USA during the GATT Kennedy Round negotiations of the 1960s, which opened the door for the United States to export its oilcake in exchange for its acceptance of European protectionist measures favorable to French and German cereal producers – with an implicit agreement not to develop soybean cultivation in Europe (Diry, 1987). When the Europeans tried to loosen the grip of this compromise by using substitute crops, they introduced rapeseed into the crop rotation, but then realized that rapeseed could not replace soybean for animal feed because of technical problems (acidity of the feed, lack of palatability for poultry) and the lack of a production tool of sufficient size capable of producing both oil and oilcake. In this dynamic, Sofiproteol was founded by four professional organizations of the value chain (FOP, ONIDOL, UNIP and Prolea)[1] and is similar in its structure to agricultural cooperatives developing an industrial tool.

The biofuels-chemicals activity of the group is concentrated in three firms: Diester, Novance and Oleon. Diester (founded in 1992), because of its quasi-monopoly situation in France during the 1990s, has become synonymous with biodiesel through the brand "Diester". In a 1990 interview, the director of Sofiproteol stated that the oilseed value chain could be saved by the development of non-food uses, but only with the support of the French government. This support took the form of: (1) direct subsidies; (2) an obligation on oil companies to incorporate some biodiesel (produced by Diester) into their liquid fuels in order to cope with the increase in biodiesel production; (3) massive support for research programs aimed at adding value to the by-products of biofuel production which have enabled oilseed producers to survive. It should be noted that these research programs, based on forms of public–private partnerships, have benefited Sofiproteol through its research subsidiary Novance, created in 1996, and have enabled it to position itself as a European leader in oleochemicals.

Oleochemistry refers to both the science of processing vegetable oils and animal fats and the industries that have historically been derived from them (the first being those of soaps and candles, before applications in detergents, lubricants, cosmetics or pharmaceuticals). Competed during the Glorious Thirty by products from the petrochemical industry (mineral oils), oil-based products are now coming back, revitalized by the administered biodiesel markets, to explore a range of solutions aimed at winning back the markets for these petrochemical products (with biodetergents, biosolvents, biolubricants, etc.) (Carus et al., 2011). It is in this context that Sofiproteol took control of Oléon, a Belgian company with the know-how of this historic oleochemicals company. Sofiproteol now presents Oléon as being backed by Novance's research and has chosen to build Oléon's second glycerine production unit near it and the Diester production site in Compiègne.

3.1.2 Agricultural anchor or technology cluster?

As a shared tool for oilseed and protein crop producers, the aim of Sofiproteol is to "develop the French value chain for vegetable oils and proteins, to provide it with new outlets and to allow a fair distribution of value between its players" (interview top management of Sofiproteol, February 2014; author's translation). These actors are "a solid agricultural shareholder base, anchored in the heart of France's regions" (interview with Sofiproteol top management, February 2014; author's translation). It thus seeks to ensure the economic sustainability of agricultural value chains. The logic here is to group together production sites dedicated to non-food products in a "clustering approach".

The site of Compiègne (Picardy, Northern France) stands out, bringing together Saipol (Sofiproteol's subsidiary for raw material transformation), Diester and Oleon/Novance. With this large industrial complex, the Oleon/Novance Oil Chemistry is organized within the research center (supported by the State) on the energy transition Picardie Innovations Végétales Enseignement et Recherches Technologiques (PIVERT), a group of actors of various natures and locations: universities (Compiegne Technological University, Lille University), research organizations (INRAE), engineering companies (for which patents are planned), Sofiproteol, the Industries & Agro-Resources competitiveness cluster (IAR; the French bioeconomy cluster whose positions are very influential with the European Commission). Chemical companies are present in the same region as well (Rhodia, Arkema). In the same way, PIVERT federates research centers from all over France around the construction of this geographical conglomeration, as theorized by the interprofession of the value chain.

3.2 Circular economy and territorial anchoring: the case of Novamont

Novamont has been exploring the economic development of low environmental impact chemicals and bio-based plastics since the late 1980s. Various media operations, from supplying the raw material for the "green pens" for the Rio Summit in 1992 to the supply of short-life crockery for the London Olympic Games, gave Novamont a high media profile. In 1996, the company's researchers were able to find support from major institutional investors. The company set up its R&D and pilot plant in Novara, near Milan, without maintaining any special relations with the Lombardy agricultural area. It then took part in a patent war to control the emergence of biomass products, particularly against American and German firms, which lasted until 2005. The important thing to note here is that the firm's plan was to use these patents for internal industrial development.

The presence of a former minister at the head of the company attests, as in the case of Sofiproteol in France, to the firm's national anchoring. This status gives Novamont not only a real capacity for intervention (particularly with the European Commission), but also the possibility of building a "storytelling" in which the firm describes itself as a bearer of the general interest. The firm claims its business model to be coherent from an environmental point of view. This model is summarized in the expression "Novamont, the power of limits" used to clearly indicate the extent to which it has become imbued with the issue of environmental limits (Bastioli, 2008).

Studies on bioplastics show that those aiming at pure and simple substitution of fossil-derived products to "green" certain end products are likely to have the highest growth potential over the next 15 years (e.g. Karan et al., 2019). However, Novamont refuses to follow this technical-economic path, precisely in the name of its vision of a circular economy and sustainability. Novamont is therefore deliberately restricting the possible applications of its research in order to preserve the core of its project. For example, when recycling solutions exist, Novamont does not develop biosourced products that compete with recycling (Bastioli, 2008).

The firm had kept its distance from biofuels, and when it decided to take up the biorefinery theme in 2006–2007, it insisted in its transition theorization on the need for a territorialized biorefinery (Ganapini, 2013). The company located near Milan is seeking to institutionalize its relationship with local suppliers of renewable resources (such as oilseeds). At the end of 2006, the firm signed a contract with the Umbrian Association of Agricultural Producers, proposing to develop an industrial unit on the Terni site: is this nevertheless a simple local alliance linked to the dynamics of innovation?

It does not seem so because, in reality, Novamont is seeking to build, with its institutional support, a national transition strategy based on the threefold problem of reindustrialization, a circular economy and a transition to the use of renewable resources. It will thus contribute to the emergence of a national "cluster" policy. One of the national clusters (Spring cluster) selected will, of course, focus on the theme of green chemistry and the bioeconomy.

The counterpart of the public support is the State's request to the company to help revitalize bank petrochemical sites, in particular through *retrofitting* (i.e.

site redevelopment). This is the case of the Porto Torres site in Sardinia, which Novamont is seeking to revitalize through a *joint venture* with Versalis (the chemical subsidiary of the Italian petrochemical company ENI). Novamont then develops a discourse on the valorization of local non-food plants (such as thistle in Sardinia) in its circular economy strategy, in association with Coldiretti (the Italian farmers' association).

3.3 Arkema: chemical company and location according to demand

3.3.1 A historic French chemical company

Formerly known as Atofina (resulting in 2000 from the merger of the chemical activities of Elf-Atochimie, renamed Atochem in 1983, and Total-Fina), Arkema can therefore be considered as a former French chemical company. And its historical roots can be traced back in the chemical corridor with sites mainly in Lyon, Grenoble and Valencia. It still has six production and research sites (mainly around Lyon) in the Rhône-Alpes region. It is the result of the numerous restructurings in the petrochemical industry that began in the 1980s (Galambos et al., 2007) and which led to French, Belgian and Italian groups retreating into specialty chemicals (like Solvay, for example). These then sought to establish a monopoly position on the products they had historically dominated: "Specialty chemicals are different from commodity chemicals due to their higher added value, lower tonnages and the fact that there are few players on the world markets" (Arkema interview #2, 2013).

In Arkema's case, it is polyamide 11 (PA11) which is dedicated to specialty applications in coatings and the production of plastics that must resist extreme conditions (temperature, humidity, etc.). PA11 was invented in 1947 and was marketed in the 1950s by Ato Chimie under the Rilsan brand name. As indicated above, while the bio-based origin of the products was not put forward, the emergence of the bioeconomy has enabled Arkema to transform this bio-based origin into a commercial argument (Arkema's 2014 public brochure on Rilsan).

3.3.2 The expansion of Arkema's activity into bio-based oils chemistry

In 2012, Arkema acquired two Chinese companies, Hebei Casda and Suzhou Hipro Polymers, strengthening its presence in China. These companies respectively produce sebacic acid (a monomer needed to produce 6/10 polyamides) from castor oil and 10/10 polyamides. While Arkema states that the purpose of this facility is to move closer to demand (Arkema's public brochures in 2010 and 2011), the value of these acquisitions also lies in the vertical and horizontal integration of the polyamide value chain, in a context of competition with BASF and Solvay. The acquisition of Hebei Casda enables Arkema to integrate the knowledge base of the Chinese firm, which has a polyamide research laboratory, but also to integrate upstream in the polyamide value chain by controlling the production of essential chemical intermediates. In February 2014 an interview with one of Arkema's research managers confirmed that the company is seeking to move closer to the production of agricultural raw materials and is conducting trials on castor oil production to secure its supplies in competition with BASF, which is also seeking to increase its polyamide production activity. The integration of the production of another type of polyamide (polyamide 10/10) into its product portfolio is intended to broaden its range of products for their use in the production of fibers.

The strategy for developing the chemical uses of bio-based oils also involves the use of glycerol, the major co-product of biodiesel production, to replace propylene (of petroleum origin) in order to produce acrylic acid from acrolein. Initial tests have been carried out at a German test site and an industrial pilot was expected to be set up in Carling (Moselle, eastern France) in one of the world's largest acrylic acid plants. Arkema's participation in the PIVERT Institute, presented in the case study on Sofiproteol, therefore makes sense in the strategy of replacing and converting its industrial facilities to produce bio-based polymers.

3.4 Metabolic Explorer: from IP-centric strategy failures to industrial offshoring

The opening up of intellectual property rights to living organisms (Coriat and Orsi, 2002) and the "biotech revolution" have brought to light a model of economic relations based on the holding of key patents by start-ups (resulting in the overwhelming majority of cases from the privatization of public research results). Metabolic Explorer was created in 1999.

The theorization of its future economic model led it in the early 2000s to propose to partners to acquire exclusive territorial licenses (on a specific agricultural region), with the responsibility for ensuring industrialization lying with these partners. The aim was therefore to develop an operational R&D strategy for target products, with a clearly identified process, in order to deliver a process that could be mobilized by agribusiness incumbents. From a certain point of view, the vision therefore remains a national vision of value chain development, based on regional planning for the emergence of sites. The company set up in Clermont-Ferrand (central France), in what became in 1995 the "Biocluster Clermont Limagne" dedicated to agri-food and pharmaceutical biotechnologies. This cluster is notably home to the historic Auvergne seed and cereal cooperative Limagrain or Carbios, another biotechnology start-up in the bioeconomy. The members of Metabolic Explorer did not really provide us with an explanation of this location, but the information available suggests that the idea of a territorial anchorage responding to an exploration phase on a site that allows research interactions presided over this choice – in other cases clusters seek to attract start-ups corresponding to their theme in order to enrich their ecosystem (Cohendet et al., 2014).

The company experienced a first failure in the conceptualization of its business model: the firm's multi-regional licensing strategy has clearly failed. The utopia of a sequence (fundamental research in universities/industrial R&D in start-ups/national spin-off policy) that would have ultimately made Metabolic Explorer a common actor in different territories was thus invalidated. The firm's strategy then evolved towards exclusive partnership agreements within joint ventures (which is the general model proposed or even imposed by incumbents on start-ups; Befort, 2020). The advantage for the incumbents is to be able to reduce the risks associated with technological exploration. For example, in 2005, Metabolic Explorer concluded an agreement with the starch manufacturer Roquette on a process for producing methionine, which is an amino acid widely used in animal feed, but until then a product of fossil origin. This agreement stipulated that Metabolic Explorer was to take charge of the development of the process, which would then be industrialized by Roquette in the north of France, near Lille. However, in 2014, Roquette announced that it was giving up the industrialization of this process, giving Metabolic Explorer back its freedom.

The company therefore finds itself in failure, this time with a *joint venture* business model and a strategy that we can describe as a-territorialized. Since then, the company seems to have taken a new turn by seeking to carry out industrial development itself, in a direct way. A product of French research, Metabolic Explorer did not hesitate to form an alliance with Technip in the United States through a development agreement to industrialize methionine. Similarly, faced with the failure of the licensing strategy, Metabolic Explorer sought to industrialize its Texerol production process (1.3 propanediol, one of the flagship molecules for biotech start-ups in the bioeconomy) in South Malaysia in the Iskandar region starting in 2010–2011. But the construction of the site encountered difficulties which led Metabolic Explorer to abandon construction in 2014, and to grant an exclusive license to the Korean firm SK Chemicals, an agreement which has now been dissolved.

4. Discussion

4.1 The diversity of alliances and relationships to territories of bioeconomy firms

In the case of Sofiproteol, it is a question of finding new uses for all oilseed producers, based on localized problems of excess production and undersizing of the industrial apparatus. Coupled with the integration of the value chain within the firm, the latter has chosen to develop *innovation commons* (Potts, 2019) on the territory of Compiègne in northern France. The latter participates in structuring the firm's R&D, the results of which are appropriate and disseminated to all branches.

Novamont does not start from the resource, but from a knowledge base that it seeks to develop with a strong sustainability perspective and a thinking of limits. Its choices of territorial anchorage are influenced by the objective of developing ecologically sustainable industrial activities. Consequently, it develops symbiotic relations with the territory. But its alliances are less integrated than those of Sofiproteol. In fact, Novamont allies itself with producers of raw materials located on its territory, firms with complementary knowledge and with downstream companies to demonstrate its products.

Arkema is developing alliances that differ from the two previous ones because of its positioning as a producer of specialty chemicals. Thus, Arkema seeks to maintain its (near) monopoly on specific segments of the value chain. Its alliances therefore serve above all to strengthen and protect this position. Its alliances with territories are therefore a combination of historical heritage, adaptation to demand needs and a desire to position itself in the significant clusters of the bioeconomy.

Finally, the start-up Metabolic Explorer is developing its territorial anchorage in line with its strategy to position itself as a supplier of complementary technologies for *incumbents*. The firm is therefore positioning itself according to the demand for its technologies.

Table 5.1 summarizes the alliance strategies of bioeconomy actors and their relationship to territories.

4.2 Multi-level and multi-scalar alliances to build heterogeneous resources

Although the firms under study deploy heterogeneous alliance strategies, they share the common feature of developing multi-level alliances linking niche actors, regime actors and landscape actors. Yet an incumbent firm such as Novamont nevertheless deploys alliances not only with petrochemical companies such as Versalis, but also with niche actors such as thistle producers in Sardinia. Similarly, the company is developing alliances with actors in the *landscape*, enabling it to obtain regulations favorable to its activity. Sofiproteol, for its part, has established itself as a multi-level actor where it is developing the activity of a multinational firm while participating in the creation of a common innovation space aimed at generating knowledge complementary to its activity (Berggren et al., 2015).

These alliances allow the actors involved to mobilize a variety of resources, whether subsidies, public policies, private investors, external knowledge, etc. This raises the question of the policies that territories could develop to support the development of a sustainable bioeconomy rooted in the territories. The case of Metabolic Explorer shows that these niche actors, because of their economic model, seek to establish relationships based on the complementarity of their knowledge with the demand of industrialists. Due to the dispersion of knowledge, it is unlikely that the knowledge produced by a start-up is then appropriate for other established actors. If the objective is to develop the bioeconomy and enable the ecological transition of industries, territories should promote the development of open R&D infrastructures, promote the connection of actors to external value chains while aiming to develop industrial projects, which implies high capital and infrastructure investments (Barbier, 2010; MacKinnon et al., 2019).

Table 5.1 The positioning of firms in the bioeconomy according to their alliances

	Types of production	*Alliances with the territories*	*Alliances in the value chain*	*Resources mobilized*
Sofiproteol	• Food/non-food • Innovation aimed at valorizing excess resources	• National and regional anchoring thanks to a distribution of activities over the territory through production and R&D activities • Formation of territorialized innovation commons	• Full integration of the value chain steps in the firm • Some external alliances to benefit from knowledge sharing	• Public support • Knowledge developed by group subsidiaries • Knowledge of allied firms
Novamont	• Non-food (biodegradable plastics, etc.) • Innovations for producing plastics from non-food plant fractions	• Creation of industrial symbioses • Local supply • Ecological reindustrialization of territories	• Upstream alliances for the supply of raw materials • Alliances with complementary firms • Alliances with the downstream to demonstrate its products	• Institutional (former minister, legislation, etc.) • Firm-specific knowledge • Institutional investors
Arkema	• Specialty chemicals	• Anchorages according to demand location and historical clusters	• Upstream alliances for maintaining oligopolies on specific segments of the value chain	• Knowledge capital of the firm • Institutional (backcasting, etc.)
Metabolic Explorer	• Innovation/ knowledge	• Opportunistic alliances according to the possibilities of producing licenses on its technologies for industrialization	• Alliances based on the needs of other companies for complementary technologies owned by Metabolic Explorer	• Institutional investors • Risk capital • Macroactors and networks of macroactors

5. Conclusion

The question of the relationship to the territories of firms in the bioeconomy is seen mainly as a question of the availability of raw materials or knowledge or infrastructures such as clusters (European Commission, 2012; European Commission, Directorate-General for Research and Innovation, 2018; IEA Bioenergy, 2020; OECD, 2017b; Stadler and Chauvet, 2018). The perspective developed in this chapter shows that bioeconomy firms must compose their relationship to territories within multi-level and multi-scalar alliances. These alliances enable them to access the resources necessary for their strategies, whether financial or institutional resources, raw materials or knowledge.

This chapter opens up a new perspective on the development of the bioeconomy by calling for a shift away from an essentially structural perspective to an analysis of the behavior of actors in the bioeconomy (Hellsmark and Hansen, 2020). Thus, global value chain and global production network approaches could be fertile in capturing the effect of the development of bio-based production in the bioeconomy.

Note

1 The FOP represents oilseed and protein producers, ONIDOL represents oilseed producers. UNIP is the federation of protein producers, and PROLEA the funding body for French oilseed and protein producers.

Bibliography

Antonelli, C., 2009. The economics of innovation: from the classical legacies to the economics of complexity. *Econ. Innov. New Technol.* 18, 611–646. https://doi.org/10.1080/10438590802564543.

Antonelli, C., 2008. *Localised technological change: towards the economics of complexity.* Routledge.

Balland, P.-A., Boschma, R., Frenken, K., 2015. Proximity and innovation: from statics to dynamics. *Reg. Stud.* 49, 907–920. https://doi.org/10.1080/00343404.2014.883598.

Barbier, E., 2010. *A global green new deal: rethinking the economic recovery.* Cambridge University Press.

Bastioli, C., 2008. *Le materie prime rinnovabili e la transizione da economia di prodotto ad economia di sistema.* Presented at the Remise de doctorat honoris causa à Castia Bastiolo, Gènes.

Bathelt, H., Cohendet, P., 2014. The creation of knowledge: local building, global accessing and economic development: toward an agenda. *J. Econ. Geogr.* 14, 869–882. https://doi.org/10.1093/jeg/lbu027.

Bauer, F., 2018. Narratives of biorefinery innovation for the bioeconomy: conflict, consensus, or confusion? *Environ. Innov. Soc. Transit.* 28, 96–107. https://doi.org/10.1016/j.eist.2018.01.005.

Bauer, F., Coenen, L., Hansen, T., McCormick, K., Palgan, Y.V., 2017. Technological innovation systems for biorefineries: a review of the literature: technological innovation systems for biorefineries. *Biofuels Bioprod. Biorefining* 11, 534–548. https://doi.org/10.1002/bbb.1767.

Beaudry, C., Breschi, S., 2003. Are firms in clusters really more innovative? *Econ. Innov. New Technol.* 12, 325–342. https://doi.org/10.1080/10438590290020197.

Befort, N., 2020. Going beyond definitions to understand tensions within the bioeconomy: the contribution of sociotechnical regimes to contested fields. *Technol. Forecast. Soc. Change* 153, 119923. https://doi.org/10.1016/j.techfore.2020.119923.

Bell, J., Paula, L., Dodd, T., Németh, S., Nanou, C., Mega, V., Campos, P., 2018. EU ambition to build the world's leading bioeconomy: uncertain times demand innovative and sustainable solutions. *New Biotechnol.* 40, 25–30. https://doi.org/10.1016/j.nbt.2017.06.010.

Berggren, C., Magnusson, T., Sushandoyo, D., 2015. Transition pathways revisited: established firms as multi-level actors in the heavy vehicle industry. *Res. Policy* 44, 1017–1028. https://doi.org/10.1016/j.respol.2014.11.009.

Birch, K., 2017. *Innovation, regional development and the life sciences: beyond clusters*, Routledge.

Birch, K., 2009. The knowledge-space dynamic in the UK bioeconomy. *Area* 41, 273–284. https://doi.org/10.1111/j.1475-4762.2008.00864.x.

Birch, K., 2008. Alliance-driven governance: applying a global commodity chains approach to the UK biotechnology industry. *Econ. Geogr.* 84, 83–103.

Birch, K., Cumbers, A., 2010. Knowledge, space, and economic governance: the implications of knowledge-based commodity chains for less-favoured regions. *Environ. Plan. Econ. Space* 42, 2581–2601. https://doi.org/10.1068/a43191.

Boschma, R., 2005. Proximity and innovation: a critical assessment. *Reg. Stud.* 39, 61–74. https://doi.org/10.1080/0034340052000320887.

Bröring, S., Laibach, N., Wustmans, M., 2020. Innovation types in the bioeconomy. *J. Clean. Prod.* 266, 121939. https://doi.org/10.1016/j.jclepro.2020.121939.

Brown, N., Michael, M., 2003. A sociology of expectations: retrospecting prospects and prospecting retrospects. *Technol. Anal. Strateg. Manag.* 15, 3–18. https://doi.org/10.1080/0953732032000046024.

Brusoni, S., 2005. The limits to specialization: problem solving and coordination in "modular networks". *Organ. Stud.* 26, 1885–1907. https://doi.org/10.1177/0170840605059161.

Bugge, M., Hansen, T., Klitkou, A., 2016. What is the bioeconomy? A review of the literature. *Sustainability* 8, 691. https://doi.org/10.3390/su8070691.

Campagnolo, D., Camuffo, A., 2009. The concept of modularity in management studies: a literature review. *Int. J. Manag. Rev.* https://doi.org/10.1111/j.1468-2370.2009.00260.x.

Carus, M., Carrez, D., Kaeb, H., Ravenstijn, J., Venus, J., 2011. Level playing field for bio-based chemistry and materials. Nova Paper 1. https://renewable-carbon.eu/publications/product/nova-paper-1-on-bio-based-economy-level-playing-field-for-bio-based-chemistry-and-materials-–-full-version/, accessed on 10/17/2022.

Carus, M., Dammer, L., 2018. The circular bioeconomy: concepts, opportunities, and limitations. *Ind. Biotechnol.* 14, 83–91. https://doi.org/10.1089/ind.2018.29121.mca.

Cherubini, F., Jungmeier, G., Wellisch, M., Willke, T., Skiadas, I., Van Ree, R., de Jong, E., 2009. Toward a common classification approach for biorefinery systems. *Biofuels Bioprod. Biorefining* 3, 534–546. https://doi.org/10.1002/bbb.172.

Coenen, L., Benneworth, P., Truffer, B., 2012. Toward a spatial perspective on sustainability transitions. *Res. Policy* 41, 968–979. https://doi.org/10.1016/j.respol.2012.02.014.

Coenen, L., Moodysson, J., Asheim, B.T., 2004. Nodes, networks and proximities: on the knowledge dynamics of the Medicon Valley biotech cluster. *Eur. Plan. Stud.* 12, 1003–1018. https://doi.org/10.1080/0965431042000267876.

Cohendet, P., Grandadam, D., Simon, L., Capdevila, I., 2014. Epistemic communities, localization and the dynamics of knowledge creation. *J. Econ. Geogr.* 14, 929–954. https://doi.org/10.1093/jeg/lbu018.

Consoli, D., Patrucco, P.P., 2008. Innovation platforms and the governance of knowledge: evidence from Italy and the UK. *Econ. Innov. New Technol.* 17, 699–716. https://doi.org/10.1080/10438590701785694.

Cooke, P., 2004. The molecular biology revolution and the rise of bioscience megacentres in North America and Europe. *Environ. Plan. C Gov. Policy* 22, 161–177. https://doi.org/10.1068/c0344.

Cooke, P., Leydesdorff, L., 2006. Regional development in the knowledge-based economy: the construction of advantage. *J. Technol. Transf.* 31, 5–15. https://doi.org/10.1007/s10961-005-5009-3.

Coriat, B., Orsi, F., 2002. Establishing a new intellectual property rights regime in the United States. *Res. Policy* 31, 1491–1507. https://doi.org/10.1016/S0048-7333(02)00078–00071.

de Besi, M., McCormick, K., 2015. Towards a bioeconomy in Europe: national, regional and industrial strategies. *Sustainability* 7, 10461–10478. https://doi.org/10.3390/su70810461.

Diry, J.-P., 1987. La communauté économique européenne et la question du soja. *Rev. Géographie Lyon* 62, 291–312.

European Commission, 2012. *Innovating for sustainable growth: A bioeconomy for Europe.* Communication from the Commission to the European Parliament, the Council, the European Economic and Social Committee and the Committee of the Regions No. SWD(2012) 11 final. European Commission.

European Commission, Directorate-General for Research and Innovation, 2018. *A sustainable bioeconomy for Europe: strengthening the connection between economy, society and the environment.* Updated bioeconomy strategy. European Commission.

Flyvbjerg, B., 2006. Five misunderstandings about case-study research. *Qual. Inq.* 12, 219–245. https://doi.org/10.1177/1077800405284363.

Franceschini, S., Pansera, M., 2015. Beyond unsustainable eco-innovation: the role of narratives in the evolution of the lighting sector. *Technol. Forecast. Soc. Change* 92, 69–83. https://doi.org/10.1016/j.techfore.2014.11.007.

Galambos, L., Hikino, T., Zamagni, V. (Eds.), 2007. *The global chemical industry in the age of the petrochemical revolution.* Cambridge University Press.

Ganapini, W. (Ed.), 2013. *Bioplastics: A case study of bioeconomy in Italy.* Edizioni Ambiente.

Giurca, A., 2018. Unpacking the network discourse: actors and storylines in Germany's wood-based bioeconomy. *For. Policy Econ.* 101754. https://doi.org/10.1016/j.forpol.2018.05.009.

Hellsmark, H., Hansen, T., 2020. A new dawn for (oil) incumbents within the bioeconomy? Trade-offs and lessons for policy. *Energy Policy* 145, 111763. https://doi.org/10.1016/j.enpol.2020.111763.

Hermans, F., 2018. The potential contribution of transition theory to the analysis of bioclusters and their role in the transition to a bioeconomy: The analysis of bioclusters. *Biofuels Bioprod. Biorefining* 12, 265–276. https://doi.org/10.1002/bbb.1861.

IEA Bioenergy, 2020. *Bio-hubs as keys to successful biomass supply for the bioeconomy.* IEA Bioenergy Task 43 & Natural Resources Canada.

Karan, H., Funk, C., Grabert, M., Oey, M., Hankamer, B., 2019. Green bioplastics as part of a circular bioeconomy. *Trends in Plant Science* 24, 237–249. doi:10.1016/j.tplants.2018.11.010.

Langeveld, J.W.A., Dixon, J., Jaworski, J.F., 2010. Development perspectives of the biobased economy: a review. *Crop Sci.* 50, S142–S151. https://doi.org/10.2135/cropsci2009.09.0529.

Langlois, R.N., 2003. Strategy as economics versus economics as strategy. *Manag. Decis. Econ.* 24, 283–290. https://doi.org/10.1002/mde.1121.

Leipold, S., Petit-Boix, A., 2018. The circular economy and the bio-based sector: perspectives of European and German stakeholders. *J. Clean. Prod.* 201, 1125–1137. https://doi.org/10.1016/j.jclepro.2018.08.019.

MacKinnon, D., Dawley, S., Pike, A., Cumbers, A., 2019. Rethinking path creation: a geographical political economy approach. *Econ. Geogr.* 95, 113–135. https://doi.org/10.1080/00130095.2018.1498294.

Malmberg, A., Power, D., 2005. (How) do (firms in) clusters create knowledge? *Ind. Innov.* 12, 409–431. https://doi.org/10.1080/13662710500381583.

Morone, P., D'Amato, D., 2019. The role of sustainability standards in the uptake of bio-based chemicals. *Curr. Opin. Green Sustain. Chem.* 19, 45–49. https://doi.org/10.1016/j.cogsc.2019.05.003.

Morone, P., Falcone, P.M., Lopolito, A., 2019. How to promote a new and sustainable food consumption model: a fuzzy cognitive map study. *J. Clean. Prod.* 208, 563–574. https://doi.org/10.1016/j.jclepro.2018.10.075.

OECD, 2017a. *Investing in climate, investing in growth.* OECD. https://doi.org/10.1787/9789264273528-en.

OECD, 2017b. *Biorefineries models and policy.* No. DSTI/STP/BNCT(2016)16/FINAL. OECD.

Orsenigo, L., 2001. The (failed) development of a biotechnology cluster: the case of Lombardy. *Small Bus. Econ.* 17, 77–92.

Patrucco, P.P., 2014. The evolution of knowledge organization and the emergence of a platform for innovation in the car industry. *Ind. Innov.* 21, 243–266. https://doi.org/10.1080/13662716.2014.910892.

Patrucco, P.P., 2005. The emergence of technology systems: knowledge production and distribution in the case of the Emilian plastics district. *Camb. J. Econ.* 29, 37–56. https://doi.org/10.1093/cje/bei011.

Piore, M.J., 2006. Qualitative research: does it fit in economics? *Eur. Manag. Rev.* 3, 17–23. https://doi.org/10.1057/palgrave.emr.1500053.

Porter, M.E., 1990. *The competitive advantage of nations*, 10th ed. Palgrave.

Potts, J., 2019. *Innovation commons: the origin of economic growth.* Oxford University Press.

Purkus, A., Hagemann, N., Bedtke, N., Gawel, E., 2018. Towards a sustainable innovation system for the German wood-based bioeconomy: implications for policy design. *J. Clean. Prod.* 172, 3955–3968. https://doi.org/10.1016/j.jclepro.2017.04.146.

Renner, A., Giampietro, M., 2020. Socio-technical discourses of European electricity decarbonization: contesting narrative credibility and legitimacy with quantitative story-telling. *Energy Res. Soc. Sci.* 59, 101279. https://doi.org/10.1016/j.erss.2019.101279.

Saltelli, A., Benini, L., Funtowicz, S., Giampietro, M., Kaiser, M., Reinert, E., van der Sluijs, J.P., 2020. The technique is never neutral: how methodological choices condition the generation of narratives for sustainability. *Environ. Sci. Policy* 106, 87–98. https://doi.org/10.1016/j.envsci.2020.01.008.

Schmidt, O., Padel, S., Levidow, L., 2012. The bio-economy concept and knowledge base in a public goods and farmer perspective. *Bio-based and Applied Economics.* https://doi.org/10.13128/BAE-10770.

Schot, J., Steinmueller, W.E., 2018. Three frames for innovation policy: R&D, systems of innovation and transformative change. *Res. Policy* 47, 1554–1567. https://doi.org/10.1016/j.respol.2018.08.011.

Stadler, T., Chauvet, J.-M., 2018. New innovative ecosystems in France to develop the bioeconomy. *New Biotechnol.* 40, 113–118. https://doi.org/10.1016/j.nbt.2017.07.009.

Stegmann, P., Londo, M., Junginger, M., 2020. The circular bioeconomy: its elements and role in European bioeconomy clusters. *Resour. Conserv. Recycl.: X* 6, 100029. https://doi.org/10.1016/j.rcrx.2019.100029.

Strøm-Andersen, N., 2020. Innovation and by-product valorization: a comparative analysis of the absorptive capacity of food processing firms. *J. Clean. Prod.* 253, 119943. https://doi.org/10.1016/j.jclepro.2019.119943.

Truffer, B., Coenen, L., 2012. Environmental innovation and sustainability transitions in regional studies. *Reg. Stud.* 46, 1–21. https://doi.org/10.1080/00343404.2012.646164.

Vandebroucke, M., Prost, B., 1987. Le groupe italien Feruzzi: de l'agro-alimentaire à l'agro-chimie, une stratégie audacieuse de l'utilisation des produits agricoles. *Revue de Géographie de Lyon* 62, 313–337.

Vivien, F.-D., Nieddu, M., Befort, N., Debref, R., Giampietro, M., 2019. The hijacking of the bioeconomy. *Ecol. Econ.* 159, 189–197. https://doi.org/10.1016/j.ecolecon.2019.01.027.

Yin, R.K., 2014. *Case study research: design and methods*, 5th ed. SAGE.

6 Product development in the bioeconomy, the case of lactic acid and PLA

Chapters 3 and 4 showed that the bioeconomy is shaped by focusing on emblematic objects such as the biorefinery or on specific products. These products, at the institutional level, serve to illustrate visions of the future. Nevertheless, the force of these expectations comes from their material translation into objects that can be produced. The previous chapters have thus focused on the question of guiding principles, involving reflection in terms of substitution and the institutions organizing the space of competition. The aim of this chapter is to study the formation of product focus through an approach based on the economics of promises. The originality of this approach resides in a microeconomic approach to the study of the formation of these promises. Also, the objective is to account for the decision-making of actors when they make their technological choices. In order to contribute to the study of product development in the bioeconomy, this chapter is based on the following elements.

It is a question of reconstructing, over a long period, the logic of substitution that governs the development of polylactic acid. Because of its long history, it is thus possible to go back to 1780 and to study the different phases of the development of this product. However, this reconstruction is based on both the constitution of the PLA knowledge base and its implementation in the "economic development" of the product. This perspective thus aims to identify the place of R&D and the problems that the actors encounter in industrializing their products (Ellwood et al., 2022).

From a methodological point of view, this chapter is based on the collection of heterogeneous empirical materials (patents, natural science publications, company press releases and interviews). These materials make it possible to trace the evolution of PLA development over a long period of time and thus to highlight the dynamics of the formation of promises and the way in which actors go through these periods.

Section 1 is devoted to the analysis of the development dynamics of lactic acid, the precursor of polylactic acid. The second section is devoted to the dynamics of promises around the development of polylactic acid, which is now one of the most important biodegradable plastics.

DOI: 10.4324/9781003103011-6

1. Lactic acid, a basic product that comes from far away

1.1 Lactic acid and the development of industrial fermentation

Lactic acid was first used in the form of curd at the end of the 18th century in order to clean textiles. Since fermentation methods were not well developed, a form of "empirical fermentation" was used. Because of the long drying time it required, curd was replaced by sulfuric acid in the cleaning of fabrics. Curd was discovered in 1780 by Scheele, a Swedish chemist, who named it "Mjölksyra", meaning "milk acid". It was renamed "lactic acid" by Lavoisier in 1789. The product was essentially extracted from milk, however it was demonstrated in 1813 that it could also be obtained by the fermentation of beet sugar. This opened a new way of producing lactic acid from plants. We can observe here the phenomenon whereby chemistry is a research discipline applied to the substitution of one raw material by another, as described by Bensaude-Vincent and Stengers (cf. Chapter 3). This search for substitution occurred in the context of the Napoleonic Wars, whose blockades caused a shortage of sugar and led to the diffusion of sugar beet in France and Germany.

The history of lactic acid is also linked to the birth of chemistry in Germany with the chemist Liebig. He was particularly interested in plant chemistry and promoted soil fertilization. He notably inspired Marx in his reflections on the capitalist exploitation of nature (Foster, 2000). The competition between the German states within the Customs Union led to the emergence of the "Technische Hochschule" dedicated to the training of engineers and scientists for German industry. A large part of the German chemical industry thus found its origins at that time around Liebig. As early as 1845, research showed that if lactic acid was heated and then cooled, a solid yet flexible material was formed: polylactic acid. Although it was impossible to characterize this material because polymer chemistry did not yet exist, some of the processes that are used today to produce plastics from PLA had already been identified.

The interest of this period in the "chemistry of life and the causes of fermentation", to use Benninga's expression (1990), can be underlined. The knowledge base was thus formed through research on product preservation processes that sought to mobilize traditional know-how for industrialization. Fermentation was either the first step before putrefaction or a step towards preservation. The German beer industry also contributed to the improvement of the knowledge of the fermentation process by its technical progress in the modification of the fermentation methods of lagers. These are the basis for the production of lactic acid, whether it is the use of curd in the textile industry or the discovery of lactic acid production from sugar beet. Advances in lactic acid research have also focused on the use of yeast for fermentation (the first biotechnologies of scientific origin, so to speak). Their effectiveness was demonstrated by Pasteur, who also worked on lactic acid. Thus, yeast preparations specifically making it possible to produce lactic acid were developed between 1857 and 1859.

1.2 From food to solvents: the uses of lactic acid

1.2.1 The first industrial uses of lactic acid in the United States

According to Benninga (1990), the first industrial production unit for lactic acid was built in 1883 in the United States in Littleton, Colorado. Lactic acid was produced there from corn starch for different types of applications. The first use was for tanning, as with the first uses described above. The second type of product was lactic acid in liquid form intended as a substitute for vinegar. This period of "pre-industrial" chemistry is, from a certain point of view, similar to the advent of petroleum chemistry: the traditional uses have been gradually replaced by the first productions of chemistry. For example, lactic acid produced in Littleton was used as a substitute for vinegar in food preservation. However, lactic acid was also used for the production of beverages and for tanning. This use was particularly developed in Germany in the production units of Boehringer, which sought to replace tartaric acid, the price of which was rising, with lactic acid. The use of lactic acid in beverages and food (as an additive in flours and preparations for the manufacture of loaves of bread or buns, and then powdered milk) required improvements in the processes for extracting the acid: the food use required very pure products, unlike the industrial uses.

1.2.2 The use of lactic acid as a solvent during World War I

In Germany, during World War I, due to restrictions on the import of raw materials, lactic acid was widely used for food preservation. However, the lactic acid industry was also mobilized to participate in the war effort in the substitution of glycerol. Its production was becoming scarce and problematic, especially regarding the manufacture of solvents and cooling systems for vehicles and cannons from 1916 onwards. It is worth noting that lactic acid was mixed with ethanol (also derived from fermentation) in a process not dissimilar to the one used today to produce what are called "green solvents". Indeed, two papers in the emblematic journal *Green Chemistry*, which presents itself as "the home of cutting-edge research on the development of alternative sustainable technologies" (RSC, n.d.), report advances in solvents using this ethyl lactate (Aparicio and Alcalde, 2009; Pereira et al., 2011).

1.2.3 Lactic acid between the two wars

After World War I, the production of lactic acid slowly declined in France, England and the United States, while it was maintained in Germany, partly due to the strength of the German fermentation industry. Lactic acid has been challenged in particular by citric acid in pharmaceutical uses and in beverages, because the latter does not add flavor, unlike lactic acid. Nevertheless, in the field that interests us most, the lactic acid industry persists, notably by benefiting from the chemurgy movement. It was then used in the production of fibers and films, i.e., uses that are sought after today for PLA. At that time, lactic acid was transformed into methyl lactate and then into lactoprene by companies such as Dupont.

1.3 The question of raw materials: a recurring debate?

Nevertheless, the role of scientific dynamics as a determinant of a chain of knowledge on specific sectors must be put into perspective. Indeed, it can be observed that the "raw material" effects are just as important, and sometimes even more so. Lactic acid is produced by fermentation, but it can also be produced from starches or sugars. Sugar is composed of equal parts fructose and glucose, while starch, a polysaccharide, is composed of two polymers of glucose. While the results are similar, the same agricultural actors can't produce both. Sugar is rather produced by sugar beet growers while starch sugar was mainly produced by potato growers who largely dominated lactic acid production before World War I. Sugar legislation (in Germany, but also in other European countries) encouraged producers to export sugar. After the spread of sugar beet in Europe in the 19th century, small industrial processing units dedicated to sugar production were developed in France, Germany and Russia. Benninga (1990) reports that the production of German sugar began to be in surplus from 1880 onwards. In order to keep prices high, sugar exporters received compensation from domestic taxes based on the quantities of sugar exported. However, the compensation was generally higher than the taxes levied, which led to sugar being kept at a high price. As a result, sugar was not only too expensive to be processed into lactic acid, but also was not available to the German fermentation industry, which was dominant over the other domestic fermentation industries. Lactic acid was therefore produced from starch. It was mainly produced in eastern Germany where the majority of the starch and alcohol production plants were located on large farms. The shortages caused by World War I strengthened the role of this type of agriculture, especially through the production of dried potatoes for food. After World War I, Deutsche Maïzena Gesellschaft A.G. was founded to produce starch from corn. This company was none other than the subsidiary of the American firm Corn Products Refining Company, which is also a producer of lactic acid in the United States (see below). The US was a sugar importer, which made it impossible to use this raw material for the production of lactic acid. Its production was dominated by Midwestern wheat farmers because of sugar shortages, but also because of the Prohibition. During that period, much of the sugar consumed was actually purchased for the production of illegal "homemade spirits". Sugar shortages led the food industry to establish new production facilities to supply dextrose (a form of sugar obtained from wheat) in order to meet the demand. With the support of the US Department of Commerce, the chemist Newkirk worked on a process to improve the production of dextrose so as to obtain higher levels of purity than those already achieved before being hired by Corn Products Refining Company in 1920. With this process, production increased from 9,000 tons/year in 1923 to 18,000 tons/year in 1924 and reached 150,000 tons/year in 1940 (Benninga, 1990). Thus, an oligopoly was formed, as Corn Products Refining Company licensed its production process to American Maize-Products, Clinton Corn Syrup Refining Company and Penick, and Ford also developed processes. We can therefore observe a dynamic of competition on the use of raw materials between food uses (if we equate consumption alcohols with food) and non-food uses, which has led to the specialization of lactic acid production from starches. This explains why it was not sugar manufacturers but Cargill that became interested in PLA at the end of the 1980s.

1.4 The knowledge base of lactic acid

The formation of the knowledge base of lactic acid is therefore not only dependent on the dynamics of scientific advances. Naturally, progress in the understanding of fermentation, both in industrial processes and in reactions, has made its development possible, following the example of the advances made by famous chemists such as Liebig and Pasteur. The second dimension of the knowledge base is its insertion in sectors whose upstream was dominated by the agro-industries of potato starch or wheat production; within these sectors, lactic acid constituted one of the outlets with regard to the industrialization of production processes and the reorientation of chemical production imposed by World War I. A 1938 article in Fortune magazine refers to the processing unit of the Corn Products Refining Company – which formed a trust after having acquired New York Glucose – as the largest wheat refining unit in the world. Since then, various outlets have been sought in industry for all sorts of uses of lactic acid (food, pharmaceuticals, solvents, etc.). This gives way to one of the uses of lactic acid, which is poly lactic acid. Let us remember that PLA is of particular concern here because it is one of the first bio-based reference polymers claiming broad applications in plastics processing since the 1990s (Datta and Henry, 2006).

2. The development of polylactic acid: a reading through the economics of promise[1]

2.1 1930–1980s: the formation of the PLA knowledge base

PLA is made from lactic acid. Lactic acid was produced from milk before the second half of the 19th century. Since then, sugar beets and corn have replaced milk as the inputs to produce lactic acid. Lactic acid was used during World War I to produce solvents, fiber and film. This period, from the beginning of the 20th century to 1930, was the foundation of the "modern chemistry paradigm" (Galambos et al., 2007). According to these authors, the modern chemistry paradigm relies on a periodical classification of elements paving the way for systematized polymer development.

At that time, Carothers, the famous chemist who also invented nylon during the same period, developed the production process for resins made of lactic acid while working at Dupont. He applied for a first patent in 1931, which was published in 1937 (Carothers, 1937). This first patent was wide-ranging, covering different types of bio-based materials. Nevertheless, it explicitly mentioned producing flexible, elastic materials from bio-based lactic acid. Also in 1931, Dorough, a member of Carothers' team at Dupont, applied for a patent for "the production of new lactide resins. A further object is the production of new compositions of matter, particularly coating compositions comprising these resins" (Dorough, 1935). This patent clearly announced the invention of PLA (which was called "polylactide" or "lactide resins"). Whereas the main promise of PLA is now to produce "stand-alone plastics", its original aim was to enrich fiber polymers (especially made from cellulose, another bio-based material).

A third patent (Schneider, 1955) confirms this. This patent mentions the former use of PLA in blends to produce fibers and films, i.e. plastic uses. It claims to "produce polylactides which are suitable for forming tough self-supporting thin films, fibers, and the like, which are orientable by drawing" (Schneider, 1955). Hence, this patent paved the way for the production of stand-alone PLA. In 1955, PLA was a known polymer, but it was competing with other plastics, notably produced from fossil fuels, which were less expensive to produce. Nevertheless, PLA has been used as a medical device (prosthesis and suture threads) since the 1960s, produced by the firm Ethicon (Lunt, 1998). PLA was used in these applications for three reasons. First, it is easy to shape, allowing for complex designs. Second, it is resistant to shocks and tension. Third, it is biocompatible and biodegradable.

2.2 1986–2000: PLA "hype": PLA as bio-based commodity plastic

Lipinsky and Sinclair (1986) proposed to extend PLA uses outside medicine. They argued that although lactic acid was a specialty polymer, it could be turned into a stand-alone commodity polymer for the production of bio-based commodity materials in order to compete with thermoplastics in packaging, i.e. a commodity PLA to compete with Polyethylene Terephthalate (PET). The expected applications were film (for agroindustry or agriculture), plastic cups and woven ropes.

This promise was based on two features. First, the patent optimized two types of technology that could be hybridized: fermentation from biotechnology, and ring-opening from chemistry. This new technological path was expected to increase yields which had not previously been high enough to target commodity markets. Second, biomass, especially corn, was widely available because of overproduction (Befort, 2020). Therefore, the authors promised to produce a bio-based and biocompatible plastic that provided the expected functionalities of thermoplastics, including resistance to tension. Nevertheless, the authors stressed an important lock-in: fermentation used to produce PLA has a very low yield, justifying the development of the new processes mentioned above to overcome problems of purification of the liquids used to produce the fermentation. A new patent by Dupont published in 1988 focused on the production of commodity polymers for packaging and fiber applications (Murdoch and Loomis, 1988). This promise was reinforced in 1993 with a new patent (Sinclair, 1993) claiming to have stabilized a production process for commodity PLA-based polymers. This process would produce bio-based, biodegradable plastics fulfilling the expectations of the chemical industry for stand-alone commodity or mixable plastic polymers. Even if the product was bio-based, the environmental argument was not part of the fundamental formation of the promise, which was the possibility of extending use of PLA from a specialty polymer to a stand-alone commodity polymer, possibly bio-based, which could compete with existing commodity plastics without modifying the paradigm of producing disposable plastic.

Between 1995 and 2000, PLA promises peaked with regard to making economies of scale to produce commodity PLA, justifying its adoption by the chemical industry (Datta et al., 1995; Sinclair, 1996). It was during this period that the environmental argument justifying such investments emerged, especially with the promise of making a biodegradable disposable plastic. At the end of the 1990s, Lunt (1998) stated that PLA was ready to be a commodity chemical like other existing chemicals. As an illustration, PLA competed and was compared with other plastics, such as PET (Calmon et al., 1999; Ramkumar and Bhattacharya, 1998). Two researchers from Galactic, a firm producing lactic acid which launched a joint venture with Total to produce PLA, stated that "PLA (is) becoming a commodity plastic" (Bogaert and Coszach, 2000, p.287).

NatureWorks, the dominant actor in PLA production, was founded in 1997 under the name Cargill Dow, a joint venture between the agro-industrial firm Cargill and the chemical firm Dow Chemicals. NatureWorks used a ring-opening polymerization process developed in the early 1990s in expectation of producing a commodity chemical. Using this process, the firm launched its first production unit (Dartee et al., 2000).

To sum up, the promises of the PLA are as follows: it is a commodity plastic competing with existing plastics; its production costs are competitive compared with existing commodity plastics; it is fully biodegradable, and adaptable to a wide range of uses.

2.3 2000–2006: the turning point: disappointment with PLA as a stand-alone commodity polymer

The year 2000 was the peak for the promise of developing a biodegradable, bio-based commodity plastic to compete with oil-based plastics in terms of production costs. Bogaert and Coszach (2000), two researchers at Galactic, the world leader in lactic acid and precursor of PLA, drew a three-stage story of biodegradable commodity polymers. In their view, PLA was the third generation of biodegradable polymers. It would replace the first two generations of biodegradable polymers, because they "did not satisfy the public's expectations of complete degradation" (Bogaert & Coszach, 2000, p.287). Nevertheless, in the same paper, these authors point out that PLA was only biodegradable in industrial conditions, thus requiring the implementation of "*biodegradable selective waste collection*" (*Ibid.*, p.302). Moreover, these specific conditions are problematic for such promised applications as plastic film for agriculture.

Alongside this first disappointment, a second appeared: PLA was not heat-resistant (Auras et al., 2003; Garlotta, 2001). That is, PLA could not be used for applications such as plastic cups, because hot beverages usually melt PLA. To this second disappointment (Vink et al., 2003), members of the NatureWorks research team added two new ones. First, to cope with the biodegradation and heat resistance issue, producers would need to mix PLA with other polymers. That is, PLA could not serve as a stand-alone commodity polymer. Second, because of the need for these mixes, PLA might not be sustainable. The final disappointment was that despite being expected to have the same mechanical properties as oil-based plastics, PLA appeared to find it difficult to resist shocks (hindering applications like plastic bottles and cups or agricultural film) and was not gas-resistant (hindering applications like film for food) (Khare and Deshmukh, 2006).

2.4 2007–2017: back to PLA blends?

After describing the inability of PLA to achieve its expected functionalities, Khare and Deshmukh (2006) considered the option of blending PLA with other bio-based plastics. This option, replacing PLA as a stand-alone polymer with PLA-based blends, ultimately prevailed (Lim et al., 2008). Since then, the idea has been to escape from lock-in of PLA in producing blends. In 2007, NatureWorks published a paper classifying PLA blends with other materials. This paved the way to five main trajectories (Domenek and Ducruet, 2016).

First, PLA may be used with reinforcing polymers such as Biomax, produced by Dupont. These processes raise product production costs, preventing the product from being a commodity chemical. Second, PLA subtypes may be produced, making PLA heat-resistant. The firm Purac developed this type of PLA, but here again, production costs are so high that it prevents the product from being a commodity plastic (Dever, 2015). Third, PLA may be blended with other bio-based polymers, such as its direct competitor, Polyhydroxybutyrate (PHB). For example, the firm Metabolix offers a blend of PLA/PHB to improve the mechanical performance of PLA and preserve its biodegradability (Krishnaswamy and Padwa, 2013). However, this trajectory does not achieve the expected commodity prices. Fourth, PLA may be reinforced with natural fiber such as hemp, or with nanocomposites, to produce resistant materials (Graupner, 2009; Hassan et al., 2013; Hu and Lim, 2007). While these processes are efficient, even with small quantities of composites, they prevent the biodegradability of PLA. A final option is to add small quantities of PLA into common packaging plastics to claim the use of bio-based polymers.

Figure 6.1 summarizes the PLA techno-economic promises cycle.

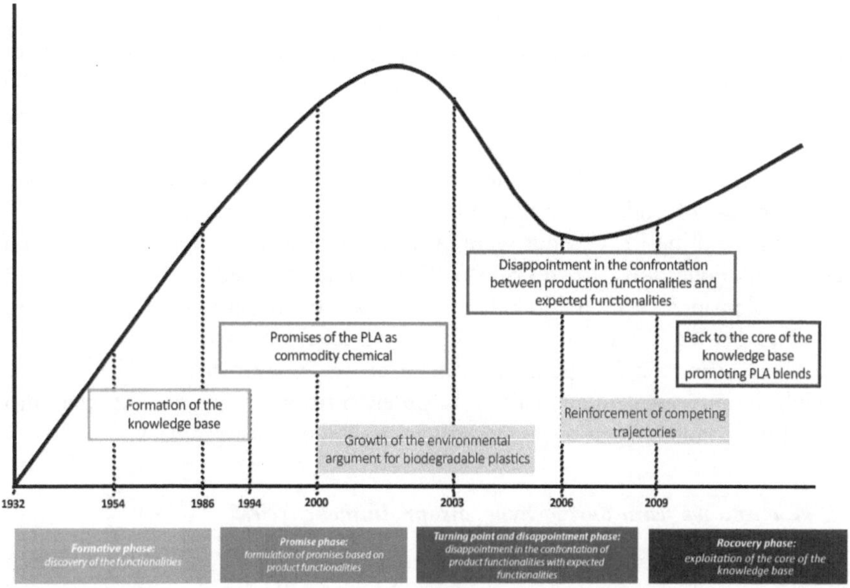

Figure 6.1 The PLA techno-economic promises cycle (Befort, 2020)

3. Discussion and conclusion

3.1 Micro-dynamic sequence of promises

This case study reveals a dynamic of product promises. The first phase comprises constitution of the knowledge base. The development of this knowledge base was typical of the modern chemical industry, which started to industrialize the production and use of PLA in blends in the 1950s and as a specialty chemical during the 1960s (Benninga, 1990; Galambos et al., 2007).

During the second period, actors formulated promises. This case study shows two sub-periods characterized by the evolution of the promises of PLA. During the first period (1986–1995), scientists promoted PLA as a competitive thermoplastic, because of low agricultural prices and rising oil prices and the advances of biotechnology, which enabled a combination of traditional chemical processes with biotechnology processes (Lipinsky, 1981; Lipinsky and Sinclair, 1986). Alongside these claims, firms like Cargill and Dupont developed new processes exploiting these scientific advances (Datta et al., 1995). In the second sub-period, while PLA was still presented as a commodity polymer, the promise turned to the environmental benefits of its biodegradability (Sinclair, 1996). In other words, the promise involved the possibility of preserving the paradigm of disposable commodity plastics.

The turning point, the third period, occurred when actual product functionalities contrasted with the expected functionalities of such polymers. The turning point was both the peak of the promise and a lasting moment demonstrating the failure of the promises to achieve expected functionalities. The turning point was followed by a period of disappointment during which the promises were rejected.

The fourth period comprised the recovery. This period featured a focus on the core knowledge base and product functionalities. New developments took advantage of the possibility of mixing PLA with other materials. It should be remembered that in the 1950s, the first uses of PLA were not as a stand-alone polymer but as a blend, due to its properties. At the same time, new technological developments using PLA blends were presented as a way to overcome identified lock-ins in applications. In the case of PLA, these included heat-resistance and mechanical properties. Consequently, the disappointment phase is a learning phase regarding the identification of lock-ins to achieve expected functionalities. It means that during the disappointment phase, actors discover that they are not able to fulfill the promised functionalities. In order to recover, they have to take into account these failures so as to preserve their credibility and legitimacy.

3.2 What do we learn during hype/disappointment cycles?

In the previous subsection, the disappointment cycle appears as the period when the extent to which a product is unable to deliver on the promise of its expected functionality is discovered. We may now examine what types of learning processes appear during the hype cycle (Antonelli, 2009; Malerba, 1992; Rosenberg, 1976). In the first phase, the knowledge base is formed by learning from advances in science and technology and learning from investigation. PLA was developed in the context of advances in polymer science in the 1930s due to the systematic analysis of chemical processes (Galambos et al., 2007). But PLA was explicitly invented in a Dupont research laboratory while the firm was developing other polymers of this type, such as nylon. Nevertheless, due to high production costs, PLA was only used as a medical device, due to its biocompatibility.

In the second phase, that of expectation, two learning configurations occurred. During the promise sub-period (see section 2.2), most learning occurred through searching and inter-industry spillovers. This was due to a combination of established chemistry knowledge and new biotechnology knowledge developed through R&D. This led to the development of new processes to achieve commodity production costs and competing processes between biotechnology and chemistry (Bud, 1991). In parallel with this expected fall in production costs, the agro-industry had massive production surpluses, reducing input prices substantially. Thus, agro-industries became interested in non-food applications, like bioplastics such as PLA, as a way of restoring their competitiveness. This corresponds to inter-industry spillover.

During the transformation of the promise sub-period (see section 2.3), learning was related to interactions with society and a growing concern for the environment, leading to the development of PLA lifecycle analysis. But learning also stemmed from the development of Pilot and Demonstration Plants (PDP) to test PLA production processes, which constituted learning by doing. Nevertheless, the use of PDP also led to the discovery of techno-economic lock-ins and the industrialization of the production process involving new research programs. This relates to learning by researching. In this phase, development is limited to exploration of the techno-economic conditions that will allow the economic viability of the exploitation of the eco-innovation (Levinthal and March, 1993; March, 1991).

The turning point and disappointment phase occurred when the product's actual functionalities fell short of its expected functionalities. Section 2.3 explains in detail how the product failed to achieve the promised functionalities. From a learning perspective, this process relates to learning by using PLA, interacting with potential customers, and inventorying all the problems of PLA.

Table 6.1 Learning in the hype cycle

Phase		*Types of learning*	*Characteristics*
Formative phase		• Learning from advances in science and technology • Learning by searching	• Development of polymer science and systematic chemical analysis • Invention of PLA alongside other polymers such as nylon
Promise phase	Formation of the promise	• Learning by searching • Learning from inter-industry spillover	• Combination of established knowledge in dedicated R&D activity • Low cost inputs
	Transformation of the promise	• Learning by interacting • Learning by doing • Learning by searching	• Promise transformed through growing concern for the environment • Development of pilot plant to test PLA
Turning point and disappointment		• Learning by using • Learning by searching • Learning by interacting	• Turning point occurs due to the difference between product functionalities and expected functionalities • Discovery of production and consumption issues through the development of PDP
Recovery		• Learning by searching • Learning from inter-industry spillover • Learning by interacting	• Back to the core PLA knowledge base • Development of PLA blends to achieve specific expected functionalities

The recovery period featured two combined dynamics. First, actors went back to the core PLA knowledge base, i.e. producing PLA blends. Second, actors developed new PLA blends aiming to achieve specific expected functionalities. Contrary to the promise phase, the goal was no longer to produce a commodity plastic fulfilling broad expectations but to satisfy dedicated applications. To do so, firms and scientists were involved in learning by studying new research projects aiming to learn from inter-industry spillover and interaction with potential customers. Hence, the main difference with the first period is the integration as a constraint in the development process of the expected functionalities of the product. Table 6.1 synthesizes each type of learning in each phase of the hype cycle.

Note

1 This section is reprinted from Befort, The promises of drop-in vs. functional innovations: The case of bioplastics, *Ecological Economics 181*, p.106886, Copyright 2021, with permission from Elsevier.

Bibliography

Antonelli, C., 2009. The economics of innovation: from the classical legacies to the economics of complexity. *Econ. Innov. New Technol.* 18, 611–646. https://doi.org/10.1080/10438590802564543.

Aparicio, S., Alcalde, R., 2009. The green solventethyl lactate: an experimental and theoretical characterization. *Green Chem* 11, 65–78. https://doi.org/10.1039/B811909K.

Auras, R.A., Harte, B., Selke, S., Hernandez, R., 2003. Mechanical, physical, and barrier properties of poly(lactide) films. *J. Plast. Film Sheeting* 19, 123–135. https://doi.org/10.1177/8756087903039702.

Befort, N., 2020. Going beyond definitions to understand tensions within the bioeconomy: the contribution of sociotechnical regimes to contested fields. *Technol. Forecast. Soc. Change* 153, 119923. https://doi.org/10.1016/j.techfore.2020.119923.

Benninga, H., 1990. *A history of lactic acid making: a chapter in the history of biotechnology, chemists and chemistry.* Kluwer Academic Publishers.

Bogaert, J.-C., Coszach, P., 2000. Poly(lactic acids): a potential solution to plastic waste dilemma. *Macromol. Symp.* 153, 287–303.

Bud, R., 1991. Biotechnology in the twentieth century. *Soc. Stud. Sci.* 21, 415–457. https://doi.org/10.1177/030631291021003002.

Calmon, A., Guillaume, S., Bellon-Maurel, V., Feuilloley, P., Silvestre, F., 1999. Evaluation of material biodegradability in real conditions-development of a burial test and an analysis methodology based on numerical vision. *J. Environ. Polym. Degrad.* 7, 157–166.

Carothers, W.H., 1937. *Linear condensation process.* US2071250 A.

Dartee, M., Lunt, J., Shafer, A., 2000. NatureWorks PLA: Sustainable performance fiber. *Chem. Fibers Int.* 50.

Datta, R., Henry, M., 2006. Lactic acid: recent advances in products, processes and technologies: a review. *J. Chem. Technol. Biotechnol.* 81, 1119–1129. https://doi.org/10.1002/jctb.1486.

Datta, R., Tsai, S.-P., Bonsignore, P., Moon, S.-H., Frank, J.R., 1995. Technological and economic potential of poly(lactic acid) and lactic acid derivatives. *FEMS Microbiol. Rev.* 16, 221–231. https://doi.org/10.1111/j.1574-6976.1995.tb00168.x.

Dever, C., 2015. *Forces et faiblesses de l'acide polylactique en plasturgie*. Presented at the Polymères biosourcés: relations structure – propriétés, Paris, France.

Domenek, S., Ducruet, V., 2016. Characteristics and applications of PLA, in: Kalia, S., Avérous, L. (Eds.), *Biodegradable and biobased polymers for environmental and biomedical applications*. John Wiley & Sons, pp.171–224.

Dorough, G.L., 1935. *Polymeric lactide resin*. US1995970 A.

Ellwood, P., Williams, C., Egan, J., 2022. Crossing the valley of death: Five underlying innovation processes. *Technovation* 109, 102162. https://doi.org/10.1016/j.technovation.2020.102162.

Foster, J.B., 2000. *Marx's ecology: materialism and nature*. Monthly Review Press.

Galambos, L., Hikino, T., Zamagni, V. (Eds.), 2007. *The global chemical industry in the age of the petrochemical revolution*. Cambridge University Press.

Garlotta, D., 2001. A literature review of poly(lactic acid). *J. Polym. Environ.* 9, 63–84.

Graupner, N., 2009. Improvement of the mechanical properties of biodegradable hemp fiber reinforced poly(lactic acid) (PLA) composites by the admixture of man-made cellulose fibers. *J. Compos. Mater.* 43, 689–702. https://doi.org/10.1177/0021998308100688.

Hassan, A., Balakrishnan, H., Akbari, A., 2013. Polylactic acid based blends, composites and nanocomposites, in: Thomas, S., Visakh, P.M., Mathew, A.P. (Eds.), *Advances in natural polymers*. Springer, pp.361–396.

Hu, R., Lim, J.-K., 2007. Fabrication and mechanical properties of completely biodegradable hemp fiber reinforced polylactic acid composites. *J. Compos. Mater.* 41, 1655–1669. https://doi.org/10.1177/0021998306069878.

Khare, A., Deshmukh, S., 2006. Studies toward producing eco-friendly plastics. *J. Plast. Film Sheeting* 22, 193–211. https://doi.org/10.1177/8756087906067324.

Krishnaswamy, R.K., Padwa, A.R., 2013. Impact modification of PLA using biobased, biodegradable Mirel PHB copolymers.

Levinthal, D.A., March, J.G., 1993. The myopia of learning. *Strateg. Manag. J.* 14, 95–112. https://doi.org/10.1002/smj.4250141009.

Lim, L.-T., Auras, R., Rubino, M., 2008. Processing technologies for poly(lactic acid). *Progress in Polymer Science* 33, 820–852. https://doi.org/10.1016/j.progpolymsci.2008.05.004.

Lipinsky, E.S., 1981. Chemicals from biomass: petrochemical substitution options. *Science* 212, 1465–1471. https://doi.org/10.1126/science.212.4502.1465.

Lipinsky, E.S., Sinclair, R.G., 1986. Is lactic acid a commodity chemical? *Chem. Eng. Prog.* 82, 26–32.

Lunt, J., 1998. Large-scale production, properties and commercial applications of polylactic acid polymers. *Polym. Degrad. Stab.* 59, 145–152. https://doi.org/10.1016/S0141-3910(97)00148–00141.

Malerba, F., 1992. Learning by firms and incremental technical change. *Econ. J.* 102, 845. https://doi.org/10.2307/2234581.

March, J.G., 1991. Exploration and exploitation in organizational learning. *Organ. Sci.* 2, 71–87. https://doi.org/10.1287/orsc.2.1.71.

Murdoch, J.R., Loomis, G.L., 1988. *Polylactide compositions*. US4719246 A.

Pereira, C.S.M., Silva, V.M.T.M., Rodrigues, A.E., 2011. Ethyl lactate as a solvent: properties, applications and production processes: a review. *Green Chem.* 13, 2658. https://doi.org/10.1039/c1gc15523g.

Ramkumar, D.H.S., Bhattacharya, M., 1998. Steady shear and dynamic properties of biodegradable polyesters. *Polym. Eng. Sci.* 38, 1426–1435. https://doi.org/10.1002/pen.10313.

Rosenberg, N., 1976. On technological expectations. *Econ. J.* 86, 523. https://doi.org/10.2307/2230797.

Royal Society of Chemistry (RSC), n.d. Green chemistry. https://pubs.rsc.org/en/journals/journalissues/gc#!recentarticles&adv, accessed 21/06/2022.

Schneider, A.K., 1955. *Polymers of high melting lactide.* US2703316 A.

Sinclair, R.G., 1996. The case for polylactic acid as a commodity packaging plastic. *J. Macromol. Sci. Part A* 33, 585–597. https://doi.org/10.1080/10601329608010880.

Sinclair, R.G., 1993. *Blends of polyactic acid.* US5216050 A.

Vink, E.T.H., Rábago, K.R., Glassner, D.A., Gruber, P.R., 2003. Applications of life cycle assessment to NatureWorks™ polylactide (PLA) production. *Polym. Degrad. Stab.* 80, 403–419. https://doi.org/10.1016/S0141-3910(02)00372–00375.

7 The case of the two other "small molecules"

Succinic acid and levulinic acid

The case of lactic acid and PLA has provided us with a long-term study that sets the analysis of the formation of chains within the dynamics of transition. Two other intermediate products have been selected here. They are considered by the actors to be good candidates for becoming precursors of a biosourced chemistry used in two types of process. PLAs are, from a certain point of view, part of the "classic" polyester family. After the fermentation step to obtain lactic acid, the polycondensation process that leads to PLA makes it a "chemosynthetic polymer" close to the traditional culture of chemists, while being rooted in the world of agro-industries.

Succinic acid has become an emblematic intermediate product of biotechnologies resulting from genetic engineering. It is a molecule that is well known to oil companies, because it was produced industrially from petroleum derivatives (acetylene and formaldehydes) for which the markets are well known. But a series of American patents have targeted it for transformation from genetically engineered enzymatic strains (it is easy to multiply competing patents as soon as even minimal differences between strains exist). The race for intellectual property will lead macro-actors to join forces with start-ups holding patents in order to explore industrial development. It is therefore a product that is at the heart of the bioeconomy of biotechnology, which offers disruptive innovations that challenge traditional value chains. The objective of producing succinic acid by means of biotechnology (biosuccinic acid obtained from glucose) at prices fairly close to those of the petroleum route seemed achievable at the end of the 1980s, with an impressive series of patents from different carriers during the 1990s. It is therefore a question of aiming for a long-term substitution for a product with known uses and markets, succinic acid already being a precursor of polyesters of fossil origin.

As for levulinic acid, it is obtained by a thermochemical conversion process of cellulosic biomass (wood, straw, corn, etc.) at high yield, obtained with co-products in a continuous process (coal and formic acid). It could be a precursor for biofuels, Bisphenol A substitutes, herbicides. It is not surprising to find it alongside succinic acid in the top 12 of the 2004 US foresight exercise, considering that it had already been identified in the 1950s as a high-potential precursor for a range of intermediate products (Leonard, 1956).

DOI: 10.4324/9781003103011-7

The aim of this chapter is to show that overcoming promises requires the deployment of specific strategies. The hypothesis presented here is that these strategies are based on the necessity of combining knowledge inherited from the past with alliances that make it possible to prepare the insertion within the division of labor. To do this, I combine the study of the techno-economic promises with the study of the formation of joint-venture agreements. The first section presents the case of succinic acid and the development of biotechnologies. The second section presents the case of levulinic acid.

1. A bioeconomy of biotechnologies: the case of succinic acid

The case of succinic acid is marked by the presence of such start-ups as BioAmber or Genomatica, which are seeking to license or industrialize the processes they implement, alongside macro-actors. The production of Bio-Based Succinic Acid (bioAS) has a direct substitution relationship with petroleum-based succinic acid, i.e. it is a drop-in molecule. In addition, the recognition by the USDA of its non-toxic character in food opens up opportunities in the complex formed by food and non-food.

Finally, concerning the drivers of firms' strategies, it seems that a powerful development driver is due to the fact that this molecule seems to be able to reach a lower production cost by a biosourced biotechnological route rather than a petrochemical one, and this very quickly (in any case, there is a place on the markets, where the conditions of purity obtained by the biotechnological route are of particular interest to the client; these conditions of purity have quickly made it possible to open up markets for bioAS, according to our interviews). The problematization of the economic space concerns the many promises of bioAS as a precursor involving positioning in the different sectors. It is therefore these positions that need to be clarified. The interest of the succinic acid case, given its insertion in the bioeconomy of biotechnologies, is that it will enable us to study specifically the development strategies of these value chains in the bioeconomy. Given the context of the emergence of succinic acid, special importance is ascribed to the analysis of the positions taken by joint ventures bringing together macro-actors such as BASF or Myriant, which is the branch dedicated to succinic acid of the Thai public chemical group PTT Chemicals, and knowledge-based companies such as Genomatica. The latter is a producer of bio-based 1.4-Butanediol (1.4 BDO), which is one of the major outlets for succinic acid.

1.1 From succinic acid production to the formation of techno-economic promises in science

The production of succinic acid is currently petroleum-based. According to the studies consulted, the production of succinic acid would amount to between 30 and 35 kt/year. This acid is used in the pharmaceutical industry (in particular in the production of vaccines), in cosmetics, in the food industry and 5% of

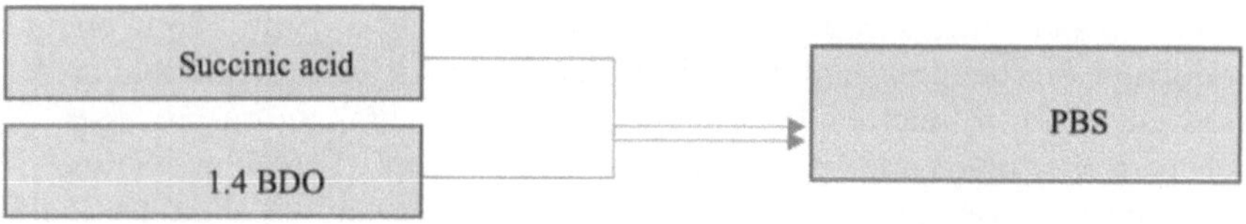

Figure 7.1 Steps in the production of PBS

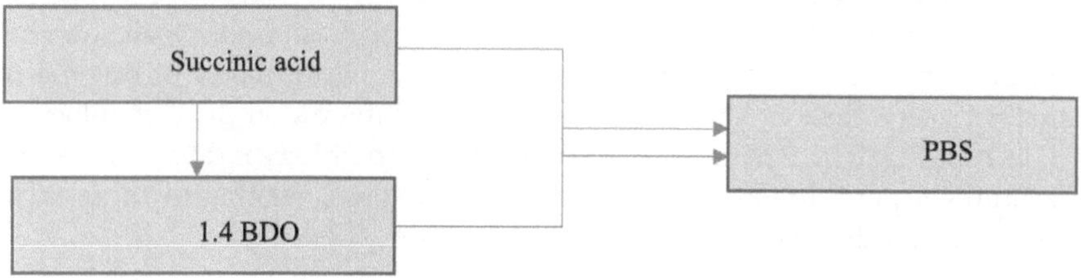

Figure 7.2 The economic model of the value chain developed around bio-based succinic acid

production output is used for the production of PolyButylene Succinate (PBS). The example of PBS will be used here. PBS is a biodegradable plastic whose properties are close to polyolefins, i.e. plastics such as polyethylenes. In the petroleum-based approach, obtaining PBS involves an oxygenation step based on a process developed by BASF during World War II (Chauvel et al., 1989). The biosourced processes seek to avoid this step by taking advantage of the presence of oxygen in the biomass. Thus, the production organization scheme offered by the actors is as shown in Figures 7.1 and 7.2.

The research question developed by the companies concerns the fastest or most economical way to move towards PBS, knowing that one can either produce succinic acid, then 1.4-BDO (step by step) or, as claimed by Bioamber or Genomatica, eliminate some steps (one step in the reaction). There is a desire to produce succinic acid for the production of PBS, meaning that there is a substitution of petroleum chemistry (succinic acid and 1.4 BDO) in order to develop new uses for PBS. The viewpoint discussed here is that the problem for industrialists is therefore to determine whether they give priority to producing PBS so as to open the way to polyesters, or whether they wish to have a succinic acid production unit leaving room for greater versatility for succinic acid itself, as discussed in Figure 7.2, or whether they consider 1.4 BDO to be their core platform.

1.2 A trajectory of promise rooted in biotechnology

1.2.1 The 1980s: the formation of the promise of industrialization and commercialization of white biotechnologies

The first references on the anchoring of succinic acid in biotechnologies date back to 1980. Zeikus (1980) refers to it in the introduction to his contribution to the research carried out from the 1930s to 1950s or early 1960s on the production of chemicals and fuels from anaerobic bacteria, thus bringing the knowledge base in microbiology to the core of the thinking on processes. In their narrative, biotechnology productions should serve (1) to limit the use of petroleum in a context of increasing petroleum prices, and (2) should make it possible, through the reprocessing of wastewater, to recover long carbon chains that have already been produced.

It was at that time that the debate began on the products that could be derived from biotechnologies, including succinic acid, and above all, on the types of bacteria to be used. This indicates that the modification of bacteria is considered to be the key knowledge base to make progress on the technological lock to be lifted. The technological promise of microbiology is thus at the heart of Zekius's paper. However, there are other problems, relating to more tacit knowledge and the costs of separation/purification.

1.2.2 1992–1995: from the formulation of the promise on opportunities to the theorization of value chains

The promise of substitution for the petroleum pathway was explicitly stated as early as 1992 by Glassner and Datta who claimed, in their patent (which is apparently an extension of a 1986 patent), to have developed the first industrializable process for the biotechnological production of succinic acid:

> succinic acid and its derivatives are widely used as specialty chemicals for applications in polymers, foods, pharmaceuticals, and cosmetics. Furthermore, succinic acid is a valuable 4-carbon intermediate useful for the production of 1.4-butanediol, tetrahydrofuran, and gammabutyrolactone. Although the succinate ion is a common intermediate in the metabolic pathway of several anaerobic microorganisms, there are no examples of any prior art fermentation that produces succinate in large amounts or with high yields.
>
> (Glassner and Datta, 1992)

In the same year, two other patents were filed (Datta, 1992; Datta et al., 1992) also defending the possibility of producing succinic acid by economically viable processes. For example, Datta et al. (1992), in describing the methods and materials used, emphasize the use of low-cost wheat with A. Succiniproducens. As the name suggests, these bacteria are known to produce succinic acid by digestion of carbohydrates, i.e., during the fermentation process. The determination of the type of bacteria to be used, and their optimization, is therefore at the heart of the biotechnological process. In addition, in all three patents, the possibility of recycling part of the raw materials (mainly bacteria) to be reused in a new production cycle is mentioned.

Later, Zeikus et al. (1999) insisted on the place of succinic acid in a biosourced commodity chemistry that would take advantage of the low prices of agricultural raw materials: "commodity agricultural crops such as corn, and food processing wastes, such as molasses raffinates, are potential sources of low-cost succinic acid" (Zeikus et al., 1999, p.71). In order to do so, the authors identify three technical and economic obstacles:

> For fermentation processes to gain wide application in generating succinic acid for specialty and commodity chemical production, they must be economically attractive. Both low-cost fermentation methods and efficient product recovery and purification methods are required. *Anaerobic fermentations offer promise for the production of large quantities of low-cost chemicals because of their high yields and straightforward scale-up requirements for very large-scale fermentations.*
>
> (*Ibid.*, p.71)

The economic profitability of biotechnological processes for the production of succinic acid is therefore based on the availability of low-cost raw materials, techniques for the recovery and purification of effluents (e.g. Glassner and Datta 1992), and the possibility of developing large-scale production units. In 1999, Zeikus et al. published a new contribution justifying the interest in succinic acid by the fact that

> green technology [is] becoming more of a driving force in the chemical industry because of the current need to decrease pollution caused by petrochemical processing and the future need to replace the dwindling hydrocarbon economy with a renewable, environmentally sound, carbohydrate economy.
>
> (Zeikus et al., 1999, p.545)

The second promise made by the authors is that succinic acid

> has the potential to become *a large-volume commodity chemical* that would form the basis for supplying many important intermediate and specialty chemicals for the consumer products industries. As a commodity chemical, succinic acid could replace many commodities based on benzene and intermediate petrochemicals, resulting in a large reduction in pollution from the manufacturer and in the consumption of over 250 benzene-derived chemicals.
>
> (*Ibid.*, p.546)

Unlike lactic acid for the production of polylactic acid, actors are therefore not faced with the problem of migrating towards a commodity platform production world, because succinic acid was already a commodity platform. The tree of opportunities established in 1999 identifies opportunities in specialty chemicals, which are not targeted here, in maleic anhydride (which is a traditional outlet for succinic acid that is no longer targeted by bio-based succinic acid), and in 1.4 BDO, which makes it possible to reach the production of solvents and adipic acid. As we recalled earlier, the contributions of Jung et al. (1999) and Lee et al. (1999) develop visions in which succinic acid is considered as the chemical intermediate necessary for the production of plastics with medium added value, but which would be biodegradable. Thus, succinic acid is constructed as a molecule that would be one of the first intermediaries upstream of one or more value chains built around a discourse of sustainable development in which two production worlds are confronted: on the one hand, that of commodity chemistry in which succinic acid of fossil origin is included, and on the other hand, the need to find an emblematic outlet such as PBS which is not a commodity product.

1.2.3 From 2000 to 2007: the imposition of an emblematic molecule to coordinate value chains

Succinic acid, as mentioned above, was included in the US "top 12" list established by (Werpy and Petersen, 2004). This list was intended to "qualify" the molecules likely to make the transition to a bio-based economy. The obstacles identified by the authors were identical to those described by Zeikus and his co-authors: the need to improve reaction yields, to develop catalysis processes that are insensitive to impurities, etc., in order to reduce production costs. Thus, it appears that the outlets considered for succinic acid are other chemical intermediates. The possible, or even necessary, hybridizations with other types of technologies are not mentioned, as was the case at the end of the 1990s for the mixtures described by Lee et al. (1999). On the contrary, the authors try to qualify each of the opportunities as either commodity or specialty chemistry (Werpy et al., 2006).

It was found that the conception of succinic acid and its outlets remains relatively identical over time. Moreover, this molecule was used in the period 2004–2006 to problematize the division of labor in the industry, from the mimetic vision of a transition from refinery to biorefinery fulfilling the same objectives, as shown in this contribution by Werpy et al. above. The molecule is studied because it represents the model of a platform molecule taking over from petroleum intermediates, which can be integrated into a biorefinery using sugar extracted from low-cost agricultural raw materials (such as wheat), the first outlets for which are clearly identified. While the issue of raw materials was already present in the previous period, what is new is the rise of the discourse on a "bio-based industry".

1.2.4 From 2007: a succession of disappointments

From this point of view, the publication by (Budarin et al., 2007) brings together part of the team from the Green Chemistry Centre of Excellence at the University of York[1] and is entitled as follows: "Towards a bio-based industry: benign catalytic esterifications of succinic acid in the presence of water". This title is part of the intention to anchor succinic acid as an object of discourse construction aimed at structuring the emergence of the entire bio-based industry.

This dimension is perfectly clear in Bechthold et al. (2008, p.647): "the suitability of succinic acid as a platform chemical is based on the ease of its biotechnological production and on the huge variety of chemicals that can be produced from it by chemical conversion". Succinic acid is thus highlighted as a potential success story of the bio-based industry. The other side of the coin, however, is less cheerful:

> many problems like slow growth, high by-product formation, and low yield could be solved partially by metabolic engineering. Nevertheless, a complete suppression of the by-products has not been achieved yet. (...) The subsequent problem of the biotechnological process is product purification (downstream processing). Regarding the rising energy prices, electrodialysis may probably not be the best suited method. The power consumption is rather high for an intended bulk chemical.
>
> (*Ibid.*, p.651)

The fact that the pathway is not obvious when one leaves the laboratory cannot be better described. Indeed, each of the promised advantages of the use of succinic acid is in reality a source of technological locks. It is therefore understandable that they present this "old intermediate" as a novelty, because it is the accumulation of these locks that makes them cautious and justifies the title of their article: "Succinic acid: a new platform chemical for biobased polymers from renewable resources". Thus, since Zeikus et al.'s 1999 article, we have been witnessing the "maintenance of the promise" of succinic acid as a "new platform molecule". From our point of view, the year 2008 marked a turning point towards a phase of disappointment. For example, the paper by (Cukalovic and Stevens, 2008) can be interpreted as follows: they list all the theoretical possibilities (and obstacles to development) for succinic acid. They focus their conclusion on the fact that the most appropriate place to develop it is as a precursor to maleic acid (used in food, surfactants and pharmaceuticals). Indeed, the price and the demand of this product are increasing, along with the problem of scarcity. So one goes from a set of promises to the only one that seems credible and achievable. This impression is confirmed if we refer to the "revisited" Top 10 of Bozell and Petersen (2010). This table shows at the same time the possibilities, the extent of the commitment to industrial tools and the weakness of the estimated commercial opportunities.

It was from 2008 to 2010 that we saw the emergence of joint ventures exploring industrial development (DNP Green Technology with ARD for the Bioamber Joint Venture (JV) or Reverdia held by Roquette and DSM). The argument put forward to justify JVs is consistently that of controlling the property rights to the bacteria used. Since the 1980s, the succiniproducens bacterium has been used, but since the end of the 2000s, Bioamber has patented processes using E. Coli for the production of succinic acid.

1.2.5 From 2010: a shift in the issue to the question of which bacteria to use

As a techno-economic lock in the optimization of biotechnological processes, bacteria research is becoming a strategic issue. The review of the types of bacteria clearly shows that the actors in the biosourced succinic acid industry are taking a position by developing processes associated with proprietary bacteria (Thakker et al., 2012). Thus, the establishment of biotechnological production units reveals all its complexity: "E. Coli remains a preferred organism for testing new succinate technologies due to the extensive knowledge of its genome, proteome, availability of genetic tools, simple nutrient requirements, and facile cultivations" (Thakker et al., 2012, p.215). The management of the bacteria and its reactions is thus part of the development of this type of process, as is the promise associated with it. Indeed, the previous quote mentions technical and economic promises on a bacterium (E. Coli) to try to justify its use in processes.

Two studies show the problematization of succinic acid that was mentioned above. The first acknowledges that "recovery and purification of succinate represents a technological challenge and an economical obstacle for an efficient microbial production on a large scale. All methods used at present showed unsatisfied product yield and purity" (Cheng et al., 2012, p.313). That is to say that the promises made about the process, i.e. the purification and recycling of bacteria, remain at the status of promises and do not make it possible to fulfill the expected functionalities.

1.3 The positioning of succinic acid companies in value chains

The formation of techno-economic promises in succinic acid has been discussed previously. The first period of development of succinic acid was marked by a discourse centered on (1) the interest in the product for its chemical functionalities, (2) the possibility to valorize agricultural products whose prices were low and to reach production costs close to those of the oil method, and (3) a discourse aiming at justifying the use of renewable resources because of a decrease of fossil resources. The second period consisted in the construction of the case of succinic acid, in the scientific field, as an emblem of the economic model of a bioeconomy based on the drop-in substitution of the traditional refinery by biotechnologies. This emblematic character probably explains why the two French firms that are the most active in sugar chemistry (Roquette and ARD, which is the armed wing of the cereal and sugar cooperatives) engage in different JVs on the same model and the same pathway of succinic acid production from competing American patents.

As observed above with regard to the value chain diagrams designed in the European research programs, the division of labor is thought of here in terms of the technological obstacles that firms set for themselves, as a horizon to be overcome. These companies position themselves according to patents filed or their production assets: this is the case for BASF, which, after having invented the production process for 1.4 BDO of fossil origin in the 1940s, is currently developing a biosourced process. The aim now is to study the four emblematic companies (Bioamber, Reverdia, Myriant, Succinity) of succinic acid and to pay particular attention to their alliance strategies.

1.3.1 *The case of Bioamber: towards an assembly of technologies*

Bioamber – which has now ceased to exist – was originally a JV founded in 2008 by DNP Green Technologies, a spin-off of DNP, and ARD, the research arm of the Champagne region agricultural cooperative. That same year, the firm announced the construction of an industrial demonstration unit on the Pomacle-Bazancourt site in order to "demonstrate the technological breakthrough of the US Department of Energy's proprietary E. Coli bacterium, which is under exclusive license to DNP Green Technology" (Bioamber, 2008). The first step in the development of the JV is based on the assembling of a technology available to DNP and the possibility for ARD to develop an industrial demonstrator, making it possible to structure the Pomacle-Bazancourt site. As part of this agreement, ARD claims to have invested €21 million in the construction of a 2,000 t/year demonstration unit. The initial objective, according to ARD head of R&D, was "to validate its technology and finalize the process book in order to prepare the sale of licenses".

ARD's shares in Bioamber were purchased by DNP Green Technologies in November 2010. In the period leading up to this move, DNP appears to have "set the stage" for its action and for the development of Bioamber. On the agreement side, an agreement on the development of thawing products was concluded in December 2008 with Basic Solutions. The production of thawing products is one of the already existing outlets for bio-based succinic acid: it would have the advantage of being less corrosive than the thawing agents usually used (Weastra, 2012). Production was estimated at 350 t/year in 2010. Then an exclusive partnership was concluded in December 2009 with Sinoven Biopolymers. This second agreement placed Bioamber as the exclusive supplier of succinic acid to Sinoven, which was a PBS producer. DNP Green Technologies then took control of the company in February 2010. Finally, on the financing side, DNP also raised €12 million in October 2009 with the financial arm of Mitsui, which is one of the largest Japanese chemical firms with which Bioamber entered into further agreements.

After DNP Green Technologies purchased ARD's shares, the latter merged into Bioamber. This was followed in 2011–2012 by a period of JV formation. The most important was between Bioamber and Mitsui (with a 70%–30% split) for the construction of the first plant in Sarnia (Ontario, Canada) with an announced capacity of 10 kt/year. The second JV contracted (in September 2011) was for the construction of a PBS plant in Thailand, in collaboration with PTT PLC (the Thai state-owned petrochemical consortium very active on biotech investments) and Mitsubishi Chemicals, for which Bioamber announced it became the exclusive supplier of succinic acid in 2011. The third JV was with NatureWorks to produce PLA/PBS blends. This agreement is described by some observers as NatureWorks's way of getting its hands on the PLA/PBS blend patents that Bioamber holds.

This agreement should be seen in the context of the five license agreements that Bioamber has entered into to develop an industrial *process*. The first license is for the development of business opportunities through Dupont's patents on catalysis for the production of 1.4 BDO. The second is for Cargill's yeast, although Bioamber was founded on the use of an E. Coli bacteria developed by the US DOE. The third agreement (signed in 2011) concerns a process for the production of adipic acid, which could be an outlet for succinic acid. Indeed, it is a precursor in the production of polyamides. However, this type of outlet (polyesters and polyols) has instead been captured by Reverdia, which is the JV between Roquette and DSM. Bioamber concluded a second agreement focused on Dupont's catalysis processes with Evonik, whose facilities were used for testing. Finally, Bioamber also acquired a license from JM Davis,[2] in April 2015, on the production of 1.4 BDO and THF. The constitution of this set of agreements thus shows that Bioamber has instead worked to articulate already existing processes to constitute an industrial *process*. It also shows that from a certain point of view, business models based on a firm with property rights that it licenses (the "victorious start-up") is a failure, and that the company had to descend into the industrial arena, a place that consumes fixed capital, and where one cannot be pressed for time to obtain returns on investment: the leaders of cooperatives use for this opposite business model the very appropriate phrase of "patient capital", which is necessary for industrial development, and which is capable of overcoming the cycles of disappointment.

This assembly dynamic is also identifiable in the construction of outlets. As previously shown, biobased succinic acid is not designed to fit into the existing uses for oil-based succinic acid. It is therefore a matter for the actors to develop its properties. Thus, the first agreements (on thawing agents and adipic acid) and then those on PBS, 1.4 BDO or THF show that the company did not know what its outlets would be and was therefore forced to explore its capacities. In order to do so, Bioamber therefore sought to secure its outlets by contracting distribution agreements. For example, in January 2014, a take-or-pay agreement was contracted with Vinmar on 1.4 BDO produced in a plant to be built in North America, which was to be commissioned in 2017. In May 2014, Bioamber also signed an agreement to be the exclusive supplier of succinic acid to the PTT-MCC JV resulting from the agreement with PTT and Mitsubishi Chemicals to build a PBS plant. The firm has organized two "financing campaigns" to secure its opportunities. The first made it possible to raise funds to build the ARD industrial demonstrator, but also for DNP Green Technologies to take control of Bioamber. The second financing campaign consisted of a fundraiser in 2013 and then an IPO in 2013 as well as obtaining loans over the 2013–2014 period and grants. Thus, announcements of agreements coincided with fundraising and grant awards by the Canadian government through various agencies. In order to secure its outlets, the firm also entered into two distribution agreements in 2013. In doing so, it is transferring some of the uncertainty, and therefore the risk, associated with the development of new uses for succinic acid to a downstream intermediary in its supply chain, which has better visibility of markets and logistics – in any case, Vinmar is justifying its collaborations with emerging firms in this way.

The case of Bioamber is that of a company whose initial business model was based on intellectual property rights obtained through a license with the American DOE. The firm behaved as if it were playing on its territorial anchorage to generate its financial resources: it originated in American research, grew partially in France and then captured the subsidies granted by Canada in order to attract these types of biotechnology firms. The representation of the firm's development we established here is based on the firm's press releases as well as on the analyses of observers who, generally, partially repeat the firms' declarations. As a result, a sort of "ideal" narrative emerges which illustrates the mode of development of biotechnology firms. However, the analysis of the entry into succinic acid of the other firms will allow us to observe that Bioamber was facing intense competition, notably on the property of the processes used.

1.3.2 Reverdia: the joint venture between two macro actors

The Reverdia joint venture was contracted in 2010 by DSM and Roquette to produce succinic acid, as part of the Biohub project led by Roquette. In order to understand the current dynamics of this joint venture, this section will review the history of these two firms and their relationship with biotechnology. These two companies are macro-actors anchored in different sectors. Roquette is the fourth largest starch producer in the world (and the second largest in Europe) and DSM is an established Dutch company (founded in 1902) which, at the beginning of its history, was dedicated to coal mining and was later converted into a scientific knowledge production company.

Roquette was founded in 1925 and has remained a family company ever since. Its historical site is located in Lestrem in the Nord-Pas-de-Calais region, where its R&D activities are developed. Since its foundation, the company has been producing starch that can be used in the food industry, but also in the paper industry, and this is the purpose of the strategy on succinic acid in bio-based chemistry. The company has a history of developing patents in regard to sorbitol, for food and non-food uses, since the early 1960s. The company has a tradition of industrial secrecy, as its comparative advantage lies in the custom production of industrial solutions for its customers in the paper industry and elsewhere (e.g. pharmaceutical coatings) using more than a thousand references. Developments on sorbitols have led it, from a productive heritage particularly cultivated by Roquette, to develop a family of isosorbides.

The company has discovered, according to a presentation by Marc Roquette in 2010 at the Paris School of Management, that it must position itself in the great turning point of the use of renewable resources vis-à-vis the substitution model of the oil refinery. He therefore presents the core business of the strategic management of his company as the identification of products that will be the first to leave the oil production assets so as to enter those of renewable chemistry. In 2010, he mapped out three programs: modified starches (Gaiahub), the chemistry of sugars such as sorbitol – isosorbide – and succinic acid (Biohub), and algae, in the long run, which would make it possible to free renewable energy from the constraints of agricultural land.

The Biohub project, which began in 2006 and ended in 2015, was funded under the first call for projects launched by the short-lived Industrial Innovation Agency.[3] This agency was founded following a report by industrialist J.-L. Beffa, commissioned by President J. Chirac in 2004. Noting the decline of French industry, the aim of the report was to produce tools aimed at providing a framework for the relaunch of "major programs" such as those that had led to the development of civil nuclear power, Airbus or Concorde. Here again, one can observe the same logic that governed these major programs in France: the emergence of national champions that receive the entirety of public support (Colletis, 2012). It is therefore interesting to note that Roquette has melted into the mold of the industrial firm capable of carrying out this type of program.

As part of Biohub, the presentation of the project in April 2006 essentially mentioned the "creation of a new value chain" dedicated to isosorbide, which Roquette had already been producing since the 1950s. But the objective, if one follows the promise of a large-scale production (it was announced at 100 kt/year in 2006), was thus to generalize not only the use, but also the model, preparing other shifts in production from the petroleum paradigm to the chemistry of the renewable, as Marc Roquette stated in an interview in 2010, outlining a global vision of the bioeconomy. Isosorbide is currently used mainly in pharmaceuticals and cosmetics, but it could be used in the production of biosourced plastics (in particular to replace terephthalates).[4] Concerning this product, Roquette is developing a new production unit of 20 kt/year. If the form follows the logic of large national programs, it appears that the subsidization of this project was obtained because of a planned partnership. Indeed, the Beffa report advocated an extension of the surface of these "large programs". The presence of DSM made this hypothesis possible. But it is confirmed by the bibliographical research on Roquette's patents evoking succinic acid between 1980 and 2000. It turns out that nine patents, essentially relating to the production of paper from starch, put forward greater achievability from succinic acid, itself produced from starch (cf. Fuertes et al., 1998, 1997, 1996 for example).

THE DSM ALLY

The Biohub project is thus part of a strategy of re-exploration and valorization of the productive heritage of the Roquette firm. However, this type of strategy requires alliances with actors, thereby making it possible to organize[5] the articulation between technologies that underlies the product compromise. This is the role played by DSM. As mentioned above, DSM was a state-owned company, founded in 1905 in order to produce coal. From the 1950s onwards, it continued its diversification into chemicals, which it had begun in the 1930s with the production of fertilizers from coal. In 1952, it produced caprolactam and then polyethylene in 1959. Its diversification strategy, together with the abandonment of coal production in the early 1990s, continued upstream with the purchase of activities in the pharmaceutical sector (purchasing Andeno, a producer of precursors for the pharmaceutical industry, in 1987) and then downstream with the purchase of ACF Chemie, a pharmaceutical company, in 1991.

It was in 2005 that the topic of biotechnologies really took hold within DSM, before becoming the "Bio-Based Products and Services" unit in 2010. This change of name clearly marks the repositioning of the firm in this direction. The agreement with Roquette should therefore be understood as the result of an attempt to reposition itself on high value-added products, between technical polymers, health and biosourced products, driven in part by the exploration of biotechnologies.

BIOHUB: THE DEVELOPMENT OF AN ALLIANCE BETWEEN COMPETITION AND COOPERATION: A READING FROM THE FIRM'S PATENT PORTFOLIO BETWEEN 2008 AND 2013

At first glance, Roquette and DSM are not exactly competitors; their activities are quite distinct. However, it seems that the cooperation on succinic acid, first through the Biohub program and then through the Reverdia joint venture, has set up competition between the two firms. The collaboration between the two companies was announced in January 2008, which more or less corresponds to the time when the two companies filed patents, independently of each other. In particular, Roquette's "large-scale microbial culture process" patent (filed in 2007, published in 2009 and cited by DSM) (Segueilha et al., 2009) is next to DSM's "process for obtaining improved polypeptide expression" (Roubos and Peij, 2008). The period 2008–2013 was an active period for DSM (24 patents on succinic acid in the period) and Roquette (four patents) on the succinic acid patenting front, while the announcement of the creation of Reverdia was made in 2010.

The number of patents filed by Roquette may seem relatively limited, but we should not overlook the fact that DSM was in a period of building its portfolio of activities in white biotechnology and seemed to be moving more towards a strategy of licensing or agreements with other macro-actors (Jeannet and Schreuder, 2015). A firm must therefore have "material" to offer to ensure its strategy. The paradox lies in the fact that over this same period, both firms have filed more patents on succinic acid each on their own than in the Reverdia structure. To date, Reverdia has no patents – they all belong to DSM and Roquette.

THE DEVELOPMENT OF A SPECIFIC VALUE CHAIN SEGMENT: A FERMENTATIVE PROCESS TO OBTAIN SUCCINIC ACID...

However, the analysis of the 11 patents tells us three things. First, they can be divided into three groups. That is, the process developed within Reverdia can be considered to involve three patents: a fermentative process, a fermentation process to obtain succinic acid, and a succinic acid crystallization process.[6]

Then, each of the patents cites a portion of the patents held by Roquette and DSM. The most emblematic example is Jansen et al. (2012) who cite the patents that allow each of the two firms to position themselves in the production of succinic acid. For Roquette, it is essentially the control of the global process, whereas for DSM, the patents concern the control of the bacteria and yeasts used. Finally, one can also note the presence of patents relating to the use of E. Coli, which confirms that it is this bacterium that is used in the process.

A PROJECT THAT DEMONSTRATES THE FORMATION OF COMMON POOL RESOURCES

There is thus a constitution of common pool resources by Roquette and DSM, but the relationships that are formed are of two kinds. On the one hand, the very constitution of Reverdia is based on the cooperation between two actors, who share the ownership of the structure and who pool a certain amount of tacit or codified knowledge. On the other hand, the sharing of these resources is based on the initial production of knowledge that will be codified and above all privatized – in the form of patents – in order to (1) justify its place in the joint venture, and (2) control as much as possible the compromise formed by the sharing of resources. It is this fundamental tension in the construction of the joint venture that resembles a power struggle for the domination of the compromise. In the case of Bioamber, the tension was not sustainable and clearly the compromise ended up being dominated by DNP with the acquisition of Bioamber.

After the launch of the joint venture in 2010, the creation of a production unit with a capacity of 10 kt/year on Roquette's Cassano (Italy) site was announced. During the construction period of the plant, Reverdia worked on the demonstration of its succinic acid (Biosuccinum) on Roquette's historical site of Lestrem. We might therefore assume that the trade-off here is dominated by Roquette, but the interview of a DSM technology manager shows that the stake in Reverdia is one arm of DSM's business portfolio. That is, Roquette's takeover of its production sites could be interpreted as DSM's way of expanding its business portfolio – in line with its business reorganization – while outsourcing part of the risk. Moreover, Festel (2010) points out that DSM is one of the dominant actors in the supply of enzymes for biotechnologies.

THE FORMATION OF THE PRODUCT IDENTITY...

However, it seems that the risk is shared by both companies. Indeed, in 2012, shortly before the launch of the production unit, it was announced that Biosuccinium would be used for the production by Proviron of dimethyl succinate, which is used as a food additive, i.e. a use of the type that

Roquette and DSM have mastered. However, it was announced that same year that Helm would be the exclusive distributor of Biosuccinium in Europe. The superimposition of these two announcements shows that the identity of the product is not stabilized and that, in fact, the companies are working on the construction of these outlets, while exploring different production worlds.

Indeed, the third announcement concerns an agreement with another joint venture: Dupont Tate & Lyle, which specializes in the production of propanediol. The mixture of succinic acid and propanediol makes it possible to produce polyurethanes (such as plastics or adhesives). As for DSM, it has announced that it has acquired a license to produce butanediol from Genomatica for the purpose of producing PBT. Thus, DSM claims to green the PBT it already produces under the Arnitel brand:

> We present test results demonstrating that BDO made with Genomatica's process technology can be used as a replacement for conventional BDO produced from fossil fuels, with no adverse impact on Arnitel performance and no changes needed in DSM Arnitel production processes or equipment. We believe that the success of Genomatica process technology in providing a renewable version of a major chemical will facilitate use (...) speeding the adoption of more environmentally-friendly ingredients in a wide range of supply chains.
>
> (DSM, 2013)

Similarly to Myriant's offensive in Europe (see below), Reverdia also led an offensive towards the United States by obtaining the "bio-based" label from the USDA in 2014. That same year, Reverdia expanded its strategy by announcing the licensing of its process. Following Festel et al. (2012), this strategy permits firms to (1) diversify their revenues – which are mostly made up of product sales – and (2) participate in the diffusion of the technical process. In the case of succinic acid, the primary reason could be the latter. Indeed, the firms could quite quickly find themselves in a situation of overproduction: four production units with a capacity of 10 kt/year are under construction while the outlets for succinic acid are not assured, so the firms have an interest in disseminating their technology as widely as possible in order to integrate it into the production of outlets (such as BDO, PBS, etc.). The idea put forward here is that this is the purpose of the development of the Biosuccinnovate project led by Reverdia. This European project brings together Dutch (Wageningen University in particular), British (London Imperial College) and French (INRA) research organizations – that is to say, the major research organizations present in the vast majority of European projects – as well as two firms specializing in technical and economic analyses and life cycle assessments. But the project also includes CIMV which is specialized in lignin (see analysis of the Biocore project in Chapter 4).

CONCLUSION: REVERDIA'S STRATEGY

The construction of Reverdia was based on the pooling of patents held by both firms. Although they patented processes, they did constitute pools of resources (in the sense of Mangolte, 2006). The pooled resources that build the firm's productive assets structure Reverdia's dynamics with the tension described above. At the same time, the joint venture also constitutes a diversification of DSM's portfolio of activities and enables it to move downstream in the value chain. To some extent, in addition to producing enzymes, DSM produces the outlets for them. However, Reverdia has its own existence in which the firm is trying to build its outlets, particularly in polyurethanes. The affirmation of this outlet, which is not a commodity molecule like Bioamber's 1.4 BDO, is thus aimed at building or anchoring Biosuccinum in a world of production of specialty polymer chemicals.

Therefore, two strategies are already apparent. The first, that of Bioamber, targets the major commodity markets and involves entering into agreements to supply the succinic acid needed (e.g. for a PBS plant in Thailand). The second, that of Reverdia, aims to produce a product that could support a green premium price for example. For the moment, Reverdia has the American "bio-based" label, which not only gives it access to US government tenders, but above all guarantees the bio-based origin of the product in the light of the US evaluation standard. DSM uses the argument of biosourced succinic acid to build the identity of its PBT produced with the Genomatica process. Similarly, the Dutch firm is seeking to build a portfolio of high value-added activities, hence its shift from "traditional" chemistry to biotechnology. Contrary to the strategy of hegemony in joint ventures such as Bioamber, we have here a set of tensions and complementarities that result from the collective construction of value chains for medium- and high-added-value products.

1.3.3 Myriant, a strategy aimed at hegemony through "open-innovation" diffusion

Myriant is an American firm that was founded in 2005. No information is available about its existence before 2009. At that time, Myriant presented itself as a "privately-held science and technology company leading the development and commercialization of next generation biorefineries for the production of high-value bio-based chemicals from renewable feedstock, through the use of its proprietary biocatalyst technology" in the perspective developed by H. Ford: "In 1934, Henry Ford predicted that biochemistry would unite agriculture and industry. At Myriant Technologies, we have realized this vision – next-generation biorefineries where a pound of sugar can replace a barrel of crude" (Myriant, n.d.).

EXPLORATION OF THE E. COLI PLATFORM

Myriant has positioned itself on two molecules: lactic acid and succinic acid. The announcement of the production of commercial samples was made in

2009. As the following quotes show, Myriant's entry strategy is based on the exploration/exploitation of its catalysis technology mainly from E. Coli. This is the trend observed in its patents for succinic acid. The firm filed three patents in 2009 that pertain to the development of modified E. Coli strains (Gong et al., 2012), the behavior of E. Coli strains producing organic acids (thus, among other things, succinic acid) (Grabar et al., 2012),[7] and a method for purifying water containing succinic acid (Gerberding and Singh, 2011).

During the period 2009–2013, the firm developed various succinic acid production processes while testing the 1.4 BDO production process developed by J.M. Davy, which is the same process Bioamber used. The patents filed over this period (Hermann et al., 2012; Yocum et al., 2013 for example) all deal with exploring *E. Coli* fermentation and have relatively broad claims to "organic acids". However, each of them mentions the production of succinic acid.

A FIRST AGREEMENT WITH SHOWA DENKO ON PBS SUBSTITUTION

In June 2012, two agreements were announced by Myriant. First, Myriant's succinic acid was selected for Showa Denko for the production of PBS. In doing so, Myriant succeeded in becoming a supplier to an old firm (founded in 1939) of Japanese chemistry. Showa Denko was the first company to produce PBS in 1993. Thus, after having launched polymers mixing PBS/starch and PBS/starch/PLA, the firm tried to make PBS itself biosourced by Myriant's succinic acid which would be used by Natur-Tec, a firm specializing in the production of plastic films (de Guzman, 2012) (see Figure 7.3).

AND A POSITION ON POLYOLS THANKS TO AN "OPEN INNOVATION" MODEL

The second agreement involves the production of a bio-based adhesive from Dupont Tate & Lyle's 1.3 PDO and Myriant's succinic acid by DaniMer. But this operation was also carried out in Europe with the Italian chemical firm Piedmont. On this occasion, the companies made available to producers of polyols the following formulation:

> Under a strategic collaboration between Piedmont, DTL and Myriant, the three companies have agreed to an "open innovation" concept by which the polyol formulations will be made available to polyol producers and the urethane industry at large. This means that polyol customers will be able to

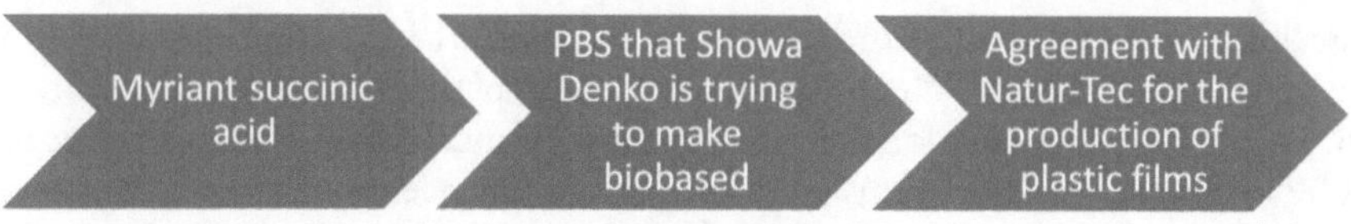

Figure 7.3 Succinic acid die segment held by Myriant

> purchase polyols produced from DTL's Susterra® propanediol and Myriant's Bio-Succinic Acid from Piedmont as well as from other polyol producers. Piedmont will manufacture the initial polyol product samples and will offer commercial supply of the polyol products to the market.
>
> (Myriant, 2012)

After an initial demonstration with DaniMer, Dupont Tate & Lyle and Myriant have joined forces with Piedmont to take a stand in the upstream part of the polyols chain, opening up the formulation to downstream manufacturers, i.e. potential future users, to whom Piedmont is able to provide samples. Polyols are very much upstream of the chemical industry and make it possible to produce polyurethane foams and polyesters, i.e. insulating foams, adhesives and plastic fibers. Thus the firms try to constitute their formulation as the heritage of the polyols industry by organizing the diffusion of the formulation. However, we note an evolution in the strategy of the firms. Myriant was built as a producer of succinic acid, but it needs to build outlets and thus to go downstream of the chains, even if it means allying with other firms.

AND THE FORMATION OF CO-DEVELOPMENT AND DISTRIBUTION AGREEMENTS

At the same time, Myriant was following a "classic" mode of development. Its plant was commissioned in May 2013. In 2013, it entered into marketing agreements with Bayegan for the Middle East, Eastern Europe and Africa. Concerning Austria, Germany and Switzerland, a deal was made with BCD Chemie. And for the rest of Europe, an agreement was made with Azélis in 2014. That same year, Myriant also became Oxea's succinic acid supplier for the production of its plastics; it seeks to be phthalate-free. Myriant has also signed a co-development agreement on this type of plastic with UPC and the Japanese chemical company Sojitz. Myriant's strategy is therefore twofold. On the one hand, it is developing its succinic acid produced in Louisiana, and on the other hand, it is organizing its distribution through marketing and co-development agreements and the distribution of the formulation of derivatives of its products.

1.3.4 Succinity: another form of competition-cooperation

AN AGREEMENT BETWEEN TWO COMPETITORS

Succinity is a joint venture that was established in 2012 by BASF and Corbion Purac (formerly CSM). These two firms are competitors in the production of PLA, but they cooperate on this acid. After a period of collaboration between 2009 and 2012, the two firms announced their alliance and the customization of a production site owned by Corbion Purac in Spain. This site was commissioned in 2014 and has an announced capacity of 10 kt/year.

THE PATENTS OF BOTH COMPANIES

Corbion Purac's patents on succinic acid are mainly related to the production of bakery products, i.e. the core of its production assets. Yet, the case of BASF is more complex. The first database search on the company's patents on succinic acid yielded 8,970 results. The query was then narrowed down using the following combination: "basf" AND "succinic acid" AND "bio-based". That is, the scope of patents on succinic acid was limited to those relating to the possibility of producing bio-based succinic acid or producing derivatives of this acid.

The results of this search make it possible to better understand BASF's strategy. All of the patents identified pertain to the production of succinic acid derivatives, primarily 1.4 BDO, GBL and THF, polyesters and polyols. The first uses of butadiene (or 1.4 BDO) were developed by BASF during World War I in order to produce synthetic rubbers. A BASF patent (Broecker and Schwarzmann, 1977) is cited 45 times by Genomatica in its patents. Genomatica is a start-up company that has developed a 1.4 BDO production process which it has patented to Novamont and BASF. The number of citations for Genomatica's patent spans the period 2011–2015, during which time BASF pursued its strategy of filing patents on the downstream part of the succinic acid value chain.

FOR A BUSINESS PORTFOLIO STRATEGY

Therefore, BASF is indeed pursuing a strategy of portfolio activity in line with its production assets. Thanks to the joint venture agreement with CSM, it is establishing itself in the succinic acid sector, while retaining the possibility of withdrawing from the joint venture all the more easily since the investments were made on a production site of Corbion Purac, which, let us remember, is seeking to develop its activities in non-food products. But in doing so, it is taking a position in the downstream of the succinic acid sector, i.e. polyurethanes and polyesters, thus adding biosourced products of this type to its portfolio of activities with Ecovio for example. This polymer is used, as a demonstration, in the production of biodegradable plastic bags. Unlike Myriant, which is demonstrating the possibility of producing polyols by opening up access to the product's formulation without industrializing it, BASF is taking advantage of its "firepower" to keep its business portfolio strategy open and to manage its business segments.

CONCLUSION: FROM THE PARADOX OF INTELLECTUAL PROPERTY TO TERRITORIAL ANCHORING

While a first approach to the opportunities, from the point of view of the promises of the scientific literature, insisted on either PBS, 1.4 BDO, GBL or THG, it turns out that the majority of the opportunities explored and constructed by the firms essentially concern polyurethane or polyesters. This means that the firms have a thorough management of the value chain segments, contrary to what the technical and economic promises might suggest.

In the case of 1.4 BDO, two different approaches have been outlined. The first was used by Bioamber: in building the industrialization of its succinic acid production process, it was forced to offer, or at least demonstrate, outlets. In another case, that of Genomatica, it is directly the production of 1.4 BDO that is the object of the technology developed and the value proposition of the firm. This therefore brings to the fore two different ways of managing the 1.4 BDO segment. As for the other firms, they are each developing an approach to polyurethanes and polyesters. It is thus in this field that competition is built, using heterogeneous strategies. The first strategy is that of Reverdia. It constitutes more than a temporary "truce" between Roquette and DSM whose competition on succinic acid is possible if one looks at the production of patents by each of the firms. Nevertheless, contrary to a conventional approach to patents based on the paradox of intellectual property (Foray, 2009), patents can also be considered as a legitimate call for collaboration.

The solution to this paradox, at least temporarily, was the pooling of resources. This probably does not mean that competition no longer exists between the two firms – in other words, the search for the domination of the compromise that takes the form of a joint venture – but that it is neutralized in a very specific space, in which the firms probably share the work on upstream primary processing (Roquette) and downstream specialty outlets (DSM). The case of Reverdia also illustrates a strategy of "large projects" which supports national agro-industrial champions, in the image of what Sofiprotéol was able to develop (cf. Chapter 5). Myriant's strategy, at least in its narrative, is to have built a slow industrialization based on patents and on public capital (USDA loans, for example). But here again, in order to build its presence in the industry, Myriant has to develop, through agreements – again a compromise – a temporary truce to build a community of users in "open-innovation". These strategies of internationalized industrial groups take place in national spaces. For instance, Reverdia was backed by Roquette, on the basis of public funds, as was Myriant in the United States. The diffusion of the formulation of polyols between Dupont Tate & Lyle, Piedmont and Myriant took place in Europe and not in the United States, where the firm was supported by the public authorities. Conversely, Reverdia claims to be eligible for US government contracts. Similarly, Reverdia does not have a distributor in Europe but does have one for other regions of the world, while Myriant does not have one for America but does have one for the rest of the world. These two cases are ideal: each is very much linked to public programs to support the emergence of a bioeconomy, but what about Bioamber and Succinity?

Regarding Bioamber, the firm was a nomadic firm. Initially based on an exclusive license from the US DOE, its development and demonstration were carried out in France, before production was relocated to Canada and, eventually, a second factory was built in Thailand. The vagueness about the form of

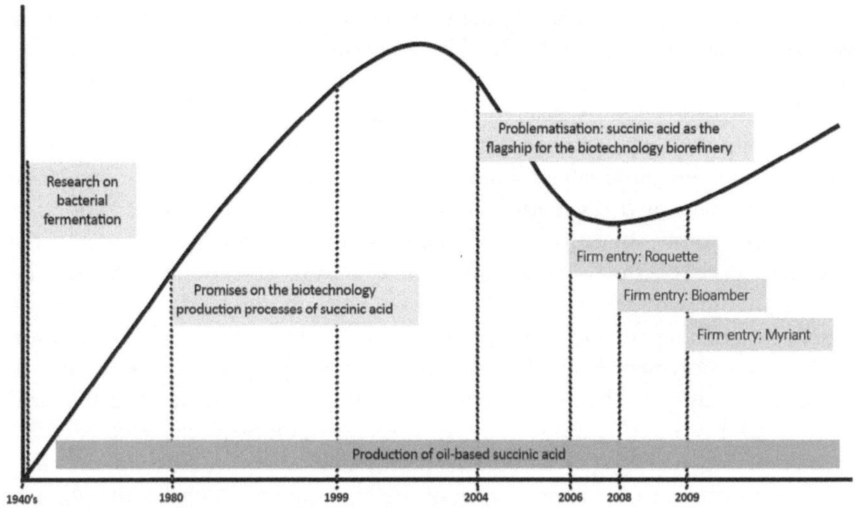

Figure 7.4 The techno-economic promises of succinic acid

this plant, its production, who would have owned it, etc., testifies to the economy of promises in which Bioamber is rooted. If the other firms also develop promises, they build a relationship with the territory, if only in terms of managing the diffusion of their processes or products. In Bioamber's case, the image of the "winning start-up" emerges, one that seeks rapid growth and aims to become the world leader in its sector and to enter the stock market. However, is Bioamber actually a "winning start-up"? On the one hand, it has been noted that its model is based on license assemblies, and on the other hand that it has had to secure flow cooperations. This is how the evolution of Bioamber's model should be understood, as it has taken the measure of the alliances necessary to ensure its development. Finally, the case of Succinity shows that BASF is not really developing a relationship with territories concerning succinic acid as it has maintained production on the Purac Corbion site, but is consequently mobilizing downstream, in the production of plastics which will be added to its portfolio of activities.

Figure 7.4 summarizes the development of succinic acid.

2. Levulinic acid, a product at the heart of the biorefinery transitional object?

Levulinic acid, as systematically recalled in all the articles devoted to it, is considered in the US inventory of building blocks of 2004 as one of the promising intermediates of the Top 12 (see Chapters 1 and 3), likely to serve as a building block for a set of other intermediates (in this case other building blocks). For example, it is mentioned among its (many, as always) possible applications as a starting material for producing succinic acid – making it an alternative pathway to the biotechnological pathways, the expectations and promises of which were discussed in the previous section. The hypothesis put forward here is that levulinic acid owes its place at the time of the institutional construction of the top 12 and to the support granted by the American government to a process, that of Biofine, which at the time was undergoing pre-industrial development.

The role of levulinic acid should therefore be considered not so much in terms of its share of the scientific literature – a sign of high expectations and promise, of course – but in terms of its contribution to the construction of the collective space of the bioeconomy in the minds of economic actors and experts. In the same way that PLA, along with modified starches, was the flagship intermediate of the 1990s (as the bearer of the promise of the transition of bio-based polymers from a niche and specialty polymer status to that of commodity polymers challenging traditional chemistry), and that succinic acid garnered a lot of media attention in the 2000s (as an emblematic product of the capacity of biotechnologies to replace petroleum-based products in the long term to contribute to the construction of the bioeconomy), what is the place of levulinic acid?

The interpretative hypothesis reached here is the following: the specific place occupied by levulinic acid stems from the issues related to the biorefinery. The biorefinery provides the plan of action to transform agricultural raw materials into "something". This "something" may be biofuels, but these are under discussion. Here, the focus is on the fact that they are discussed from an economic point of view. For it regularly appears that they are too expensive, and that defending subsidies is not always politically sustainable. Similarly, what is questionable about biofuels is the use of food fractions for non-food purposes. The biorefinery object therefore needs a broader system of promises to exist.

2.1 The Biofine process: making a biorefinery credible at the crossroads of chemurgy and petrochemistry

In the Biofine process, levulinic acid is the product of high-pressure cracking of lignocelluloses used as a cheap source of material, by means of a strong acid technology, to make their sugars (hexoses) available and cause the formation reaction. Then, what remains is to separate the levulinic acid from the solvent and to purify it. Together with its co-product formic acid (which can be used for formaldehydes), it offers the possibility of a wide spectrum of applications in both specialty and commodity products, pesticides/herbicides and biofuels. Based on the interviews carried out for this study, the promise is that the Biofine process would accept a variety of low-cost or environmentally imageable resources (municipal waste, wood industry residues, agricultural waste, etc.). If we want to place levulinic acid in the history of chemistry, to measure the degree of novelty of the promises about levulinic acid and to identify the context in which these promises were made, it is worth identifying key literature reviews at different times. The first publication dates from 1956 and lists all the possibilities offered by succinic acid as a commodity chemical in industrial and engineering chemistry (Leonard, 1956). The 1981 paper by Veal and Whalley criticizes the idea that we can move towards a substitution of fossil fuels by ethanol quickly, and concludes, after having inventoried its possible uses, as follows: "a good starting point might be to reexamine some of the work *on the levulinic acid which was done 30–40 years ago*" (Veal and Whalley, 1981, p.56, emphasis added). The 2000 paper by Bozell et al. reviewed the possibilities of levulinic acid as a chemical platform and described the Biofine process (a company created in 1987 on the basis of patent portfolios on levulinic acid, which, in the framework of a project with NREL that began in 1996, is exploring the applications of levulinic acid from its process). It is this paper that is used in the 2004 American foresight exercise. This study also benefits from a paper by Hayes et al. (2006) which will be published in the encyclopedia on biorefineries. It is a plea for the thermochemical approach and the Biofine process contains energetic notations on the difficulties faced by biotechnological routes – and consequently the benefits brought by the "levulinic acid promise". Finally, the journal *ChemSusChem* published a review by Pileidis and Titirici (2016) with a suggestive title if one follows the hypothesis of this study: "Levulinic acid biorefineries: new challenges for efficient utilization of biomass".

2.2 The historical trajectory of levulinic acid: an American story

Industrial production emerged in the 1940s and 1950s, in particular under the impetus of Staley, as shown by the book that serves as a review of the literature published by the firm in 1943. This firm was initially an agricultural company of soya and wheat, which developed thereafter, among others, the production of levulinic acid. The latter is transformed by a thermochemical process applied notably to starch (Meyer, 1945; Moyer, 1942). Quaker Oats, an American food company founded in 1901, was also one of the first to develop a production unit for a precursor of levulinic acid, furfural, as early as 1922 for phenol-furfural resins (which can therefore be classified in the large family of formaldehydes). By using its agricultural residues, its oat hulls, the company created a "circular" biorefinery before its time. It also filed a patent on the production of levulinic acid in 1953 (Dunlop and Wells, 1957).

The 1940s and 1950s were a turning point in the production of levulinic acid. Leonard's (1956) contribution follows on from Staley Manufacturing Company's (1943) research by making an inventory of productions from levulinic acid: esters of levulinic acid as a plasticizer, preparation of active chemical intermediates (following on from Meyer, 1945), emulsifiers, pesticides and food supplements. This same article, as well as the patents cited above, would be considered by Schraufnagel and Rase (1975) as being at the origin of the technological trajectory of levulinic acid production: "Commercial production using an autoclave began in the United States in 1940 by A.E. Staley Co. using dextrose as feed and HCI as the acid (Meyer, 1945)" (Schraufnagel and Rase, 1975, p.40).

2.3 Biofine's patent family

It is in this context that we should consider the support of the American government to the Biofine company (Hayes et al., 2006). Thus, the first patents filed by Biofine for the production of levulinic acid from lignocellulose can be found as early as 1990 (see Table 7.1). For example, Fitzpatrick (1990) specifies a process for the production of furfural and levulinic acid from lignocellulose by a thermochemical process. It is important to realize that the development of levulinic acid is embedded into a long-term technological trajectory, as shown by the references of previous patents identified by the examiner of his patent, and those of patents citing the 1990 patent.

It can be noted, from that time, that what was at stake was to include this process in the traditional uses of levulinic acid: "Furfural is used primarily in lubricating oil manufacture and in making resins. Levulinic acid is also used to make resins, and, in addition, plasticizers, fragrance products, and pharmaceuticals" (Fitzpatrick, 1990, p.1). That is, precisely the possibilities imagined and the products produced 50 years earlier if one follows the compilation on succinic acid of the R&D department of the Staley Manufacturing Company dating (probably) from 1942 and which mentions the implementation of its – already – new large-scale production process of levulinic acid.

Table 7.1 The trajectory of patents cited in the 1990 Biofine patent (Fitzpatrick, 1990)

Patent cited	*Date of publication*	*Submitter*	*Title*
US3258481	1966	Crown Zellerbach Corp	Preparation of levulinic acid from hexose-containing material
US3701789	1972	Commw of Puerto Rico	Process for jointly producing furfural and levulinic acid from bagasse and other lignocellulosic materials
US4237226	1980	Trustees of Dartmouth College	Process for pretreating cellulosic substrates and for producing sugar therefrom
US4469524	1984	St. Lawrence Technologies Limited	Continuous process and apparatus for modifying carbohydrate material
US4497896	1985	St. Lawrence Technologies Limited	Fermentation of glucose with recycle of non-fermented components
US4578353	1986	St. Lawrence Reactors Limited	Fermentation of glucose with recycle of non-fermented components

2.4 Institutional support for process identity development

2.4.1 Institutional support for projects

The support of the American government first occurred through the implementation of a project aimed at accompanying the industrialization of the Biofine process as early as 1995, as established in the report written by Biometics (2002). This engineering firm managed the construction and data collection on the production unit implementing the Biofine process. The project also included the participation of the Great Lake Chemical Corporation and the New York State Department of Energy which was involved in supporting Biofine. The construction of the demonstration and production site began in 1996 and testing was conducted as of 1997. In the narrative, the goal is to use lignocellulose from biomass:

> the Biofine process allows the possibility of using biomass as a feed to a bio-refinery. Using the process, the biomass feed can be fractionated into levulinic acid, formica cid, furfural, and a hydrophobic (bone dry) char which is suitable for gasification to synthesise gas.
>
> (Biometics, 2002, p.13)

Later in the report, it is stated that the lignocellulose used comes primarily from pulp and paper production waste, followed by municipal waste and finally forestry residues.

The second point of interest in this report is that it specifies the proportions for each of the products obtained in a way that shows that the interpretation of the situation is dominated by levulinic acid and not by the other co-products, which are precisely considered as co-products when the opposite reasoning could be made. Indeed, the production of levulinic acid also makes the production of furfural possible, which is also part of the Top 10 list (Bozell and Petersen, 2010; Bozell et al., 2000).

2.4.2 Supporting the Green Chemistry Presidential Award and making promises

During the project, the firm was also supported by the US government by receiving the Green Chemistry Presidential Award in 1999. Then, Bozell et al. published in 2000 the study on levulinic acid, defending the Biofine process in the journal *Resources, Conservation and Recycling* (Bozell et al., 2000).

In this contribution, the authors defend levulinic acid as an additive for fuels allowing them to make fuels partially biosourced thanks to MTHF which is a derivative of levulinic acid. This use is defended because of the possibility of blending it directly at the refinery site, unlike ethanol:

> because it is miscible with gasoline at all proportions and hydrophobic, MTHF could be blended at the refinery and transported by pipeline. In

> contrast, ethanol must be added later in the distribution process because contamination with water can cause phase separation.
>
> (Bozell et al., 2000, p.232)

Regarding the application in DALA, i.e. herbicides, the authors believe that "DALA is completely biodegradable with a broad spectrum of activity rivaling and possibly exceeding that of Monsanto's Roundup" (Bozell and Petersen, 2010, p.232). Finally, levulinic acid is also described as a potential component of diphenolic acids, a large family of acids with very broad applications, which had been supplanted by bisphenol A due to its lower cost, in polycarbonates. This inventory of uses, including biofuels, does not exceed what was already written in the 1950s.

2.4.3 …which are part of a long-term strategy of maintaining technological expectations

This demonstrates that what is at stake is the maintaining of a promise. The construction of the narrative aimed at demonstrating the value of the Biofine process does indeed inscribe the potential of the biorefinery in that of levulinic acid. In other words, the success of the biorefinery depends on the levulinic acid industry, as Hayes et al. (2006) argue, hence the importance given to its outlets. Biofine stages the lignocellulosic biorefinery by framing it as an opportunity to break out of the food–non-food competition pitfalls over resources. This contemporary debate should not obscure the fact that the technology is part of the long, even very long, history of high-temperature acid hydrolysis technology:

> research and development efforts and attempts to commercialize biomass hydrolysis technology began in the early 1900s. (…) The Quaker Oats Company began production of furfural in the United States in the 1920s and until recently was the major world producer of furfural from agricultural residues. Furfural is produced from agricultural sources including corncobs, oat hulls, rice hulls, cereal grasses, and sugar cane bagasse.
>
> (Katzen and Schell, 2006, pp.129–133)

Moreover, after insisting on the novelty of the process ("the process involves high-temperature acid-hydrolysis in two reactors and one of the most advanced and commercially viable lignocellulosic-fractionating technologies currently available" (Hayes et al., 2006, p.139), the firm's actors now point to its rusticity, the possibility of anchoring it on under-used sites and, an amusing detail if one remembers the violence of the identity crisis in chemistry, the fact that the process is chemical and not biotechnological.

As shown previously, it is the process that makes it possible to access levulinic acid that is offered rather than the molecule itself. This is how the previous diagram constructs the modularity of the process with two reactions that can be controlled and that make it possible to reach precise intermediates. This hypothesis is confirmed by the following quote:

> In a complete Biofine plant, additive processing may then occur, depending on the final products required. For example, syngas production from the Biofine char (a dry, powdery material of calorific value comparable with that of bituminous coal, and composed of the residual materials in the Biofine Process which has value as a fuel and as a soil additive) can be conducted in a gasification unit or the LA can be esterified with ethanol to produce ethyl levulinate.
>
> (Hayes et al., 2006, p.145)

The product is thus constructed as being able to be integrated into existing production sites or to participate in the organization of the profitability of an industrial site by reusing certain flows.

2.4.4 Industrialization of the process in Italy

The process was industrialized in the mid-2000s. Thus, Hayes et al. (2006) state that an industrial site located in Caserta in Italy was to industrialize the process. A market study by the Nova-Institute showed that an Italian firm called Green Future had been producing levulinic acid since 2008 but did not communicate about it. This same firm, Green Future, was also located in Caserta. In November 2015, an Italian firm, GF Biochemicals, claimed to have developed a process to make levulinic acid directly from biomass: "GFBiochemicals is the only company to produce levulinic acid at 'commercial scale directly from biomass" (n.d.). This level of production (8 kt/year) would have been reached after having been used as an industrial demonstration since 2008. In the company's communication, there is no mention of Green Future, or even of a possible name change. However, the location of Green Future and the location of the GF Biochemicals production unit in Caserta (Via delle Industrie, Caserta) suggests that it is the same company. The second question that arises about GF Biochemicals' production is whether it has, as it claims, developed a process, or whether it is licensing the Biofine process. My investigation of patents from Green Future or GF Biochemicals did not return any results on registered patents. In contrast, some of its personnel (R. Parton, B. Engendahl and A. de Rijke) previously worked at DSM and filed some patents on levulinic acid (Jacobs et al., 1997; Parton et al., 2014, 2013; RIJKE et al., 2014). Thus, GF Biochemicals reportedly industrialized the Biofine process at its production site in Italy. This makes it the second production facility (after Biofine's demonstration facility in South Glen Falls, New York) using this process.

This detour into GF Biochemicals could have been omitted, as the company does not appear to significantly alter the landscape. Nevertheless, the fact that it has held a significant place in the media since Leonard (1956) testifies to the fact that actors, in order to make the field exist as a space for mobilization, need

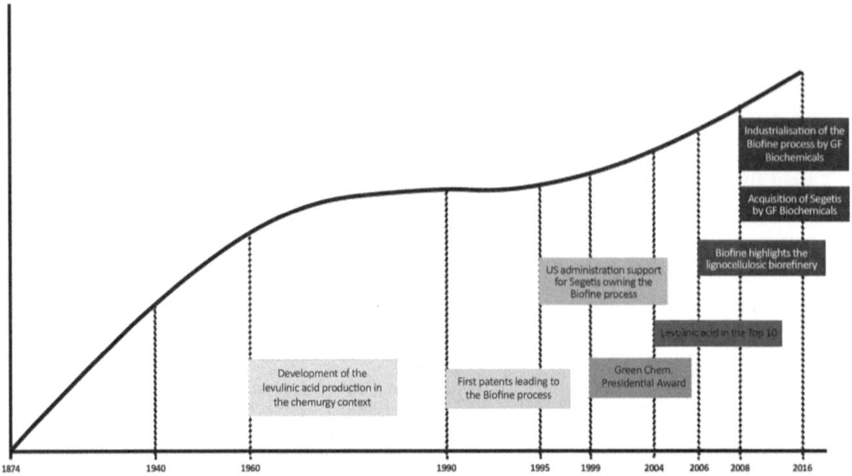

Figure 7.5 The techno-economic promises cycle of levulinic acid

to renew the promises of levulinic acid. While what qualifies levulinic acid is its inclusion in the various inventory lists of "molecules of the future" and its presence in the work of Kamm et al. (2006), and thus in the field of contemporary biorefinery.

The fact that all of these opportunities are found in the extensive 2016 review in *ChemSusChem* with a particular focus on obtaining succinic acid from levulinic acid – i.e., by a "non-biotech" pathway – draws attention to a particular point. The bioeconomy of the third type is constructed as a field in which the actors of the biochemical and thermochemical pathways compete, while at the same time collaborating to create institutional arrangements that are favorable to them and that contribute to the closure of the field. In this space, the insistence on levulinic acid is a marker of the field used in variable legitimization and credibility devices: (1) to indicate the possibility of a "bio-based economy" since it has already occurred; (2) to indicate that it is possible to overcome biomass recalcitrance, since the Biofine process is there – in this case to treat non-food fractions of biomass; (3) to indicate that there is a sufficiently versatile platform molecule to cover a range of needs from a sufficiently rustic process; and last but not least (4) to avoid doing genetic engineering.

Figure 7.5 summarizes the development of levulinic acid.

3. Conclusion

The case of levulinic acid shows how deeply the bioeconomy of the biorefinery is embedded in the productive heritage of petrochemistry, since as early as the 1920s there was significant activity around the problem of acid hydrolysis to make it. The work published by the Staley Manufacturing Company (1943) shows that the same type of recurrent dynamics is present. An industrial production capacity for the platform molecule was established in 1940. It was therefore necessary to ensure that a community of users would focus on it. The company's R&D department therefore produced this work, which documents all the possible uses and invites collaboration. In this respect, the remarkable stability of the promises concerning the opportunities offered by the versatile platform molecule could be noted, as shown by the comparison between Bozell et al. (2000) and Leonard (1956). The case of succinic acid exposes a very similar dynamic, only it does not do so by illustrating the independence of the biotech sector, as its promise to be a general-purpose technology like computer science might suggest. On the contrary, to move beyond the laboratory stage, biotech firms of the bioeconomy must (1) demonstrate the potential efficacy of their products, and (2) develop alliances with existing companies capable of bearing the cost of process industrialization.

Chapter 6 has shown the different phases, at the microeconomic level, of the cycles of technical and economic promises. It highlighted that, at the same time as they formulate promises, actors are caught up in learning logics. That is to say, at the same time as they are discovering obstacles, they are identifying opportunities that they could exploit. Chapter 7 has thus underlined the fact that the rebound phase is not the "end of the story" but a new stage in which actors continue to draw on their knowledge inherited from the past. Nonetheless, while this knowledge is re-interrogated in the promise phase, it is also integrated into the firms' economic model. This entry of several firms into one field leads to competition between them, but also to the competitors producing products of fossil origin.

Notes

1 One of the world's leading research centers for green chemistry.
2 Which also has a licensing agreement with Myriant.
3 This agency lasted from 2005 to 2008.
4 It should be noted that Roquette has a patent on large-scale production (Segueilha et al., 2009) which is also cited by DSM in its patents on succinic acid.
5 Moreover, this is what ADEME calls "technology bricks" in the 2016 call for projects "Plant-based chemistry and bio-based materials".
6 That is to say, to obtain succinic acid in a solid state.
7 The patents were published in 2011–2012 but were indeed filed between November and December 2009.

Bibliography

Bechthold, I., Bretz, K., Kabasci, S., Kopitzky, R., Springer, A., 2008. Succinic acid: a new platform chemical for biobased polymers from renewable resources. *Chem. Eng. Technol.* 31, 647–654. https://doi.org/10.1002/ceat.200800063.

Bioamber, 2008. *Bioamber announces world's first bio-based succinic acid plant: helping to reduce dependence on fossil fuels.* http://investor.bio-amber.com/2008-12-16-Bioamber-announces-world-apos-s-first-bio-based-succinic-acid-plant-helping-to-reduce-dependence-on-fossil-fuels, accessed 10/30/2015.

Biometics, 2002. *Commercialization of the Biofine technology for levulinic acid production from paper sludge* (Final technical report). US DOE.

Bozell, J.J., Moens, L., Elliott, D.C., Wang, Y., Neuenscwander, G.G., Fitzpatrick, S. W., Bilski, R.J., Jarnefeld, J.L., 2000. Production of levulinic acid and use as a platform chemical for derived products. *Resour. Conserv. Recycl.* 28, 227–239. https://doi.org/10.1016/S0921-3449(99)00047–00046.

Bozell, J.J., Petersen, G., 2010. Technology development for the production of biobased products from biorefinery carbohydrates: the US Department of Energy's "Top 10" revisited. *Green Chem.* 12, 539–554.

Broecker, F.J., Schwarzmann, M., 1977. *Manufacture of butanediol and/or tetrahydrofuran from maleic and/or succinic anhydride via ⊠-butyrolactone.* US4048196 A.

Budarin, V., Luque, R., Macquarrie, D.J., Clark, J.H., 2007. Towards a bio-based industry: benign catalytic esterifications of succinic acid in the presence of water. *Chem. Eur. J.* 13, 6914–6919. https://doi.org/10.1002/chem.200700037.

Chauvel, A., Lefebvre, G., Chauvel, A., 1989. *Synthesis-gas derivates and major hydrocarbons, petrochemical processes.* Éditions Technip.

Cheng, K.-K., Zhao, X.-B., Zeng, J., Zhang, J.-A., 2012. Biotechnological production of succinic acid: current state and perspectives. *Biofuels Bioprod. Biorefining* 6, 302–318. https://doi.org/10.1002/bbb.1327.

Colletis, G., 2012. *L'urgence industrielle!*, Retour à l'économie politique. Le Bord de L'eau.

Cukalovic, A., Stevens, C.V., 2008. Feasibility of production methods for succinic acid derivatives: a marriage of renewable resources and chemical technology. *Biofuels, Bioprod. Bioref.* 2, 505–529. https://doi.org/10.1002/bbb.105.

Datta, R., 1992. *Process for the production of succinic acid by anaerobic fermentation.* 5143833.

Datta, R., Glasser, D.A., Jain, M.K., Vick Roy, J.R., 1992. *Fermentation and purification process for succinic acid.* 5168055.

de Guzman, D., 2012. To succinity and beyond! Green Chemicals Blog, 5 October. http://greenchemicalsblog.com/2012/10/05/to-succinity-and-beyond, accessed on 11/23/2020.

DSM, 2013. *Achieving high bio-based content in DSM arnitel copolyesters.*

Dunlop, A.P., Wells, J.P.A., 1957. *Process for producing levulinic acid.*

Festel, G., 2010. Industrial biotechnology: market size, company types, business models, and growth strategies. *Ind. Biotechnol.* 6, 88–94. https://doi.org/10.1089/ind.2010.0006.

Festel, G., Detzel, C., Maas, R., 2012. Industrial biotechnology: markets and industry structure. *J. Commer. Biotechnol.* 18, 11–21.

Fitzpatrick, S.W., 1990. *Lignocellulose degradation to furfural and levulinic acid.* US4897497 A.

Foray, D., 2009. *L' économie de la connaissance*, Nouv. éd. entirement ref. et mise à jour. ed, Repères Economie. La Découverte.

Fuertes, P., Delmotte, A.L., Dreux, J.-L., 1998. *Cationic polysaccharides esterified by a discarloxylic acid anhydride substituted with a branched carbon chain.* US5731430 A.

Fuertes, P., Delmotte, A.L., Dreux, J.-L., 1997. *Composition and process for sizing paper.* US5647898 A.

Fuertes, P., Delmotte, A.L., Dreux, J.-L., 1996. *Composition and process for sizing paper.* EP0742316 A1.

Gerberding, S.J., Singh, R., 2011. *Purification of succinic acid from the fermentation broth containing ammonium succinate.* WO2011082378 A3.

GF Biochemicals, n.d. About us. www.gfbiochemicals.com/company/#about-us, accessed 12/14/2019.

Glassner, D.A., Datta, R., 1992. *Process for the production and purification of succinic acid.* 5143834.

Gong, W., Dole, S., Grabar, T., Collard, A.C., Pero, J.G., Yocum, R.R., 2012. *Engineering microbes for efficient production of chemicals.* EP2501797 A2.

Grabar, T., Gong, W., Yocum, R.R., 2012. *Metabolic evolution of escherchia coli strains that produce organic acids.* EP2501798 A2.

Hayes, D.J., Fitzpatrick, S., Hayes, M.H.B., Ross, J.R.H., 2006. The biofine process: production of levulinic acid, furfural, and formic acid from lignocellulosic feedstocks, in: Kamm, B., Gruber, P.R., Kamm, M. (Eds.), *Biorefineries: industrial processes and products.* Springer, pp.129–162.

Hermann, T., Reinhardt, J., Yu, X., Udani, R., Staples, L., 2012. *Improved fermentation process for the production of organic acids.* CA2807102 A1.

Jacobs, P.A., Parton, R., Rane, V.H., Renard, M., Tas, D., Van, B.W., 1997. *Chiral solid catalyst, its preparation and its use for the production of substantially enantiomerically pure products.* WO1997014500 A1.

Jansen, M.L.A., Segueilha, L., Verwaal, R., Louchart, M., 2012. *Dicarboxylic acid production process.* CA2811539 A1.

Jeannet, J.-P., Schreuder, H., 2015. *From coal to biotech: the transformation of DSM with business school support.* Springer.

Kamm, B., Gruber, P.R., Kamm, M. (Eds.), 2006. *Biorefineries – industrial processes and products: status quo and future directions.* Wiley-VCH.

Katzen, R., Schell, D.J., 2006. Lignocellulosic feedstock biorefinery: history and plant development for biomass hydrolysis, in: Kamm, B., Gruber, P.R., Kamm, M. (Eds.), *Biorefineries: industrial processes and products.* Springer, pp.129–138.

Lee, S.H., Lim, S.W., Lee, K.H., 1999. Properties of potentially biodegradable copolyesters of (succinic acid-1,4-butanediol)/(dimethyl terephtalate-1,4-butanediol). *Polym. Int.* 48, 861–867.

Leonard, R.H., 1956. Levulinic acid as a basic chemical raw material. *Ind. Eng. Chem.* 48, 1330–1341. https://doi.org/10.1021/ie50560a033.

Mangolte, P.-A., 2006. Brevets et émergence de l'industrie cinématographique, une étude comparative États-Unis-Europe (1895–1908). *Ann. Hist. Sci. Soc.* 61.

Meyer, W.G., 1945. *Manufacture of levulinic acid.*

Moyer, W.W., 1942. *Preparation of levulinic acid.*

Myriant, n.d. Homepage. https://web.archive.org/web/20090830195553/http://www.myriant.com/company.htm, accessed on 10/16/2022.

Myriant, 2012. *Piedmont Chemical launches 100 percent renewable polyester polyols leveraging renewable chemicals from DuPont Tate & Lyle Bio Products and Myriant Corporation.* www.prweb.com/releases/2012/12/prweb10193537.htm, accessed on 10/17/2022.

Parton, R.F.M.J., Janssen, M.C.C., Engendahl, B., De, V.J.G., 2014. *Process for the preparation of formylvaleric acid and adipic acid.* CA2896843 A1.

Parton, R.F.M.J., Rijkers, M.P.W.M., Kroon, J.A., 2013. *Continuous production of furfural and levulininc acid.* US8426619 B2.

Pileidis, F.D., Titirici, M.-M., 2016. Levulinic acid biorefineries: new challenges for efficient utilization of biomass. *ChemSusChem* 9, 562–582. https://doi.org/10.1002/cssc.201501405.

Rijke, D.A., Hangx, G.W.A., Parton, R.F.M.J., Engendahl, B., 2014. *Process for the isolation of levulinic acid.* WO2014087013 A1.

Roubos, J.A., Peij, V.N.N.M.E., 2008. *Procédé pour obtenir une expression de polypeptides améliorée.* WO2008000632 A1.

Schraufnagel, R.A., Rase, H.F., 1975. Levulinic acid from sucrose using acidic ion-exchange resins. *Ind. Eng. Chem. Prod. Res. Dev.* 14, 40–44. https://doi.org/10.1021/i360053a009.

Segueilha, L., San, K.-Y., Bennett, G., Martinez, I., 2009. *Procédé de culture microbienne à grande échelle.* WO2009083756 A1.

Staley Manufacturing Company, 1943. *Levulinic acid; a literature reference.* Division of Research Development, A.E. Staley.

Thakker, C., Martínez, I., San, K.-Y., Bennett, G.N., 2012. Succinate production in Escherichia coli. *Biotechnol. J.* 7, 213–224. https://doi.org/10.1002/biot.201100061.

Veal, F.J., Whalley, L., 1981. Renewable resources as chemical feedstocks. *Conserv. Recycl.* 4, 47–57.

Weastra, S., 2012. *Determination of market potential for selected platform chemicals.* Bio-ConSepT FP7 Project.

Werpy, T., Frye, J., Holladay, J., 2006. Succinic acid: a model building block for chemical production from renewable resources, in: Kamm, B., Gruber, P.R., Kamm, M. (Eds.), *Biorefineries: industrial processes and products.* Springer, pp.367–379.

Werpy, T., Petersen, G., 2004. *Top value added chemicals from biomass.* US Department of Energy.

Yocum, R.R., Hermann, T., Yu, X., 2013. *Fermentation of glycerol to organic acids.* CA2841461 A1.

Zeikus, J.G., 1980. Chemical and fuel production by anaerobic bacteria. *Annu. Rev. Microbiol.* 34, 423–464. https://doi.org/10.1146/annurev.mi.34.100180.002231.

Zeikus, J.G., Jain, M.K., Elankovan, P., 1999. Biotechnology of succinic acid production and markets for derived industrial products. *Appl. Microbiol. Biotechnol.* 51, 545–552. https://doi.org/10.1007/s002530051431.

Conclusion

Post-fossil economy and transition: making the future happen today

1. Using renewable resources, a necessary but not sufficient condition for the transition to a post-fossil economy

This book takes as its starting point the question stemming from political economy aiming to characterize the historical forms of capitalism. The perspective of the ecological transition questions the capacity of capitalism to become ecologically sustainable. Instead of asserting one or the other position, this book chooses to embrace the tension between overcoming capitalism and reproducing capitalism as one of the dynamics of the transition. In keeping with the perspectives of the political economy of capitalisms (Amable, 2009; Boyer, 2015; Boyer and Saillard, 2002), the study of the evolution of capitalism must be based on the concrete forms of accumulation and its evolution. Hence, the fossil economy emerged at the time of the industrial revolution through the increasing consumption of fossil resources. The transition to a post-fossil economy, a concept put forward in the introduction to the book, theorizes the process of transition by which the use of fossil resources is substituted by the use of renewable resources, anchored in a thinking of planetary limits.

As shown in Chapter 3, the substitution in the transition refers both to material dimensions (the use of new processes, for example) and to immaterial dimensions. Consequently, the study of the ways in which actors theorize and organize the substitution, with regard to the fossil economy, makes it possible to feed the debate on the transformation or overcoming of capitalism in the ecological transition. Nicholas Georgescu-Roegen's original bioeconomy project thus provides a vision of the future of an economy (1) anchored in social systems, and (2) in balance with the availability of natural resources (Georgescu-Roegen, 1975; Giampietro, 2019; Mayumi, 2001). The development of today's bioeconomy, as defined in Chapter 1, which holds the promise of the substitution of fossil resources by biomass, is an emblematic area for observation. The development of the contemporary bioeconomy is positioned far upstream of contemporary value chains. In the fossil era, the book has shown that the turn of the 1930s corresponds to the moment when the search for substitution of artisanal products, potentially of renewable resource origin, by products from fossil resources began (Benninga, 1990; Galambos et al., 2007). This changeover is a key moment because the constraint of raw materials

DOI: 10.4324/9781003103011-8

emerges as a guiding principle in the allocation of resources for the innovation process. It is this approach of seeking substitution via raw materials that we find today in the debate on the transition to a post-fossil economy. Consequently, the sole argument of the use of biomass is not a sufficient criterion for assessing whether a bioeconomy project is part of a post-fossil economy, since it may be shared by actors with contradictory positions, in their attempt of imposing their vision.

Going back to the criteria that reflect the rationality and values of the actors at stake makes it possible to determine whether they are indeed seeking to break with the fossil economy. A given bioeconomy is therefore not necessarily contradictory to the fossil economy when it seeks to copy its model of the division of labor or the mode of consumption of its products, as is the case with the bioeconomy of the biorefinery. From the point of view of substitution, it is not obvious that the development of the use of biomass will lead to the substitution of fossil resources, but it could extend it by helping to legitimize the use of renewable resources, as is the case with PLA-based plastics (see Chapter 6). The development of these "green" products could generate green growth. Instead of replacing fossil fuel growth, this growth would complement it, making the discourse on ecological transition acceptable to capital.

2. The foundations of the activity of an economy in transition

The economy of the future is taking shape today. Therefore, the transition is a key stage in which the conflicts that will generate tomorrow's economy develop. This is the result put forward in this book. The ecological transition is an economic period in itself, since it questions the logic of resource allocation in order to bring about an economic system whose legitimacy, based on sustainability, will be imposed by the group of actors who will become dominant. The transition process brings into play problems of innovation and production that must be framed by an institutional architecture. These problems are expressed in the form of controversies around visions of the future held by the actors and their coalitions. In the transition, there is thus a blend of (1) controversy over past activities (should they be maintained, transformed or abandoned?), (2) activities aimed at structuring the transition period, and (3) the emergence of new activities that will belong to the future economy.

The issue of representations has the advantage of making it possible to discuss the promises and attempts of actors to capture the space of the transition. Assuming the role of representations in resource allocation strategies, paradoxically, brings into play the role of the materiality of production and of institutions in economic life. This leads to develop two results that open the way to new research on the political economy of the ecological transition. On the one hand, the aim is to show how the theorization of the field in the transition by the actors themselves helps to shape its future. On the other hand, this conclusion offers a grammar of mesoeconomic spaces in the transition based on the concepts put forward in Chapter 2 and the results of the book.

2.1 The theorization of the field by the actors themselves: the bioeconomy as a field of conflict and cooperation with multiple borders

Chapters 3 and 4 have focused on the actors' theorization of the bioeconomy field. Indeed, these theorizations have contributed to giving direction to collective actions at a given time. It has been shown here that the dominant representation of the bioeconomy which has been constructed in Europe in recent years is not formed from processes (the use of processes resulting from the biotechnological revolution and based on the economic promises of the biosciences) as in the version advocated by the Organisation for Economic Co-operation and Development (OECD) and its International Futures Programme, 2009. But it is from the raw material (the biomass), constructed as a unique object,[1] that the European Commission constructs the space of the bioeconomy; "The Bioeconomy refers to the sustainable production and conversion of biomass into a range of food, health, fibre and industrial products and energy. Renewable biomass encompasses any biological material (agriculture, forestry and animal-based including fish)" (BECOTEPS, n.d., p.4).

The bioeconomy has thus emerged as a space within which actors are addressing the issue of "new uses for biomass". The bioeconomy space is sometimes reduced by political and economic actors to only non-food uses for materials, chemistry and energy (McCormick and Kautto, 2013). The "biologization" of industrial processes (National Research Council of the National Academies, 2015) in the sense of advances in genetic engineering-based biosciences is second only to the ecological issue in the intentions of the most important actors. They were originally driven by the problems of agricultural surpluses, although the oil shocks and the discourse on peak oil opened up opportunities for action. The theorization of the field by the actors naturally borrows from these two registers (biotech revolution and sustainable development). But it invites us to go beyond the arguments currently used to legitimize it. This is not the first theorizing exercise of its kind. The example of the *chemurgy* of the 1930s invites us to pay attention to the tools of coordination for developing mesoeconomic spaces: oriented states of the art, technological demonstration platforms, research projects, product identity standards and, above all, *backcasting* exercises.

This book also shows that the movement towards the name "bioeconomy" cannot be separated from the one that generated it from another material, but also semantic and conceptual, construction. From the second half of the 1990s, it was a narrative of the biorefinery that began to delineate the space thus constructed, based on exercises aimed at shifting the non-food uses of biomass from the value chains of fossil molecules. This has conditioned the development of the exploration of biomass uses around small molecule chemistry based on sugars. The chemistry of sugars is merging with this chemistry of small molecules to provide biosourced carbon for the same uses as fossil carbon. For example, the American state of the art on large molecules has attempted to fit these products into the workings of petrochemical chemistry on the basis of the promise of functionalities that they could achieve (*cf.* in particular the Top 12 by Werpy and Petersen, 2004).

The intensity of the institutional construction of this space, which will be translated into roadmaps for the researchers called upon to remove the technological barriers on this trajectory, cannot be denied or neglected. In the European case, this book shows that it has been done in particular through the European Commission's support for projects explicitly dedicated to the formation of the knowledge bases necessary for the strategic thinking of private biorefinery actors, and to their influencing actions, such as the FP6 Specific Support Action (Biorefinery Euroview and Biopol).[2] Nevertheless, they should not be reduced to simple political lobbying actions, because these actions are only a consequence of the actors' problems. They aim to build the institutional framework for reproducing and projecting common-pool resources into the future by enriching them with new attributes.

While the problematization of the bioeconomy based on biorefinery dominates the vision of biotechnologies or that of a post-fossil economy, the diversity of representations of the bioeconomy is still present (Gravitis and Suzuki, 1999). The constitution and dynamics of space cannot therefore be conceived as the product of a single type of linear strategy, but as a learning process in which actors seek to complete the bases of their cognitive, institutional and material resources. One cannot consider either that this space has a "center" even if one of the points made here is that the biomass and its uses are a structuring factor. This study has shown that the actors present in the field think of their value chains according to their respective positions. An actor with a certain type of biomass seeks the processes that make it possible to valorize it and the products that make it possible to sell it; but an actor involved in processes or chemical intermediates has little interest in the original biomass that he seeks to compete with. Similarly, manufacturers of products that are subject to regulations, such as wood panel manufacturers, observe the portfolio of solutions available to them in order to substitute formaldehydes. Hence the interest shown in the decomposition of value chains that actors seek to theorize, with which the following subsection will deal, for the concrete analysis of the configurations linking raw materials, processes and products, as well as the discourses intended to make them legitimate and credible in the field.

At the national level, it is possible to explain the differences in definitions of bioeconomy models according to the dominant industries that have controlled the definition of national roadmaps. This study has shown that actors are dominated and oriented by institutional arrangements, but at the same time they seek to invest in existing arrangements and produce new ones. The value chain models developed in demonstration projects aimed at building them, such as Eurobioref, Biocore or Suprabio (see Chapter 4), form localized compromises. They inscribe regularities in the mode of operation in a field linking products, actors and procedures. It is, for example, this method of the "economic model of value chains" that has been adopted by the European Commission in the setting up of a PPP with the actors of the bioeconomy, and for which it has given the direction to the former director of the EUROPABIO biotechnology lobby in Brussels. Thus, beyond the different models developed, the battle is that of institutionalizing the selection mechanisms of the principles of evaluation and judgment: these will dictate which actors, products and organizations are credible and legitimate to be part of the bioeconomy field.

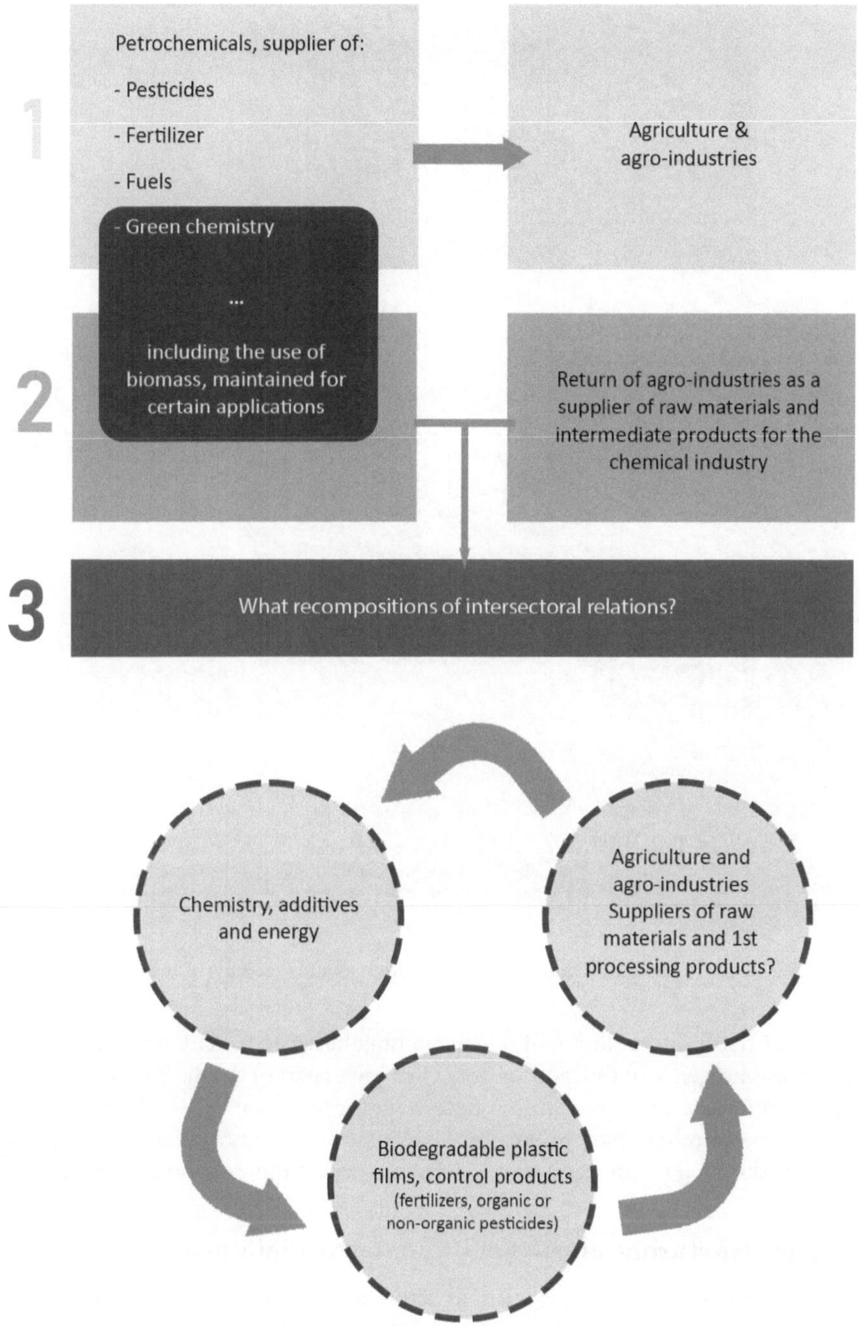

Figure 8.1 The evolution of the relationship between agriculture and petrochemistry

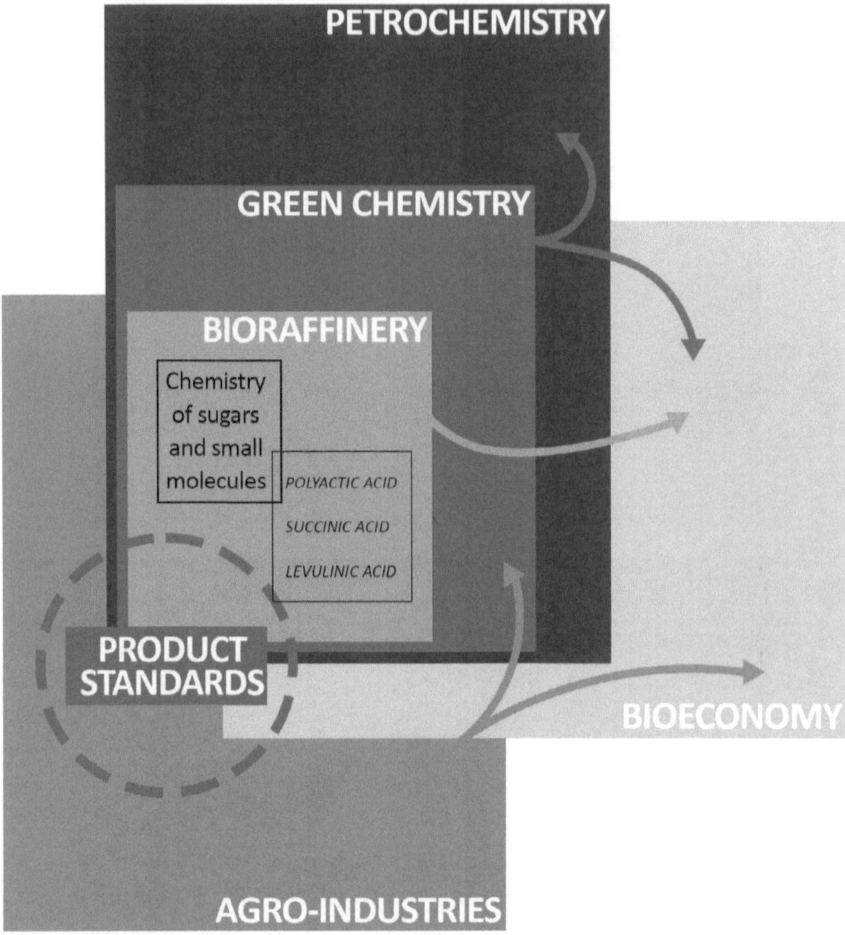

Figure 8.2 A static representation of the intertwining fields creating the bioeconomy

Figure 8.1 traces the evolution of the relationship between agriculture and industry up to the emergence of the bioeconomy. The lower part of the diagram should not lead us to believe that agriculture is becoming the sole supplier of chemicals, but that the use of renewable resources is developing in chemistry. Figure 8.2 "takes over" by showing the bioeconomy as a space in which different issues overlap.

3. The structuring of the field by intermediate products

The findings of this study suggest that actors invest material and cognitive and institutional resources in the exploration of product trade-offs (molecules, materials or technologies), but that it is the conversion of biomass into key intermediate products that structures the field of the bioeconomy. From this point of view, the bioeconomy can be seen, through its problematization by actors, even more than chemistry, as an "industry of industries". Its downstream boundaries are in fact delimited by the fact that the bioeconomy offers to deliver these intermediates to specialty chemicals, materials manufacturers or energy suppliers. For this reason, three major intermediates that have held (and continue to hold) particularly strong promise have been selected for Chapters 6 and 7. The aim was to resituate these products in their key role in the constitution and dynamics of the bioeconomy field. Indeed, it is the narratives about these great intermediaries that have taken turns to open up the bioeconomy from the trap and crisis of legitimacy of biofuels. It should be remembered that biofuels had been classified by historical authors of ecological economics as an emblematic example of environmental innovation (Faucheux and Nicolaï, 1998, 2011).

Actors had to find some form of response to the criticisms about biofuels, presenting the bioeconomy of biorefinery in a different light from that of agrofuels. This study has singled out three major biomass intermediates for the promises and the role of "gatekeepers" towards the bioeconomy that the actors themselves have assigned to them. It is necessary to bear in mind that the study of these intermediates must beware of media effects. From this point of view, these major intermediaries are in competition with each other in terms of being candidates to be precursors in chemical reactions. But they are also in competition as ways of exploring new sectors with other strategies that avoid the fractionation stage (cracking of the biorefinery) to produce them. It is therefore under the sole aspect of the role in the constitution of the field that they have been mobilized for this study. Polylactic Acids (PLA) are one of the major polymer families, which from the late 1990s are presented as the "royal road" to the development of the use of biomass. The actors discovered that the application technologies were necessarily a complex field, in which it was necessary to realize, beyond the promises, combinations of technologies and compromises between functionalities to obtain viable products. This study therefore set out to understand why they were so important in the field. This study has found that the development of PLA was the result of a long-term dynamic. Derived from lactic acid, this product has been well known since the beginning of the 20th century. A knowledge base in starch fermentation to obtain lactic acid was therefore established very early on. The modification of this precursor to obtain plastic fibers was carried out as early as the 1930s in the context of widespread exploration of macromolecules. After being used as an additive in plastics, PLA was used for the production of medical devices from the 1960s onwards. What is the role of PLA in the bioeconomy? From the 1980s onwards, actors sought to address the problems of biomass, which had withstood the "cheap oil era", by returning from a specialty chemistry to a commodity chemistry (consumer plastics). Indeed, PLA, like other biomass products, was positioned in highly specialized niches – in this case, biocompatible medical materials.

To do this, the actors sought to demonstrate that PLA could be used on its own, i.e. that it was possible to move away from the hybridization techniques that had been used during the 1930s and 1940s. The actors' learning process over the period 1986–2015 was guided by three challenges: to produce PLA continuously, to achieve production costs that would enable them to reach the price levels of commodity polymers, and to manage competition with other candidates for bio-based plastics. PLA will therefore be the product of reference for actors in the agro-industry field looking for solutions for the disposal of mass agricultural surpluses – the first of these being the grain and oilseed trader Cargill, which in the 1980s was the world's leading agri-food company. They argued that it was possible to make commodity chemicals from agricultural products with PLA.

The case study on succinic acid made it possible to verify the role of large intermediates as a model for specific development. Succinic acid was produced industrially via fossil fuels, from petroleum derivatives (acetylene and formaldehyde). Its industrial outlets already existed. So the promise of succinic acid grew in the bioeconomy as researchers explored biotechnological processes to substitute petroleum-based succinic acid with bio-based succinic acid. There are three reasons for the rush to succinic acid. First of all, bio-based succinic acid very quickly reaches production prices that are very close to those of petroleum-based products – or even directly competitive under specific purity conditions. It is therefore a platform molecule that could validate the petroleum substitution strategy that is at the heart of the bioeconomy. Then, the production process, based on patented modified bacteria, is emblematic of the bioeconomy based on biotechnology, which the OECD was promoting. The point was to be present in the patent war, which was supposed to ensure an immediate competitive advantage in biotechnology. The major actors in the French agro-industry have waged this war by buying out licenses on competing American intellectual property rights, the field of patentability of small variants in genetic or enzymatic manipulations being highly extensible. Finally, since succinic acid is a possible precursor – from a theoretical point of view – of a whole series of other chemical intermediates, the large chemical firms, each established in positions of dominant oligopoly on one or more products, are faced with the question of the possible circumvention of the patents of the dominant competitor on a product, by using a new (biotechnological) pathway to reach its major key intermediate. The regulation of change therefore follows this logic of exploring substitution strategies. And the importance of biotech succinic acid in the construction of the bioeconomy must be understood as the ability of the bioeconomy based on biomass and biorefinery to integrate the promises of the biotechnological revolution, and thus to capture the public subsidies linked to the preparation of the "third industrial revolution".

Finally, the case of levulinic acid has made it possible to identify the fact that intermediate products are not simply objects of research and innovation dynamics, but also "focal points" around which the problematization of the bioeconomy is built. Indeed, this study has observed that levulinic acid was linked to the constitution of the biorefinery, which was struggling to prove its potential economic viability from biofuels alone. The levulinic acid occupied in the period 1985–1995 the place of the key platform molecule in which learnings to be carried out can be projected, starting from thermochemistry.[3]

The question is: Why? Because the versatility of this platform molecule has been recognized since the early 1940s, and it has been rediscovered with each wave of interest in biomass – as shown by publications from the early 1980s, when the term biorefinery first emerged. Levulinic acid thus proves the credibility of the biorefinery at times when it goes through periods of disappointment. It is therefore not surprising, after having seen it hold the spotlight at the end of the 1990s (the Biofine process biorefinery) to see it reappear in a major state of the art of the journal *Green Chemistry* in 2016 (Lima et al., 2016), reaffirming all the promises of levulinic acid. Its final section is devoted to the processes which make it possible to obtain succinic acid from levulinic acid, proof if it were needed that the bioeconomy cannot be mistaken for the biotechnological way.

4. Promise dynamics and field structuring

The study of these commitments to material resources has shown two impacts on the construction of the field. The first concerns the question of technological choice, which this study sought to endogenize. That is, technological choice and its corollary lock-ins can be read as the product of endogenous dynamics of existing technological trajectories. A technology or an intermediate product has no meaning in itself. A unitary technology only makes sense in economic activity if it can be combinatory, complementary and cumulative (Antonelli, 2014; Befort, 2021; Pavitt, 1998).

Technological lock-ins do not therefore exist in an absolute way but are constructed over the course of the actors' actions as locks on their trajectories. Thus, the regulation of change can be read in trajectories that are regimes, that is, stable ways of approaching the question of the production of knowledge necessary for action, and in particular for the creation of new activities. Consequently, it is the mode of knowledge development that makes actors identify the obstacles that interest them in the deployment of their productive activities. And this is what leads them to make promises about the lifting of these barriers in order to attract holders of other technologies to the cooperative actions necessary for the development of products. This is why firms often announce the formation of co-development agreements with an emblematic downstream user: it is a condition for building the credibility of their technological choices. The selection of technologies then proceeds from the construction of criteria for estimating the increasing returns to the adoption of technologies, which it has been seen are linked (particularly in the case of PLA) to the history and the world of production into which the product is projected. The analysis of the transition from the point of view of the study of the formation of techno-economic promises invites us to understand the processes of innovation and technological change as cyclical processes of hope and disappointment (Borup et al., 2006) that the actors try to manage (as shown in Chapters 5, 6 and 7).

In the first phase, the technical and economic promises concern the lifting of the technological locks identified in this same promise. These promises then justify orienting learning along this trajectory. Typically, the promises made at the end of the 1980s were concerned with the development of a bio-based polymer capable of competing with fossil-based polymers in commodity chemistry. The second phase is that of disappointment resulting from the failure to remove the locks identified and thus to pass the test of the confrontation between the chemical functionalities of the product and the expected functionalities. In the case of PLA, this period corresponds to the moment when the actors are forced to recognize that the polymer is not heat resistant and that the management of its end-of-life requires the setting up of industrial structures, invalidating the promise of a disposable plastic in household compost. The phase of disappointment then gives way to the re-exploration of common-pool resources and the exploration of new product hybridizations that lead to the formation of new promises.

The formulation of these promises engages change, because it aims to make productive projects credible and legitimate. Consequently, the field exists as an inclusion of actors, but also because its representations are embodied in material objects carried by productive projects. Thus, the fact that projects are contested or supported legitimizes their existence, but also legitimizes the existence of the field as a relevant space for action. Nevertheless, the narratives of promises are also stories of heritages that we identify when we place them in their historicity. The stake identified here for the actors is finally that of their productive identity, which justifies, from their point of view, keeping their own technological trajectories open despite the disappointments.

5. A "grammar" for the mesoeconomic analysis of ecological transition

5.1 Some starting points for a method

This research supports the idea that these empirical results make it possible to draw lessons to constitute a "grammar" for mesoeconomic analysis based on the structure–strategy dialectic. This analysis, taking up here Bourdieu or the contributions of the French school of régulation (Boyer and Saillard, 2002), has as its starting point the consideration of mesoeconomic analysis as a structural approach: the field constituted has a structure that it is necessary to identify. But in a second step, it is necessary to consider that this structure is given by the interactions between actors. From this point of view, the actors' strategies have degrees of freedom that they use in the structure of the field. And the strategies are never strictly reproduction strategies, because they are also strategies of change, which must in turn be considered as reproduction strategies. These two dialectical relationships (structure–strategy and reproduction–change) thus make it possible to describe the strategies of innovation and the production of novelty as strategies of reproduction that will lead to changes in the field: the production of tannin foams follows processes that are certainly new, yet are inscribed in old regimes.

The second point of departure for a mesoeconomic analysis lies in the need to value both the representations and the material dimensions in economic analysis. Before going any further, let us clarify that while their presentation is kept separate, it is obvious that in reality the material and representational dimensions are linked, and some objects can have both dimensions at the same time. For example, the "biorefinery" artifact refers both to a technical, material object such as production units (which are often demonstration units in reality) and illustrates the possibility of organizing the substitution of oil by plants as a term-to-term substitution of fossil carbon by carbon of renewable origin. It is the fact that there are reports being produced (and thus material objects) that allows us to identify that documents constructing "visions for the future" play a role in the field as the production of actors with interests in seeking to orient the structure of the field. In order to orient this structure, they need to objectify their visions of the functioning of the field and of this future. The representations refer here to the way in which the actors represent the functioning of the space of regulation: which products are qualified to belong to the space? What are the devices that make it possible to identify these products (cf. the controversy over the definition of the technical standard for evaluating the bio-based content of the product)? What are the raw materials to be used? What are the technologies? And so on.

However, these problematizations are carried by communities of actors with divergent interests. The field is thus formed by the representations and commitments of actors who are intertwined and whose outcome is a space with multiple boundaries. The material dimensions refer to production units, technological platforms, products, technologies, etc. This set of artifacts makes it possible to explore new technologies and new products. In order to study these dimensions, it is necessary to open the black box of technologies: these are the result of strategic positioning by actors and must therefore be studied as such. This requires a thorough investigation of technoscience in order to identify the regimes of ecological transition in which technologies are embedded.[4] In the same way, in the regulation of change, objects should not be considered as fixed – this is the advantage of the approach in terms of compromise between intrinsic functionalities of the product and expected functionalities. Products are objects under construction. Actors explore the ways of making compromises and it is the regularities in these explorations that this study proposes to observe. This approach thus claims the production of an anchored theorization. That is, the elaboration of concepts in the mesoeconomic analysis starts from the regularities observed and from what the actors express about these regularities.

5.2 Borders and diversity within economic spaces

5.2.1 Borders and instability of economic spaces

The material and symbolic dimensions are developed in fields defined by the relations that the actors seek to maintain: collective construction of demonstrative projects, joint venture agreements, etc. However, these are not peaceful relationships, but rather power relationships that determine the structure of the field over time. For example, the Eurobioref, Biocore and Suprabio projects have responded to the European Commission's injunction to develop the transition to "TRL" levels of maturity close to industrial development. By being selected, these projects determine the dominant forms in the structure of the field. In so doing, they also influence the future shape of the field: the new structure that is formed when projects are selected and developed has an impact on the way production is organized. Thus, members of these projects explained during the interviews for this study that the purpose was not simply to demonstrate their projects, but also to prepare the ground for the establishment of the Biobased Industry PPP. These projects translate into "macro-sectoral" institutional arrangements that guide change and reproduce contradictions in new forms.

As a field, the economic space is thus constituted by the structure of the relations established or not between actors, which are materialized in localized institutional arrangements. These arrangements will then translate the representations of functioning adopted by groups of actors linked to each other. However, not all of them are linked: this is why there are multiple boundaries as represented in the second diagram of this conclusion. The boundaries of the field are the result of a process of construction of the legitimacy of belonging to the field through investment in institutional arrangements. The consequence is, of course, that the actors have to control and take charge of a part of the field that they can build on their assets and control. This control will therefore concern the allocation of subsidies, the definition of favorable public policies, etc. If we return to the institutional order of the field, whose purpose is to describe the rules of operation, its stability – if we follow Jullien and Smith (2008) – could only be an exception to common situations of instability and contestation of the order of the space.

5.2.2 The analysis of the productive dynamics in the change

The boundaries of the economic space are not only defined by institutional arrangements. They are also defined by production activities or the exploration of new technologies and products. The difficulty in empirically studying such dynamics in transition lies in the object itself, i.e. change. This difficulty can be overcome by taking as a starting point the strategies of reproduction in change. That is to say, by considering that technological exploration is guided by productive heritages that it is necessary to identify on the basis of technological exploration activities – which, it should be remembered, requires an in-depth investigation, particularly in the area of the technique.

The formation of the productive structure and its transformations are structured by two influences, which the actors link together technological choices and organizational choices. The question of technological choices refers to the actors' involvement in productive heritages. These heritages make it possible for actors to identify the technological locks that they can remove and the guiding principles that direct the way they produce knowledge. As far as organizational choices are concerned, actors must succeed in making internal compromises in their business models, but also external compromises with either upstream or downstream suppliers. But these organizational choices, as the conclusion of section 3 shows, are not unique and depend on the strategies of the actors and their positions. Chapter 5 shows that actors can either seek to constitute themselves as macro-actors capable of influencing the field (such as the large agribusiness firms), or seek to organize exploration around their technologies. These strategies can then proceed to attempt to diffuse through licensing strategies, in other words, by focusing on a particular product. The notion of ecological transition regimes then makes it possible to account for the articulation of these two choices. To do this, it is possible, on the one hand, to identify the complex systems of resources constituted and mobilized by the actors (what are the knowledge bases?) and the productive structures (what are the production worlds of the products?). On the other hand, it is possible to identify, from these first two results, the cycles of promises and disappointments and the management of these phases by the actors by comparing the expected functionalities and the functionalities of the products. This study has thus arrived at a representation of strategic behaviors within the field that can be translated into Figure 8.3.

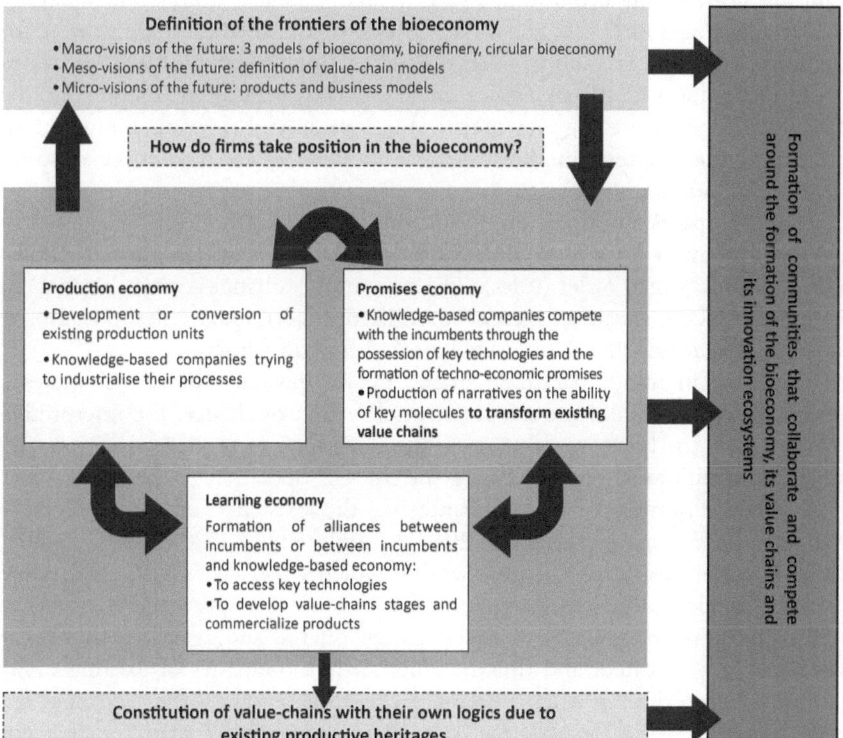

Figure 8.3 The actors projecting themselves into different economic worlds, based on multi-level representations of their collective action space

Figure 8.3 was drawn up from original documents of a heterogeneous nature; it seems that this is a lesson to be learned for mesoeconomic analysis. Because this analysis is dedicated to the way in which spaces are differentiated on the basis of tensions and stakes in collective action, it seems necessary to assume that the actors also think about this differentiation and try to give it meaning. From this point of view, the cognitive rules they give themselves form institutions (different from legal institutions), which produce rules and regularities. Geels (2004) and Scott (2014) rightly emphasize this point in their work on regime dynamics in transitions to sustainability. The difficulty that this study had to resolve in order to describe an economy in the making was therefore to tie together documents that were often of technical origin, announcements of industrial achievements, company creations or joint ventures in an analytical scheme that would account for the regulation of change. The investigations carried out in the course of this study have therefore sought to account for the institutional arrangements and the logics of production, exchange and consumption that constitute the ecological transition regimes.

The synthesis that has just been presented could lead the reader to criticize the *ad-hoc* nature of the concepts and empirical approaches used. This is a common criticism in economics (Carcillo and Reiffers, 2001). However, as Wilber and Harrison (1978) show, this is one of the methodological bases for institutional economics, and *a fortiori* for mesoeconomics: from the foundations of the recognition of the dynamics of differentiation between mesoeconomic spaces, which generate regimes specific to these spaces, it seems important to understand the "pattern models" specific to these spaces and to reconstruct them within a narrative approach.

Economic spaces and their transformations in the transition can be studied in two dimensions: their productive structure (a system of exchanges or transactions) and their institutional order (rules). The system of exchanges or transactions, in the light of Geels, is not only constituted by production activities, but also by consumption norms that define the expected functionalities.

If we bear in mind that these spaces are the products of actors' strategic actions, and if we think in terms of the organization of change, the interpretive hypothesis on the behavior of actors is that they seek to produce, intentionally or not, an institutional order defining the rules of operation of the space – i.e., of resource allocations – and guaranteeing the existence of these actors as themselves in this space (Antonelli, 2014; Musiolik et al., 2020; Nieddu, 2007). These spaces are places of initiatives within which actors (1) seek to collectively express their demands, expectations, difficulties; and (2) appreciate the type of skills to be implemented, the services already offered and available, those that will need to be created, and thus recompose the boundaries of existing organizations. Given the results concerning the role of products, these changes are achieved through the formation of communities interacting at different levels (Cohendet et al., 2020, 2014), whether within the firm, between firms or at the industry level. At this point, then, we have elements that make it possible to describe the overall dynamics of economic space formation (the multiple and conflicting boundaries of the system) and its internal dynamics related to its heterogeneity. These elements of internal dynamics are supported by "complex resource systems" (Allaire, 2013; Malerba, 2002). Here, knowledge bases are part of complex systems of resources, systems arranged by the actors themselves according to their productive legacies. To a vision in terms of a unified, homogeneous knowledge base, a preference is given to that of a variety of knowledge bases whose stabilization is also an issue in sectoral dynamics, and *a fortiori*, in emerging regulatory spaces. These knowledge bases, like the complex systems of resources and the organization of economic spaces, are controversial universes, places of contestation and confrontation for the domination of the compromises that will stabilize the space.

The productive logics (of production, exchange and consumption) under construction are inherited from the past, and this heritage guides learning and the production of knowledge. The actors will therefore confront and cooperate around a certain number of objects that crystallize the formation of links between these actors from inherited elements and projected into the future (collective productive legacies) and build and exploit the opportunities opened up by the destabilization of existing regimes and the emergence of new regimes.

The systems constitute collective resources for actors, and are part of what has been designated here as productive legacies. Following the results which highlight a plurality of logic, it is not a question of considering a *unique regime*, but a plurality of regimes coexisting in the same space. Their number is certainly not infinite; it is inscribed in the materiality of the transformation processes, and in the finite number of solutions that scientists and technologists explore for the economic actors.

The strategies of actors must be read as strategies for reproducing communities in particular spaces. The role of long-term coordination in the dynamics of change has been highlighted by Liebowitz and Margolis (1995), who emphasize that returns do not benefit a single holder, but the community carrying the technology. In other words, the question for the political economy of the ecological transition is no longer the construction of the narrative of the emergence of a dominant technology, based on a Schumpeterian entrepreneur, but the description of the strategies of actors to impose themselves in a controversial universe and to exist in the future. For, as Jullien and Smith (2008) and Nieddu (2000) show, the stabilization of controversies is an issue of anchoring and thus stabilizing the universe of actors.

6. Prospects and challenges of the post-fossil economy

The new phase of capitalism that the ecological transition constitutes exhibits a key characteristic of these periods: the recomposition of the mesoeconomic division of labor. Let us recall that "The Glorious Thirty" were the time of the formation of Fordist sectors whose forms were challenged by the emergence of sectoral, territorial or national systems (Schot and Steinmueller, 2018). From this point of view, Geels's (2004) critique of sectoral systems of innovation bears witness to this evolution and translates it into a research question that is to grasp the formation of these new spaces.

Today, the bioeconomy is not the only emerging mesoeconomic space. There is also the circular economy, the social economy and the "collaborative economy", whose boundaries are also blurred and whose capacity to respond to the challenge of the ecological transition is questioned (Martin, 2016). The result is a plural post-fossil economy whose foundations could rest on the ability to combine the principles of these different economies in a dual model. On the one hand, these spaces are constituted by core organizations whose activity consists in providing the technologies and services that make these economies work. From this perspective, the producers of algorithms provide the technologies that make intermediaries work (Evans and Schmalensee, 2016; Teece, 2018). In the perspective developed throughout this book, the use of these technologies can be achieved within the framework of organizations such as cooperatives, etc. promoting a fair transition. On the other hand, these core organizations are complemented by companies in sectors that will continue to exist (energy, agriculture, etc.). In this context, these companies will have to adopt logics from these mesoeconomic spaces that they can use to transform themselves. The specific period of the emergence of the bioeconomy provides a grammar for studying the emergence of this plural economy that would be the post-fossil economy. Nevertheless, it appears that this particular moment is the beginning of a slow process of both space formation and positioning of this space in relation to other new spaces.

Notes

1 What we can consider as the refraction in a dominant vision of the action of multiple actors.

2 Influential action including on the Commission itself. It is not given to all to be able to have the Commission itself finance lobbying actions. Nevertheless, this seems to be the case for Europabio (European association representing the biotechnology, health, agriculture and industry industries) if we follow the Corporate European Observatory, a Brussels-based NGO (CEO, 2013).

Between 2005 and 2012, EuropaBio was involved in several research projects funded by the FP7-KBBE, with Clever Consult, a consulting firm on the bioeconomy created by its director of the industrial biotechnology department; it was thus able to provide the Commission with reports, communication materials and the usual "success stories" of companies that fed into the 2012 European Commission communication cited in the general introduction. We should therefore note the very active involvement of industrialists in defining European research priorities, particularly its technology platforms. This is not without conflict with research agendas carrying antagonistic visions of the bioeconomy, which will only get very minimal shares of European funding, such as the FP7-CREPE project (2008–2010). (Schmidt et al., 2012) report on these strong tensions in the relationship between what they call the *technoscientific paradigm* and civil society.

The influence of agribusiness and the biotech industry in the process of institutionalization of the bioeconomy by the European Commission is thus robustly documented.

3 We recall that biorefineries are to some extent like automobiles (with diesel and gasoline) driven by two types of processes, some thermochemical (the Fischer-Tropsch process used by the Germans during World War II or the South Africans to cope with the effects of the apartheid boycott), others based on fermentation where industrial enzymes can be deployed – most often derived from classical biotechnologies, but for others from the work of the genetic engineering revolution. Obviously, the actors in each of the two paths promise to be more efficient than the other, but this is only true in each case locally for specific combinations of raw materials, processes and products.

4 Within this framework, interdisciplinary collaborations allow for the enrichment of analysis through the construction of tools for the production of economic knowledge by observing the practices of actors in the sense given by Wilber and Harrison (1978).

Bibliography

Allaire, G., 2013. *Les communs comme infrastructure institutionnelle de l'économie marchande.* Rev. Régulation Capital. Inst. Pouvoirs.

Amable, B., 2009. *The diversity of modern capitalism*, Reprinted. ed. Oxford University Press.

Antonelli, C., 2014. *Localised technological change: towards the economics of complexity.* Routledge.

BECOTEPS, n.d. *The European Bioeconomy in 2030.* www.epsoweb.org/file/560, accessed on 05/09/2022.

Befort, N., 2021. The promises of drop-in vs. functional innovations: The case of bioplastics. *Ecol. Econ.* 181, 106886. https://doi.org/10.1016/j.ecolecon.2020.106886.

Benninga, H., 1990. *A history of lactic acid making: a chapter in the history of biotechnology, chemists and chemistry.* Kluwer Academic Publishers.

Borup, M., Brown, N., Konrad, K., Van Lente, H., 2006. The sociology of expectations in science and technology. *Technology Analysis & Strategic Management* 18, 285–298. https://doi.org/10.1080/09537320600777002.

Boyer, R., 2015. *Économie politique des capitalismes: théorie de la régulation et des crises.* La Découverte.

Boyer, R., Saillard, Y. (Eds.), 2002. *Regulation theory: the state of the art.* Routledge.

Carcillo, S., Reiffers, V., 2001. La critique d'ad hocité en économie. L'exemple des théories de la croissance. *Louvain Econ. Rev.* 67, 197–223.

Cohendet, P., Grandadam, D., Simon, L., Capdevila, I., 2014. Epistemic communities, localization and the dynamics of knowledge creation. *J. Econ. Geogr.* 14, 929–954. https://doi.org/10.1093/jeg/lbu018.

Cohendet, P., Simon, L., Mehouachi, C., 2020. From business ecosystems to ecosystems of innovation: the case of the video game industry in Montréal. *Ind. Innov.* https://doi.org/10.1080/13662716.2020.1793737.

Corporate European Obervatory (CEO), 2013. Transformation needed for transparency: Looking towards the lobby register review. CEO, 26 February. http://corporateeurope.org/news/transformation-needed-transparency-looking-towards-lobby-register-review, accessed on 10/16/2022.

Evans, D.S., Schmalensee, R., 2016. *Matchmakers: the new economics of platform businesses: how one of the oldest business models on earth powers the most incredible companies in the world.* Harvard Business Review Press.

Faucheux, S., Nicolaï, I., 2011. IT for green and green IT: a proposed typology of eco-innovation. *Ecol. Econ.* 70, 2020–2027. https://doi.org/10.1016/j.ecolecon.2011.05.019.

Faucheux, S., Nicolaï, I., 1998. Les firmes face au développement soutenable: changement technologique et gouvernance au sein de la dynamique industrielle. *Rev. Déconomie Ind.* 83, 127–146. https://doi.org/10.3406/rei.1998.1704.

Galambos, L., Hikino, T., Zamagni, V. (Eds.), 2007. *The global chemical industry in the age of the petrochemical revolution.* Cambridge University Press.

Geels, F.W., 2004. From sectoral systems of innovation to socio-technical systems. *Res. Policy* 33, 897–920. https://doi.org/10.1016/j.respol.2004.01.015.

Georgescu-Roegen, N., 1975. Energy and economic myths. *South. Econ. J.* 41, 347. https://doi.org/10.2307/1056148.

Giampietro, M., 2019. On the circular bioeconomy and decoupling: implications for sustainable growth. *Ecol. Econ.* 162, 143–156. https://doi.org/10.1016/j.ecolecon.2019.05.001.

Gravitis, J., Suzuki, M., 1999. *Biomass refinery: a way to produce value added products and base for agriculture zero emissions system.* Presented at the International Conference on Agricultural Engineering, Beijing, China.

Jullien, B., Smith, A. (Eds.), 2008. *Industries and globalization: the political causality of difference, globalization and governance.* Palgrave Macmillan.

Liebowitz, S.J., Margolis, S.E., 1995. Path dependence, lock-in, and history. *J. Law Econ. Organ.* 11, 205–226.

Lima, T.M., Lima, C., Rathi, A., Gawande, M., Tucek, J., Urquieta-Gonzalez, E., Zboril, R., Paixao, M., Varma, R., 2016. Magnetic ZSM-5 zeolite: a selective catalyst for the valorization of furfuryl alcohol to y-valerolactone, alkyl levulinates or levulinic acid. *Green Chem.* à paraître.

Malerba, F., 2002. Sectoral systems of innovation and production. *Res. Policy* 31, 247–264.

Martin, C.J., 2016. The sharing economy: a pathway to sustainability or a nightmarish form of neoliberal capitalism? *Ecol. Econ.* 121, 149–159. https://doi.org/10.1016/j.ecolecon.2015.11.027.

Mayumi, K., 2001. *The origins of ecological economics: the bioeconomics of Georgescu-Roegen.* Routledge.

McCormick, K., Kautto, N., 2013. The bioeconomy in Europe: an overview. *Sustainability* 5, 2589–2608. https://doi.org/10.3390/su5062589.

Musiolik, J., Markard, J., Hekkert, M., Furrer, B., 2020. Creating innovation systems: how resource constellations affect the strategies of system builders. *Technol. Forecast. Soc. Change* 153, 119209. https://doi.org/10.1016/j.techfore.2018.02.002.

National Research Council of the National Academies, 2015. *Industrialization of biology: a roadmap to accelerate the advanced manufacturing of chemicals.* National Research Council.

Nieddu, M., 2007. Le patrimoine comme relation économique. *Econ. Appliquée* 60, 87–104.

Nieddu, M., 2000. Science et dynamiques économiques, le cas des biopolymères. *Sci. Société*, 87–104.

Organisation for Economic Co-operation and Development, OECD International Futures Programme (Eds.), 2009. *The bioeconomy to 2030: designing a policy agenda.* Organization for Economic Co-operation and Development.

Pavitt, K., 1998. Technologies, products and organization in the innovating firm: what Adam Smith tells us and Joseph Schumpeter doesn't. *Ind. Corp. Change* 7, 433–452. https://doi.org/10.1093/icc/7.3.433.

Schmidt, O., Padel, S., Levidow, L., 2012. The bio-economy concept and knowledge base in a public goods and farmer perspective. *Bio-Based and Applied Economics*. https://doi.org/10.13128/BAE-10770.

Schot, J., Steinmueller, W.E., 2018. Three frames for innovation policy: R&D, systems of innovation and transformative change. *Res. Policy* 47, 1554–1567. https://doi.org/10.1016/j.respol.2018.08.011.

Scott, W.R., 2014. *Institutions and organizations: ideas, interests, and identities*, 4th ed. SAGE.

Teece, D.J., 2018. Profiting from innovation in the digital economy: enabling technologies, standards, and licensing models in the wireless world. *Res. Policy* 47, 1367–1387. https://doi.org/10.1016/j.respol.2017.01.015.

Werpy, T., Petersen, G., 2004. *Top value added chemicals from biomass*. US Department of Energy.

Wilber, C.K., Harrison, R.S., 1978. The methodological basis of institutional economics: pattern model, storytelling, and holism. *J. Econ. Issues* 12, 61–89. https://doi.org/10.1080/00213624.1978.11503505.

Index

Page numbers in **bold** refer to figures, page numbers in *italic* refer to tables.